Published by Bassline Publishing
www.basslinepublishing.com

All design and layout by Bassline Publishing

Copyright © Bassline Publishing 2023

ISBN 13: 978-0-9933727-4-2

Notation Legend

The Stave: most music written for the bass guitar uses the bass clef. The example to the right shows the placement of the notes on the stave.

Tablature: this is a graphical representation of the music. Each horizontal line corresponds with a string on the bass guitar, with the lowest line representing the lowest string. The numbers represent the frets to be played. Numbers stacked vertically indicate notes that are played together. Where basses with five or six strings are required, the tablature stave will have five or six lines as necessary.

Notes shown in brackets indicated that a note has been tied over from a previous bar.

Repeats: the double line and double dot bar lines indicate that the music between these bar lines should be repeated. If the music is to be repeated more than once, a written indication will be given i.e. 'play 3x'.

1st & 2nd Time Endings: these are used for sections that are repeated, but which have different endings. The first ending is used the first time, the second is used on the repeat. The first ending is ignored on the repeat, only the second is used.

Slap: the note is slapped with the thumb.

Pop: the note is popped with either the first or second finger.

Thumb Up: played with an upstroke of the thumb.

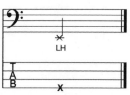

Fretting Hand: played by hammering on with the fretting hand.

Harmonic: note is played as a harmonic by lighting touching the string above the fret indicated.

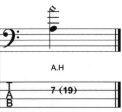

Artificial Harmonic: fret the lower note and tap the string over the fret shown in brackets.

Trill: alternate between the notes indicated by repeatedly hammering-on and pulling-off.

Vibrato: the pitch of the note is altered by repeatedly bending and releasing the string.

Hammer-On: only the first note is struck. The second is sounded by fretting it with another finger.

Pull-Off: Only the first note is struck. Lift the fretting finger to sound the second fretted note.

Slide: play the first note, then slide the finger to the second.

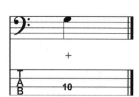

Picking Hand Tap: note is tapped with a finger of the picking hand. If necessary, the finger will be specified.

Fretting Hand Tap: note is tapped with a finger of the fretting hand. If necessary, the finger will be specified.

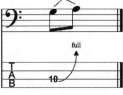

Bend: note is bent upwards to the interval indicated. ½ = half step, full = whole step.

Bend and Release: note is bent up to the interval indicated then released to the original note.

Ghost Note: note is a pitchless 'dead' note used as a rhythmic device.

Accent: note is accentuated, or played louder.

Staccato: note is played staccato - short.

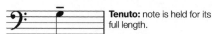

Tenuto: note is held for its full length.

p piano - played very softly
mp mezzo-piano - played moderately quietly
mf mezzo forte - played moderately loud/strong
f forte - played loud/strong

D.C al Coda: Return to the beginning of the song and play until the bar marked Coda. Then jump to the section marked Coda.
D.S al Coda: Return to the sign, then play until the bar marked Coda. Then jump to the Coda.
D.C (or D.S) al Fine: Return to the point specified, then play until the Fine marking. Stop at this point.

CONTENTS

INTRODUCTION

Welcome to *Giants of Bass*, a pair of books that form a comprehensive study and analysis of some of world's most influential bass players. In writing these titles, I have endeavoured to cover the most iconic bassists from a wide range of genres, so whether you're a funk fan, a rocker, an aspiring session bassist or a progressive metal enthusiast, there will be something here for you. For each artist you'll find plenty to keep you busy: each has a detailed biography, a selected discography, an analysis of their tone and playing technique and finally, a piece of music written in their style.

These books are actually a very extensive rewrite of *Giants of Bass*, a book that I originally wrote for Sanctuary Publishing back in 2004. The original version – of which I was very proud at the time – was a well-received title and since its release I always endeavoured to stock it on my website. However, in 2014 I was informed by the original publishers that the print run of the book had been exhausted and there was no intention to print any further copies. The copyright to the book therefore reverted to me and I decided that I would give it a brief appraisal to see if I was still happy with it, then republish it through my own publishing company, Bassline Publishing.

Upon reading *Giants of Bass* for the first time in ten years I quickly realised that it was going to require more work than I had initially thought. The main issue was that I felt that the biographies for each player were far too short and were now out of date. The majority of the musicians featured had done significant things with their careers in the time since the first book, and I wanted to be able to reflect those developments. Sadly, some of the artists such as Jack Bruce and Duck Dunn had also passed away and this too needed to be reflected. Having taken the decision to rewrite the book, I decided to use the opportunity to add in some additional artists who I hadn't been able to include the first time around. After all, it seems illogical to have a book purporting to cover the instrument's most influential users, yet not feature legendary bassists such as Rocco Prestia, Marcus Miller, Carol Kaye,w and Victor Wooten. I'm pleased that these artists and a few more are now part of these revised books.

Turning my attention to the audio, I discovered that although I was largely happy with the compositions that I had written to represent the artists, the recordings themselves left a lot to be desired. The originals were done on a very small budget and so I had programmed the majority of the drum and keyboard parts myself. In the years since these were recorded, technology has of course moved on significantly and the recordings now sounded extremely dated. The opportunity to re-record them meant that not only could I use the many amazing musicians that I have worked with in the intervening years, but I could also record them using more appropriate instruments, many of which I had been unable to source back in 2004.

What had initially started out as a simple republishing job had by now turned into a very extensive rewrite, one that I devoted all of my time to for an entire year. Somewhere along the way I realised that the finished book was going to be considerably bigger than the original (double in size in fact) and so I made the decision to split it into two volumes: 60s and 70s and 80s and 90s.

So, that's how the *Giants of Bass* books came to be. It's genuinely been a labour of love for me and although the writing process at times seemed like it would never end, I feel that the final result has been worth it. I learnt a lot in researching and writing these books and I hope that you will learn just as much when studying from them. As ever, I would be delighted to hear your thoughts and answer any questions that you might have. Please feel free to send emails to stuart@basslinepublishing.com.

Stuart Clayton
January 2017

When most people begin playing an instrument, they are typically inspired to start by having heard or seen another musician doing their thing. Our heroes are our guides, showing us things we want to learn, suggesting paths we could take. As a teenager, I was inspired to start playing by bassists such as Mark King, Billy Sheehan, Flea, Stuart Zender and Duck Dunn. I transcribed everything I could by these bassists, learnt every song, every lick. I devoured every scrap of information about them I could find, from magazine articles to tuition videos. It was a journey of discovery, a hugely enjoyable process that kept me so inspired that I practised for hours every day. As I studied my favourite players and learnt from them, my own playing began to develop: I started writing my own riffs and songs, developing my own sound. Eventually I stopped sounding like them and began to sound like ME.

For each of the bass players featured in this book I have endeavoured to include detailed information about their career, as well as a list of their best-known recordings. I've written extensively about the equipment that they have used, and I've offered advice on how to get close to their tone. Finally, I've broken down their playing styles and analysed them in painstaking detail. I've then used this information to compose and record a piece of music written in their style.

The intention here is not to turn you into a clone of any of these players, rather to give you the tools you need in order to understand what makes them sound the way they do. In studying these amazing bassists, you will undoubtedly be inspired to take what you learn and begin using it to create your own music/follow your own path.

For each artist in this book I have included the following:

BIOGRAPHY

For each artist I have written an exhaustively researched biography which covers their career to date. I have also included a selected discography, detailing the albums that represent their best work and which specific tracks to check out. For some artists, it was more appropriate to write a list of their essential tracks – this was usually required for those who are predominantly session players and who therefore didn't necessarily have many of their best songs on one album. Either way, when studying an artist, I strongly recommend also listening to as much of their material as possible. If you are seeking to emulate their style, this will be a considerable help.

GEAR ANALYSIS

I've also written an analysis of the basses, effects and amplifiers used by each bassist. In some cases, this might be about a single instrument – James Jamerson for example did the majority of his work on a Fender Precision. On the flip side, John Entwistle used a huge number of basses over the course of his career. In either case, I felt it was important to cover this in as much detail as possible.

PLAY-ALONG TRACKS

For each artist I've composed an original piece of music, written in their 'style'. Writing these pieces required an extensive amount of research: for each artist, I transcribed several of their key pieces, learning to play them as accurately as I could. In doing so, I was able to recognise common elements of their playing – chord progressions that they favoured, note choices that they often made etc. I then attempted to compose a piece in the same vein, something that recalled all of the common elements of their playing style.

There are two tracks available for each artist: one with recorded bass and one without. The audio for these pieces can be downloaded from the Bassline Publishing website, free of charge. To download, head to www.basslinepublishing.com and log into your account (if you don't have an account, you'll need to set one up, but it's free to do so). Once logged in, head to the 'Free Stuff' link on the main menu. The audio files can be found listed next to the bonus content for this book. Right click and select 'Save As' to download.

PERFORMANCE NOTES

There are extensive performance notes for each piece in this book. These will be invaluable to you, particularly when studying some of the more complex lines.

SOUND ADVICE

I've included detailed notes on the instruments and effects that I used to record the tracks. Where possible, I used the same kind of instrument that the artist is known for using. In the few instances that I was unable to do this, I used the most appropriate substitute available to me. I have also given some advice here about how best to get close to the desired tone, using whatever instrument that you have at your disposal.

It's important to note that if your aim is to mimic the sound of a particular artist, then having the right equipment will only get you so far. An artist's tone is about more than which brand of bass or amplifier they use: Flea still sounds like Flea whether he uses a Music Man, a Modulus or a Fender for example. You therefore also need to think carefully about note choices and technique. I've referenced these factors throughout the performance notes, but also included a few important 'style tips' in a sidebar for each artist.

ACKNOWLEDGEMENTS

The *Giants of Bass* project has been the biggest and most demanding that I've ever undertaken. In the process of writing the book itself – not to mention recording and mixing all of the accompanying audio tracks – I've had a lot of help. I'm eternally grateful to the following people:

MUSICIANS

Andy Sutor, Charlie Griffiths, Dan Goldman, Dan Moore, Dan Waghorn, Fjokra, Jamie Hunt, Jason Bowld, Mark Whitlam, Martin Greenlee, Simon Woods-Tucker, Steve Banks, Stuart Ryan, Gary Mitchell, Tom O'Grady and Will Beavis.

ARTIST PHOTOGRAPHY

The artist photography used throughout this book is credited below. Bold numbers refer to the page on which the image appears.

8 Cliff Burton © Tony Mottram/Avalon
20 Tim Commerford © Avalon
22 Tim Commerford © Startraks Photo/Rex/Shutterstock
28 Flea © Sipa Press/Rex/Shutterstock
30 Flea © Avalon
32 Flea © Chris Schwegler/Avalon
40 Stuart Hamm © Eric Cui
42 Stuart Hamm © Stuart Hamm
56, 59, 62, 64 Mark King © Steve Perks
58 Mark King © David Redfern/Getty Images
60 Mark King © Tina Korhonen Photography
72, 74 Michael Manring © Philippe Lissart
82 Marcus Miller © Michaela Cuccagna/Avalon
84, 86 Marcus Miller © Sire Guitars
85 Marcus Miller © Guillemin/Dalle/Avalon
98 John Myung © Christie Goodwin/Getty Images
110 Pino Palladino © Startraks Photo/Rex/Shutterstock
112 Pino Palladino © Dimitis Legakis/Rex/Shutterstock
120 Billy Sheehan © Tina Korhonen Photography
122 Billy Sheehan © Avalon
134 Sting © Jeff Kravitz/FilmMagic/Getty Images
137 Sting © Starstock/Avalon
138 Sting © Startraks Photo/Rex/Shutterstock
146 Victor Wooten © Robert Knight Archive/Getty Images
148 Victor Wooten © Grigor Fris
160 Stuart Zender © Tina Korhonen Photography

INSTRUMENTS

I'd like to thank Adrian Ashton for lending me his Music Man, Höfner and Gibson EB-3 basses, Mike Brooks for the use of his Alembic and Jonathan Worgan for the Music Man Bongo. I'm also very grateful to Ellio Martina for the Bass Mute, to Martin Sims for sending me the gorgeous Lionheart fretless bass and to James Millman for setting up my basses where needed.

INSTRUMENT PHOTOGRAPHY

The photography of the different bass guitars shown in this book is credited below. Bold numbers refer to the page on which the image appears.

11 Rickenbacker 4001 © Nigel Osbourne/Getty Images
23, 33 Music Man StingRay © Andy Casey Photography
43 Kubicki Ex Factor © Stuart Clayton
61 Jaydee Supernatural © Andy Casey Photography
75 Zon Hyperbass © Zon Guitars
87 Fender Marcus Miller Signature Jazz © Fender
101 Music Man Bongo © Stuart Clayton
113 Music Man StingRay © Nigel Osbourne/Getty Images
123 Yamaha Attitude © Andy Casey Photography
139 Fender Precision © Nigel Osbourne/Getty Images
149 Fodera Yin Yang Deluxe Series III © Fodera
162 Warwick Stuart Zender Signature © Warwick

THANKS ALSO TO...

Thanks are also due to Joe Zon at Zon Guitars, James Millman at Millman Guitars, Grigor Fris at BasstheWorld.com, Corey Brown at No.Treble.com, Paul Robinson, Freddie Draper, Nathan Raphael, Simon Troup, James Uings, Joel McIver, Tom Farncombe at Music Sales, Daniel Edmonds, Tom Powell, Kev Beardsley and Simon Woods-Tucker. Finally, I'd like to thank my amazing wife Laura for all of her help in making this book look fantastic, as well as her usual love and support.

GIANTS OF BASS

Volume 2: 80s & 90s

CLIFF BURTON

There can be little doubt that Metallica's Cliff Burton is one of the most influential bassists to have emerged from the heavy metal/thrash genre. A gifted musician, Burton possessed a solid understanding of theory, harmony, and melody in addition to his phenomenal bass skills. He was instrumental in Metallica's early development, and his sudden death in a tour bus crash in 1986 devastated both the band and his many fans. Burton's contributions to rock/metal bass playing are far-reaching, and to this day he remains an inspiration to bassists all over the world.

Cliff Burton was born on 10th February 1962 and was raised in Castro Valley, just outside of San Francisco. After showing an interest in his father's classical music collection, he began taking piano lessons as a child, something that would prove to be enormously beneficial to him later on. In his early teens he discovered rock music, specifically bands such as The Eagles, Aerosmith, The Blue Oyster Cult and Lynyrd Skynyrd. Sadly, when he was just 13, tragedy struck his family when his older brother suddenly passed away from a cerebral aneurysm. This life-changing event inspired Cliff to want to do something important with his life and further fuelled his love of music. Shortly after his brother's death, he took up the bass guitar and began taking lessons with local tutors. After an initially slow start, he began to make progress and would practice for hours and hours at a time. As he improved, he outgrew several of his tutors, finally finding a worthy mentor in jazz bassist Steve Doherty, who taught at ABC Music, a local music shop. Doherty would play a crucial part in Cliff's musical development, encouraging his love for classical music, but also teaching him about harmony, melody, and odd time signatures.

to read music and began studying the work of classical greats such as Bach and Beethoven. Cliff was a dedicated and diligent student and continued to practice extensively throughout his teens, progressing rapidly on the instrument. Through his studies, he also developed an interest in bassists such as jazz-fusion icon Stanley Clarke, prog-rocker Geddy Lee and rock bassists such as Geezer Butler, Steve Harris and Lemmy.

Cliff's first band was EZ Street, a local group who played experimental music largely built out of extended jam sessions. This group – which subsequently changed its name to Agents of Misfortune – was to be Cliff's musical home for the next few years.

In 1980, he graduated from Castro Valley High School, determined to make a living from music. His parents, proud of his schoolwork and musical achievements to date, agreed to support him for four years whilst he tried to forge a career in music. In 1982, he joined a San Francisco-based hard rock/glam band called Trauma, who were experiencing some local success. By this point, Cliff had begun to develop a wild, improvisational style of playing that was fast, melodic and lead guitar-like. During Trauma's shows, he would often take an extended solo spot, playing distorted lead bass solos whilst head-banging enthusiastically. His on-stage persona and extravagant playing soon helped him develop a name for himself and he quickly became one of the main focal points at the band's live shows.

Later in 1982, Trauma travelled south to Los Angeles to shoot a five-song promo video (which can now be seen on YouTube) and play some gigs, one of which was at the Whiskey a Go-Go club. In the audience that night were James Hetfield and Lars Ulrich of the newly formed thrash metal group Metallica. The band had begun to experience some limited success but were having misgivings about their bass player, Ron McGovney. Upon witnessing Burton on-stage, the pair resolved to recruit him for Metallica. Their offer certainly appealed to Cliff, who was by this point beginning to feel stifled by Trauma's insistence on pursuing a more commercial path than he was comfortable with. But although keen to work with Metallica, Cliff was reluctant to leave his hometown and move to L.A. After a few weeks of phone calls and meetings during which James and Lars attempted to convince him, Cliff delivered an ultimatum: move to San Francisco and he would join. As the thrash metal scene seemed to be developing more in San Francisco than it was in their hometown, the band agreed.

Cliff played his first show with Metallica on 5th March 1983. His approach to the bass – and his on-stage persona – turned out to be a perfect fit for the band. Metallica's energetic live shows continued to win them new fans, many of whom had become enthusiastic supporters through their widely circulated demo tape No Life 'til Leather. One such fan was Jon Zazula, a New York record store owner who invited the band to New York, so that he could help them sign to a major label. The band therefore rented a van and drove across the country to meet with Zazula. Upon arrival, James, Lars, and Cliff made the decision to fire their lead guitarist Dave Mustaine, whose excessive drinking was beginning to prove a significant negative factor within the group. Replacement lead guitarist Kirk Hammett, who was known to the band through San Francisco-based group Exodus, was flown out to audition for the role. Dave Mustaine of course later went on to form Megadeth, another hugely successful thrash metal band.

Finding a label that would take a chance on Metallica proved challenging and so Zazula eventually began his own, Megaforce Records. In May 1983, he rented time in a local studio and the band began recording their debut album. Released in July that year, the resulting album Kill 'Em All proved hugely popular with their fan base and would later go on to be regarded as the one of the most pivotal albums in thrash metal. Although all of the material had been written before Cliff joined, the album is notable for the track '(Anesthesia) Pulling Teeth', a live, improvised bass solo which was a superb showcase for the band's new bassist. Unsurprisingly, this track earned Cliff countless new fans, and to this day is studied intently by aspiring metal bass players all over the world. Featuring his trademark fuzz/wah sound, the solo clearly illustrates Cliff's love for both classical music (through the use of Bach-like arpeggio motifs) and heavy metal, with its wild, upper register solo lines. His technical proficiency was evident throughout the rest of the album as well – after all, there would have been few bassists who could match Hetfield's blindingly fast rhythm guitar work using conventional fingerstyle technique. Cliff's influence was to quickly extend far beyond his bass playing however: with his understanding of music theory he was able to influence Hetfield and Ulrich's song writing significantly, resulting in music that would extend beyond thrash, later coming to feature slower, classical-influenced passages that would differentiate the band from the other thrash metal bands who were prevalent at the time.

The band toured throughout the remainder of the year, relocating to Sweet Silence Studios in Copenhagen, Denmark in early 1984

TOP TRACKS

'(Anesthesia) Pulling Teeth'
Metallica – Kill 'Em All

'Seek and Destroy'
Metallica – Kill 'Em All

'Creeping Death'
Metallica – Ride the Lightning

'For Whom the Bell Tolls'
Metallica – Ride the Lightning

'The Call of Ktulu'
Metallica – Ride the Lightning

'Battery'
Metallica – Master of Puppets

'Master of Puppets'
Metallica – Master of Puppets

'Welcome Home (Sanitarium)'
Metallica – Master of Puppets

'Orion'
Metallica – Master of Puppets

'Damage. Inc'
Metallica – Master of Puppets

to begin recording their second album. This time around, Cliff was able to exert a greater influence on the writing process, with six of the album's eight tracks including him as co-writer. Whilst the resulting album *Ride the Lightning* featured plenty of the fast thrash metal the band was renowned for, it also demonstrated significant musical development: 'Fade to Black', the band's first ballad, proved something of a shock to their fan base initially, whilst their improved use of guitar harmonies and lead vocal melodies began to set them aside from other metal bands. Cliff turned in stellar bass performances throughout the album, but the stand-out tracks for his fans were undoubtedly 'For Whom the Bell Tolls' and album-closer 'The Call of Ktulu'. 'Bells' features a lead bass intro melody and an aggressive, strummed power chord bass figure throughout. 'Ktulu', an almost nine minute-long instrumental, has a distorted lead bass solo running through the first few minutes. Unfortunately, the album was mixed with the bass at a relatively low volume, meaning that some of Cliff's playing on these two songs is often overlooked. In recent years, the isolated audio of his part on 'For Whom the Bell Tolls' has surfaced on the internet, allowing his fans to clearly hear his playing with far greater clarity.

Ride the Lightning was a hugely successful album for Metallica and

YOU MIGHT ALSO LIKE...

If you're a fan of Cliff's bass work, be sure to check out the following bassists:

○ **John Paul Jones**
Giants of Bass: 60s - 70s

○ **John Entwistle**
Giants of Bass: 60s - 70s

○ **Billy Sheehan**
See page 120

within two months of its release, led them to sign a major record contract with Elektra. The band began to tour for long stretches at a time, significantly expanding their fan base wherever they went. As their popularity grew, Cliff became one of the leading figures in rock/metal bass playing.

In late 1985, Metallica returned to Copenhagen to record their third album. Considered by many of their fans to be their best work, *Master of Puppets* was another significant step forward both musically and lyrically. The band had by now evolved into a tight, well-rehearsed thrash metal machine and their song writing had developed well beyond the more basic material of their debut recording. The album's opening track 'Battery' featured a gentle acoustic guitar intro which evolved first into a powerful assault of harmony guitars, then into one of their fastest and most aggressive songs to date. The title track 'Master of Puppets' is notable for both James Hetfield's development as a lyricist, as well as for an extended middle section which clearly shows Cliff Burton's classical music influences. Aside from powerful songs throughout, the album is regarded as Cliff's defining contribution to the band largely because of the song 'Orion'. This eight-minute instrumental features Cliff at his best: the intro consists of multi-tracked, distorted bass chords, whilst the middle section features a slow, folk-like melodic bassline in 6/8 time. After the lead guitars play harmony lines above this line, Cliff plays a lead bass solo, so guitar-like that many fans simply assumed that it *was* a guitar solo. Like 'For Whom the Bell Tolls', the isolated audio for this piece has now surfaced on YouTube, meaning that it is possible to hear the brilliance of Cliff's lines on this piece clearly. The final track on the album, 'Damage. Inc' also includes an intro comprising multi-tracked harmony bass chords, a part which was apparently influenced by Cliff's studies of J.S. Bach.

With the release of *Master of Puppets* in March 1986, Metallica were fast becoming one of the world's biggest metal bands. The first to be released under their new record deal with Elektra, the album reached #29 on the Billboard 200 Chart and would later become the first thrash

metal album to achieve platinum status. Following the release of the album, the band toured as a support act for former Black Sabbath vocalist Ozzy Osbourne. This led to them reaching an even wider audience, again expanding their fan base considerably. At the end of the tour, Metallica flew to Europe to continue promoting their new album.

Sadly, *Master of Puppets* was to be Cliff's final album with Metallica. On 27th September 1986, the band's tour bus crashed when travelling through Sweden. Whilst several members of the band and crew were injured, the accident claimed the life of Burton, who was flung from the window of the bus and then crushed when it fell onto him.

Cliff was subsequently mourned by both the band and his many fans, with tributes pouring in from across the world. For many Metallica fans, Cliff had been the soul of the band and things would never be the same. 'Orion' was played at his memorial service and his ashes were scattered by his family at the Maxwell Ranch, where he had often rehearsed as a teenager. Metallica later paid tribute to Cliff with the release of *Cliff 'Em All*, a video compilation of bootleg footage. The band's next album, 1988's *...And Justice for All* would feature the song 'To Live is to Die', an instrumental piece that included a brief, spoken poem that had been written by Burton.

After a hiatus and much soul searching, Metallica reasoned that Cliff would have wanted them to continue on their journey. After extensive auditions, they recruited Flotsam and Jetsam bassist Jason Newsted and resumed touring and recording. Within a few years they would go on to become the world's biggest metal band with the release of their self-titled 1991 album. Today, thirty years after Cliff's passing, the band is still going strong, with their tenth album *Hardwired... To Self-Destruct...* released in November 2016.

In the thirty years since his death, Cliff's huge impact on both the band and the bass guitar have not diminished, with many aspiring young bassists continuing to look to his legacy as they pursue their own dreams of metal stardom.

BASS GUITARS

Cliff's first bass was a dark red Rickenbacker 4001 with triangle inlays, similar to the bass shown opposite. This instrument was purchased in 1982 and was used on the first two albums that he recorded with Metallica. It was modified by Chuck Martin (a guitar shop owner and friend of Cliff's) to include a Seymour Duncan Stratocaster pickup beneath the bridge piece. This modification – which was not easily visible – enabled Cliff to achieve a better lead bass sound. When the band came to record *Kill 'Em All*, their first album, the instrument was modified further, with the Rickenbacker's bridge pickup replaced with a Seymour Duncan stacked jazz pickup, which was a dark red colour similar to that of the instrument itself. The bass position pickup was also replaced with a Gibson EB-1 pickup. Producer Paul Curcio had a friend perform these repairs and reportedly still has the original pickups that were removed from the bass. Cliff used his Rickenbacker throughout the tours to promote both the band's first album and the follow-up, *Ride the Lightning*. This bass has remained with Cliff's family but can now be seen on display in the Rock and Roll Hall of Fame.

Feeling that the Rickenbacker would not stand up to sustained touring, Cliff briefly used a black Alembic Spoiler bass in 1985, inspired partly by jazz-fusion icon Stanley Clarke, a known user of Alembic basses. This instrument was later stolen, and so he bought an Aria Pro SB-1000 bass. With Metallica's popularity rising, Aria gave Cliff an endorsement, initially sending him three basses. His preferred instrument was a black model with gold hardware, which was reissued as a tribute to Burton in the mid-2000s. He used his Aria basses to record *Master of Puppets* and continued to tour with them until his untimely death in 1986.

Little is known about Cliff's preferred string brand or gauge, but it is widely thought that he used a lighter than average set of .035-.095 in order to facilitate string bending.

EFFECTS

Cliff pursued a distorted, lead bass sound even when with the band Trauma. In this early part of his career, he achieved this using a Bass Balls Autowah and a Big Muff fuzz pedal. He later used a Morley fuzz/wah pedal, which quickly became a key part of his sound. Good examples of the fuzz/wah can be heard on the tracks 'For Whom the Bell Tolls' and 'The Call of Ktulu' from the *Ride the Lightning* album – be sure to check out the isolated bass track for 'For Whom the Bell Tolls', which is widely available on YouTube. Morley now make the Cliff Burton Tribute Series Power Fuzz Wah pedal.

AMPLIFICATION

During the early part of his time with Metallica, Cliff used a Randall 300-Watt amplifier and Randall 1x18 and 2x12 cabinets. By the time of the *Ride the Lightning* album, he was using a Mesa Boogie 400+ amplifier with Mesa Boogie 4x12 and 1x15 cabinets. He continued to use this setup throughout the *Master of Puppets* tour.

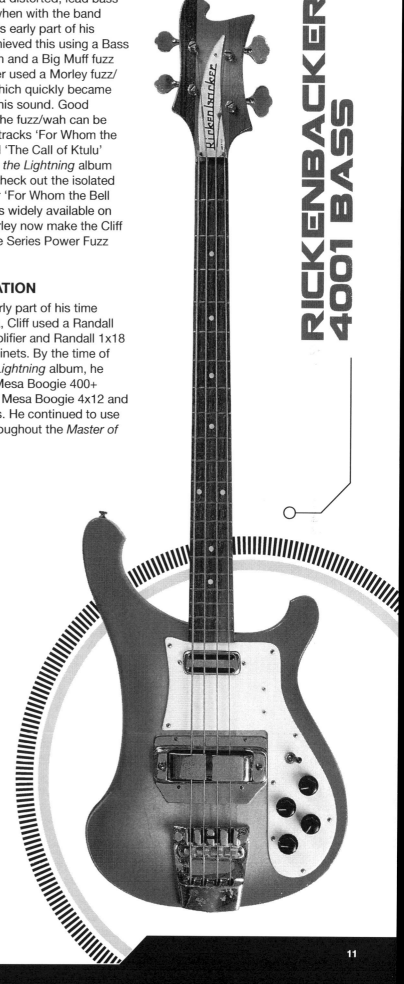

RICKENBACKER 4001 BASS

PERFORMANCE NOTES

'Master of Metal' is a fast-rock track written in the spirit of Metallica's much-loved *Master of Puppets* period. This piece features all of the classic Metallica ingredients, including those that bassist Cliff Burton was largely responsible for, such as the use of odd time signatures, harmony guitar lines and the use of different musical styles within one composition. Naturally, it also includes a bass solo.

The piece opens with a two-bar intro that establishes the quick tempo. Note that the last note of the second bar is B♭, the diminished fifth interval from the root, E. Metallica – and most other hard rock/metal bands – use the diminished fifth extensively in their writing as its sinister sound fits perfectly with the style.

At letter A, the main riff begins. This is similar in style to the verse riff from 'Master of Puppets' and is essentially a series of eighth notes on the open E-string, punctuated with different, accented tones every three notes. These accented notes work downwards through the E blues scale (E- G-A-B♭-B-D-E) before hitting an F at the end of the second bar. This F is a half step away from the root note E – again, half step intervals are often used in this style of music as they can sound quite sinister. The line restarts in the third bar but ends in a very different way in the fourth: with a bar of 5/8 time. Because 5/8 has a eighth note-based pulse rather than a quarter note, it feels like the groove 'trips over itself'. This can be a difficult part to play rhythmically, and I advise that you study both the included audio version and the Metallica song 'Master of Puppets', which also features this concept. Again, note the diminished fifth interval between the F and the B in this bar.

At bar 7 the groove remains the same whilst the drums drop into a half time feel. At bar 11, the 'a tempo' direction returns the piece to the original feel.

At letter B a new, much simpler section begins. The bassline here is played off of the open A-string,

hitting E and F notes, the latter of which is then held for a complete bar. Note the use of harmony guitars here, this was one of the key musical ingredients that Cliff Burton brought to the band thanks to his understanding of music theory.

At C we return to the main groove, this time without the 5/8 bars. This sets up the transition into the bass solo, at letter D.

The bass solo begins with the same groove from letter D, played an octave higher and with a fuzz pedal – on the recording I used the Morley Cliff Burton Tribute Series Power Fuzz/Wah pedal (See Fig.1). Because you will no longer be using the open E-string, the string crossing required here is more challenging – practice this part slowly, it's harder than it looks. After three iterations of this part, there is an ascending line in bars 37-38. This part climbs up the E blues scale using groupings of three notes. At bar 39 an arpeggio-based part begins – this line was inspired by the classic Cliff Burton bass solo 'Anesthesia (Pulling Teeth)', found on the first Metallica album *Kill 'Em All*. During this section, E minor, D,

C and B arpeggios are played. For the E minor, I recommend fretting the E at the fourteenth fret of the D-string with the second finger – this will allow you to reach the G at the twelfth fret with your first finger and the B at the sixteenth fret with your fourth. When the chord changes to D, fret the D with the second finger, the F♯ with the first and the A with the fourth. This same fingering can then be used for the C and B chords. Note that the first time through the sequence you will play the B major arpeggio phrase in bars 45-46, marked with the first time ending. The second time through, you will play the second time ending, which contains an ascending line that will take you into the upper register of the bass. When playing the first bar of this phrase, I recommend starting with the first finger of your fretting hand on the B at the ninth fret of the D-string. This will enable you to play all of the notes in this bar using the finger-per-fret method. Take care to play the hammer-ons as written here – at this tempo they provide a much-needed break for your picking hand. In the second bar of this phrase (bar 48) you will be playing an ascending figure using slides. As you will have

Fig. 1: The Morley Cliff Burton Tribute Series Power Fuzz/Wah Pedal

STYLE TIPS

- Fast unison riffs with guitars
- Use of odd time signatures
- Harmony guitar lines
- Distorted, lead bass solo
- Use of arpeggio figures

ended the previous bar with your fourth finger on the G at the twelfth fret of the G-string, you will need to use this finger for all of the notes in this bar, sliding it upwards as far as the nineteenth fret. You'll then need to quickly switch to put your first finger on this note for the beginning of bar 49.

The fingering for the next couple of bars is a little unusual, and quite tricky: play the D at the nineteenth fret with your first finger and use the third to hammer-on to the E at the twenty-first. Pull off back to the D, then slide the first finger down to the C at the seventeenth fret. The D can then be played with the third finger and the A on the string below with the second finger. The first finger will now be in position to slide downwards from the C to the B at the sixteenth fret. Use the second finger to fret the G which slides up to the A, and the first to play the C. The second finger should then perform the slide from the A up to the B, putting the first finger in place to play the D, starting the phrase again. The same fingering will work for the next two bars in the sequence, with the final two E's being fretted with the second finger.

For the descending line in bars 55-56 I recommend the following: fret the D at the nineteenth fret with the first finger and use the third to perform the hammer-on to the E at the twenty-first fret. Pull-off to the D, then slide the first finger down to the C. Hammer-on to the D, pull-off

back to the B, then slide the first finger down to the B at the sixteenth fret. In the next bar, start with the first finger fretting the B and perform the hammer-on and pull-off before sliding this finger down to the A. After hammering-on and pulling-off again, slide the first finger down to G, then to F$\sharp$.

In bar 57 a new ascending phrase begins. I recommend starting with your first finger fretting the E at the fourteenth fret of the D-string. You'll be able to stay in this position for much of the next six bars. For the descending triplet line in bars 63 and 64, start with your first finger on the D at the nineteenth fret. As you descend, use the first and third fingers for all hammer-ons and pull-offs that use intervals of a tone and the first and second for those that use a half step. Fingerings have been indicated above the notes in the score. This phrase ends on a D$\sharp$, briefly hinting at the E harmonic minor scale. In the next bar, a double stop chord of E at the ninth fret of the G-string and the low E is played, bringing the solo to a close.

When playing this solo, you'll need to consider fingerings very carefully and work on making all of the lines as clean as possible. Playing with fuzz/distortion shows up every little bit of fretbuzz or string noise and can be a very unforgiving sound.

At letter E a new section of the piece begins. We're now in 3/4 time at a much slower tempo and in the

key of D minor. The bassline is also far simpler during this section and outlines a simple chord progression. The line here is based around a root-fifth-octave pattern for most of the chords but note the use of the major third (C$\sharp$) for the A chord in bar 72, and the use of the ninth (G) on the F chords in bars 74 and 82. This section – which is similar to the middle section of Metallica's 'Orion' (co-written by Burton) – features another harmony guitar melody.

At letter F the key switches back to E minor and we're back in 4/4 time. This final riff – also reminiscent of one of the riffs from 'Orion' – is based off of the open E-string. The eighth note-two sixteenth notes 'gallop' rhythm is punctuated by descending chromatic phrases: E-E$\flat$-D and D-D$\flat$-C. After each of these a B$\flat$ (the diminished fifth again) is played. This is a challenging line to play at this speed and is made more difficult thanks to an unusual drum pattern.

SOUND ADVICE

This track was recorded using Aria Pro II bass. I played harder than I typically would and added a mild overdrive to the sound digitally. A small amount of compression was also added after the part had been recorded. For the bass solo section, I used the Morley Cliff Burton Tribute Series Power Fuzz/Wah pedal. The fuzz control was set almost to maximum and the wah element of the pedal was not used.

Obviously, using either an Aria Pro II or a Rickenbacker 4001 will get you close to Burton's tone, but regardless of the instrument used, I recommend favouring the neck pickup slightly and playing aggressively. You'll also need a fuzz pedal for both the basic tone and the bass solo.

Several of Cliff's isolated bass parts are now widely available on the Internet and can be heard on sites such as YouTube. Listening to Cliff's soloed part will be a big help if you are seeking to emulate his tone.

'MASTER OF METAL'

Written by Stuart Clayton

Drums: Jason Bowld
Guitar: Charlie Griffiths
Bass: Stuart Clayton

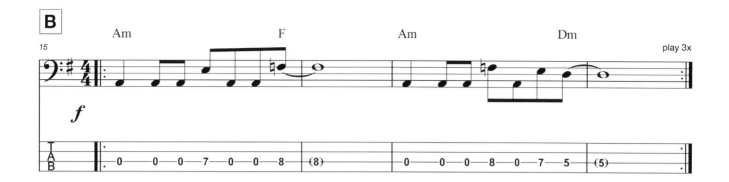

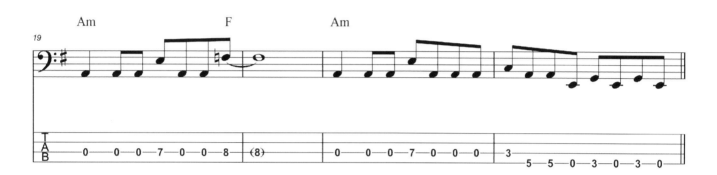

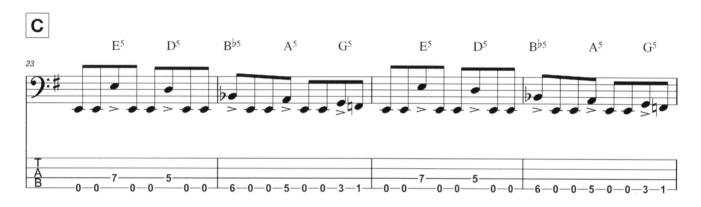

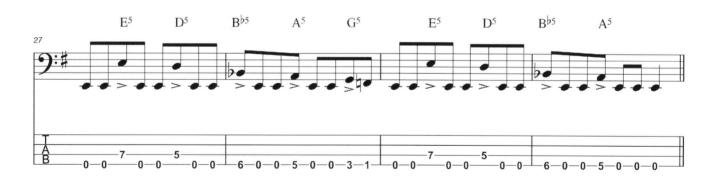

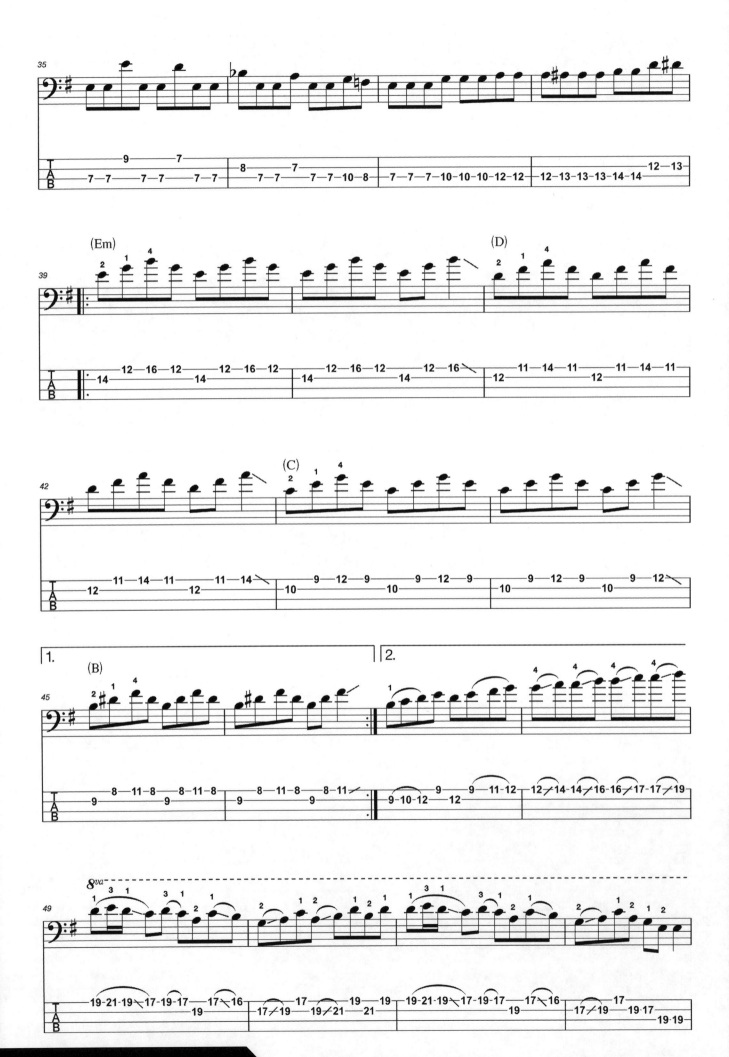

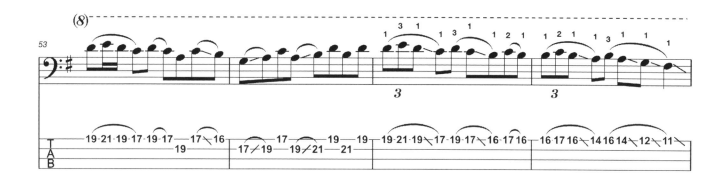

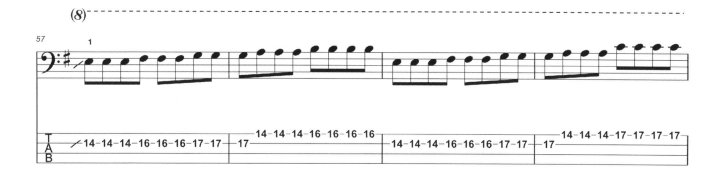

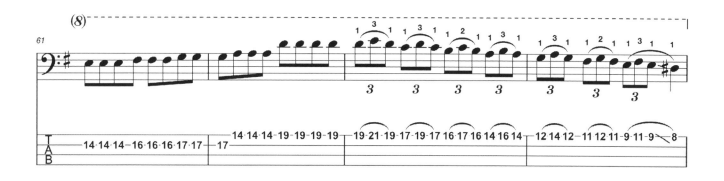

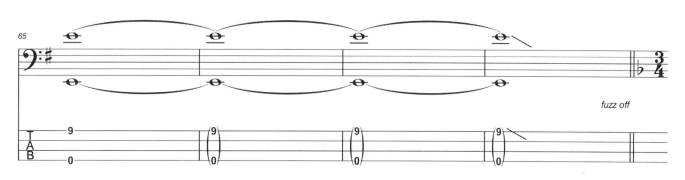

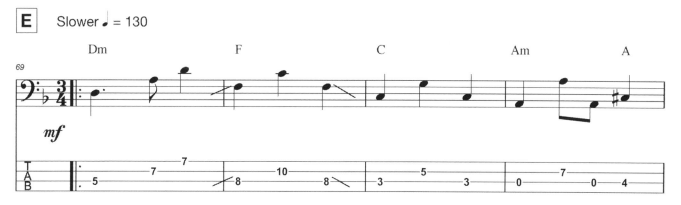

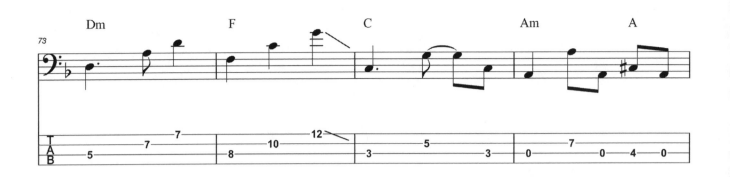

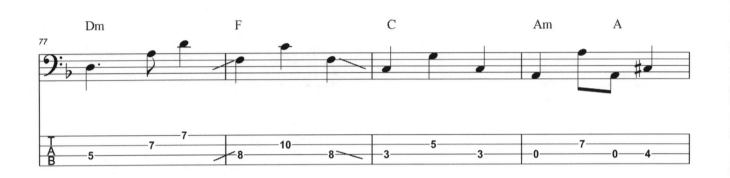

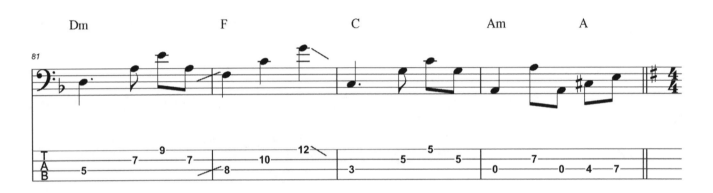

F

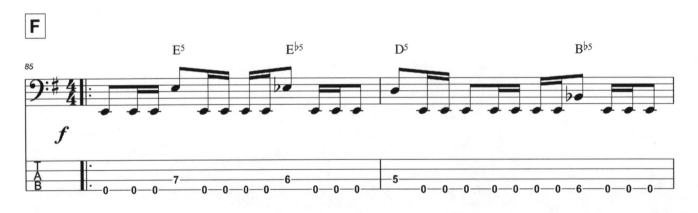

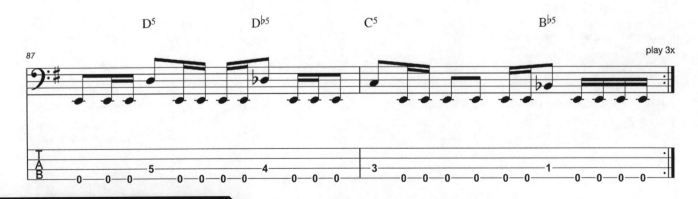

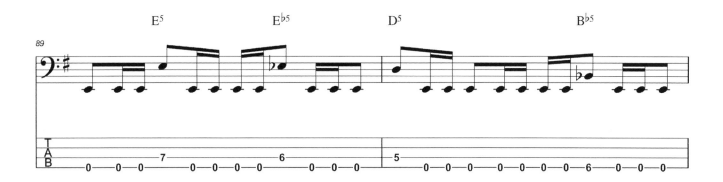

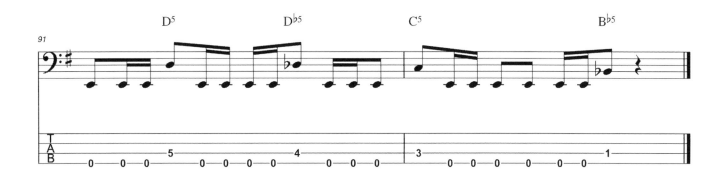

TIM COMMERFORD

The word 'uncompromising' seems to have been made for Rage Against the Machine bassist Tim Commerford. An extreme athlete with much of his body tattooed, Commerford faces every challenge head-on, whether it's off-road mountain biking, or laying down distorted, funk-fuelled grooves for some of the biggest bands in rock music. Politically outspoken, completely fearless and hailed for his unrelenting, aggressive bass style, Commerford has risen to become one of the most influential rock bassists in history.

Tim Commerford was born on February 26th, 1968. As many teenagers do, he developed an interest in music whilst at high school, initially through drumming and singing along to albums such as the Sex Pistols' *Never Mind the Bollocks* with his friend, Zack de la Rocha. He later took up the bass guitar after watching the annual rock show at his school in Irvine, California: observing that nobody ever seemed to want to play bass, he reasoned that he'd be able to gig in more local bands if he did. His initial influences on the instrument were bassists such as Sid Vicious of the Sex Pistols, Gene Simmons of KISS and Steve Harris of Iron Maiden. Later in his teens, he discovered progressive rock music and fell in love with the playing of Geddy Lee, the bassist with Rush. His own style began to develop as he taught himself by playing along with albums by his favourite artists, notably Rush's *Moving Pictures*.

After gigging in local bands for a number of years, in 1991 Commerford and his friend Zack de la Rocha were encouraged by a mutual friend to get together with guitarist Tom Morello, whose band Lock Up had just split. Realising that they would indeed work well together, the three contacted drummer Brad Wilk – who had unsuccessfully auditioned for Lock Up – and asked him to join them. In line with the left-wing political leanings of de la Rocha and Morello, the new group adopted the name Rage Against the Machine and performed their first show on October 23rd, 1991, at California State University. With their uniquely aggressive brand of hip-hop-infused hard rock, the band immediately began to cultivate a strong local following and it wasn't long before their 12-track demo tape was attracting major label interest. The band signed with Epic Records in 1992 and released their first single 'Killing in the Name' in November of that year. The uncensored version of this song features the word 'fuck' no less than seventeen times and so unsurprisingly, it received minimal promotion in the U.S. It quickly became popular in the UK and Europe however, notably after the uncensored version was accidentally played in full during the UK Top 40 Chart countdown.

The band's highly political, funk-fuelled hard rock sound quickly proved infectious, and subsequent singles 'Bullet in the Head' and 'Bombtrack' only added to their popularity. By the time the band's self-titled debut album was released in November 1993, Rage Against the Machine had become a sensation, with the album charting well around the world. Bass players quickly found plenty to love on the album, with Commerford's hard-hitting fingerstyle riffs on tracks such as 'Bombtrack' and 'Bullet in the Head' – not to mention his funky slapped line on 'Take the Power Back' – all proving hugely influential. Thanks to his off-the-wall, effects-driven solos, guitarists were equally enthralled with Morello's unique approach to the guitar. Now, over twenty years later, Commerford and Morello's innovative playing on the band's debut continues to be an inspiration for young musicians. Unsurprisingly, *Rage Against the Machine* is ranked at #368 on *Rolling Stone* magazine's poll of the 500 Greatest Albums of All Time. The band toured extensively in the year following the release of the album, appearing at Lollapalooza in 1993 and supporting Suicidal Tendencies on their tour.

Rage Against the Machine's fans had to wait until 1996 for the band's follow-up album. Preceded by the single 'Bulls on Parade', *Evil Empire* continued in the same vein, again

pairing Commerford and Wilk's unstoppable rhythm section with Morello's distinctive guitar work and de la Rocha's aggressive, politically infused vocal raps. Bass players again found plenty to get their teeth into, with the distorted riffing of 'Bulls of Parade', 'Snakecharmer' and 'Year of tha Boomerang' being undeniable highlights. The album topped the U.S. Billboard Top 200 Chart upon release, quickly rising to triple platinum status. In addition, the song 'Tire Me' won the band their first Grammy Award in 1997, for Best Metal Performance.

Rage Against the Machine released *The Battle of Los Angeles* in 1999, which was another #1 hit. The album is notable for the tracks 'Testify', 'Calm Like a Bomb' and 'Guerrilla Radio', the latter of which later won the band the 2001 Grammy Award for Best Hard Rock Performance.

Having courted substantial controversy throughout their career to date, Rage Against the Machine split following an incident at the MTV Video Music Awards in September 2000. After performing 'Testify', the band were incensed when the award for Best Rock Video went to rivals Limp Bizkit – in protest, Commerford climbed up onto part of the stage set during their acceptance speech. He and his bodyguard were subsequently arrested and were later charged with disorderly conduct. Shortly after, Zack de la Rocha announced his departure from the group. An already recorded album of cover songs – *Renegades* – was released in December 2000 and was followed in 2003 by the live album *Live at the Grand Olympic Auditorium*, which documented the band's final two shows.

Following de la Rocha's departure from the group, the remaining members decided to continue working together and began auditioning new vocalists. Seeking to avoid comparisons with de la Rocha, they resisted hiring another rapper and at producer Rick Rubin's suggestion, auditioned former Soundgarden vocalist Chris Cornell. The result was a new band: Audioslave. Pairing the aggressive Rage rhythm section with a more melodic vocalist turned out to be a winning formula, with the new group

entering the studio in May 2001 with Rubin producing. Although management squabbles briefly led to Cornell exiting the band in March 2002, he was eventually coaxed back and later in the year the band released their debut single 'Cochise'. Anchored by a classic Commerford bassline, the song was a success upon its release, as was the band's self-titled debut album, which followed later in the same year. The band's second single 'Like a Stone' was released in January 2003 and quickly became their biggest hit, topping both the Billboard Hot Mainstream Rock Tracks and the Hot Modern Rock Tracks Charts.

Audioslave's second album *Out of Exile* arrived in May 2005, preceded by the successful singles 'Be Yourself' and 'Your Time Has Come'. The album was critically well-received and went straight to the top of the Billboard 200 Chart upon release. The band's third album *Revelations* followed in September 2006. Although released to positive reviews and initially impressive sales, the band put off touring to promote it whilst Cornell and Morello considered solo projects. The band

TOP TRACKS

'Bombtrack'
Rage Against the Machine

'Killing in the Name'
Rage Against the Machine

'Take the Power Back'
Rage Against the Machine

'Bullet in the Head'
Rage Against the Machine

'Know Your Enemy'
Rage Against the Machine

'Bulls On Parade'
Rage Against the Machine –
Evil Empire

'Guerrilla Radio'
Rage Against the Machine –
The Battle of Los Angeles

'Cochise'
Audioslave – *Audioslave*

'Mountain Lion'
Future User – *SteroidsOrHeroin*

'Knucklehead'
Wakrat – *Wakrat*

split in February 2007, shortly after an announcement was made that Rage Against the Machine would reunite for a one-off show at the Coachella Valley Music and Arts Festival that April.

Following their successful show at the Coachella festival, Rage Against the Machine toured throughout 2007 and 2008. In a somewhat surprising development, in December 2009 they became the subject of an online campaign in the UK to prevent an X Factor (TV talent show) finalist achieving the coveted Christmas #1 single. With the band's expletive-littered song 'Killing in the Name' considered the most appropriate rebuttal to the perceived manipulation of the record-buying public, Rage Against the Machine were suddenly very much back in the limelight. The campaign was supported by notable musicians all over the world – including Paul McCartney, Muse, the Prodigy and Stereophonics – as well as the band themselves, who agreed to donate all proceeds from the single to

charity, as well as pledging to play a free concert in the UK in 2010. The song went on to achieve the biggest download sales total in a first week ever in the UK charts, easily reaching the number one spot at Christmas. The band subsequently played 'The Rage Factor', a free concert held in Finsbury Park, London in June 2010. Following the success of this concert, the band headlined a series of festivals around the UK and Europe that year.

Although each member of the band has indicated a willingness to record new material, to date this has not happened. The band's many fans have had to be content with the 2012 release of the 20th Anniversary Edition of their debut album and a live DVD of the Finsbury Park show.

In the absence of active projects from either Rage Against the Machine or Audioslave, in 2013, Commerford immersed himself in a new band named Future User. Predominantly a studio-based project, Future User featured Commerford – who sang lead vocals as well as playing bass – alongside keyboardist/programmer Jordan Tarlow and drummer Jon Knox. Brendon O'Brien, who had previously produced albums for both Rage and Audioslave, played guitar and produced their debut album,

SteroidsOrHeroin. The band's music – which Commerford has described as 'Progtronic' combines elements of progressive rock and electronic music, with strong melodic content. Despite a heavily produced, electronic sound, Commerford's bass plays a dominant role: 'Mountain Lion', the third single from the album is a notable highlight, featuring a demanding sixteenth note-based line at a blistering tempo of 135bpm. Commerford has stated that he adopted a three-finger picking technique in order to play the line.

Ever one to court controversy, Commerford's work in Future User has been no exception. In the band's video for their debut single 'Mountain Lion', they water-boarded tennis player John McEnroe (willingly), while Commerford injected himself with a performance enhancing drug, performed a blood transfusion and finally set himself on fire. In addition, the video for 'Voodoo Juju', features real-life footage from Commerford's spinal surgery. The video – which was intended as an indictment of the U.S. healthcare system – also featured appearances from guitarist Tom Morello and Rush members Geddy Lee and Alex Lifeson. Commerford also donated some of his own blood to manufacture the band's limited edition red vinyl release of the album.

In addition to Future User, Commerford has also been active in the band WAKRAT, an alternative punk trio that he formed with guitarist/vocalist Laurent Grangeon and drummer Mathias Wakrat. The band's debut single 'Knucklehead' was released in September 2015, with their self-titled album following shortly afterwards.

In 2016, Commerford and fellow Rage Against the Machine bandmates Tom Morello and Brad Wilk announced a new rock/rap supergroup: Prophets of Rage. The band also includes Public Enemy's DJ and turntablist DJ Lord, rapper Chuck D, as well as B-Real, lead rapper with Cypress Hill. Unsurprisingly, the new group combines the hard-hitting Rage Against the Machine sound with rapped vocals. The band released their debut EP *The Party's Over* in mid-2016.

Commerford with guitarist Tom Morello

BASS GUITARS

When Tim first began playing bass, he had a Steinberger XP2, which he had seen his hero Geddy Lee using. After finding that the instrument didn't work for him, he sold it and bought a Fender Jazz Bass. He then switched to a Music Man StingRay, which was the instrument that he did the majority of his early practice with.

By the time he recorded the first Rage Against the Machine album he was still using his StingRay bass. Whilst on tour, he purchased a second model in black to use as a backup but became frustrated at how different the two instruments sounded. This led him to switch to Fender Jazz basses, which he continued to use throughout the remainder of his time with Rage Against the Machine and during the early part of his time with Audioslave. At this stage he was favouring a Jazz bass with a maple Precision neck and a Leo Quann Badass bridge. This instrument was fitted with the pickups from the Jazz bass that he destroyed on stage with Rage Against the Machine during the MTV show in 2000. He had found these pickups in the UK during a tour and had rewound them by hand. Tim used several Jazz basses during this period, one which was tuned to the low strings of a 5-string (B-E-A-D) and which was used extensively on the first Audioslave album. Over the next few years he continued to use his Jazz basses together with Lakland instruments.

By the time he was playing with Future User in 2015 he was using Steinberger basses again, which he can be seen playing in the video for 'Mountain Lion'. He owns at least seven of these unique-looking instruments, including two L2 and four XL2 models. For the debut WAKRAT album, he used a Lakland Joe Osborn signature bass.

In 2016, Tim switched back to Music Man basses and now uses StingRay HH and HS models for shows with WAKRAT and Prophets of Rage. His only modification to the instruments has been to install a thumb rest between the two pickups. Tim takes ten of these basses on tour, with a separate model for each tuning required, each with a backup.

Tim prefers to play with a high action and uses heavy gauge Ernie Ball strings: .050-.105.

EFFECTS

After using a Marshall Guv'nor distortion pedal for many years, Tim eventually built his own distortion unit in the early 2000s. This pedal – which he continues to use – has only an on/off button and Tim has never spoken about its construction, considering his distorted tone to be a closely guarded secret.

When working with Future User Tim used a lot of different pedals including Eventide TimeFactor and PitchFactor pedals, a Markbass synth, an Akai SB1 Deep Impact, a Dirty Boy Bass Bully, a Zvex Wooly Mammoth, a Skychord Truck Loud, a WMD Geiger Counter, an Electro Harmonix Talking Machine, a Boss OC-2 Octaver and Chunk Systems Brown Dog and Agent Funk pedals. Some of these pedals were used in combination as Tim and the band experimented with synth bass sounds.

AMPLIFICATION

Tim has used Ampeg amps and cabinets for many years. His current rig consists of two amps: a mid-70s SVT with the original tubes for his clean tone, and an SVT2-Pro for his distorted tone. These are run through Ampeg 8x10 and 4x10 cabinets. Tim also owns an Acoustic 360 amp which he used during the sessions for the Future User album.

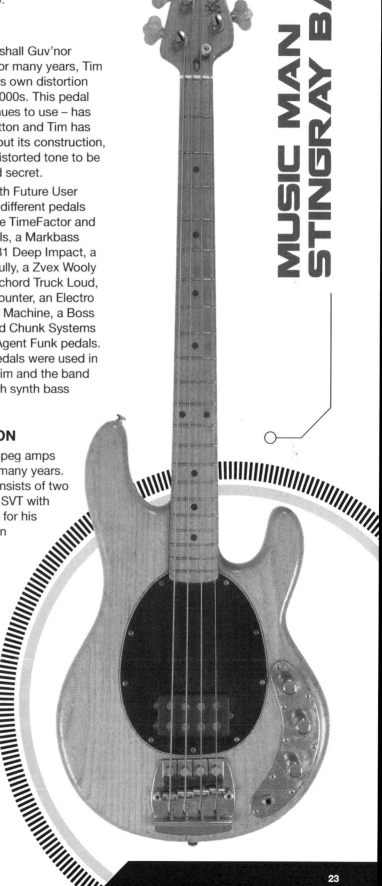

MUSIC MAN STINGRAY BASS

PERFORMANCE NOTES

'Outrage' is written in the style of the aggressive funk rock played by bassist Tim Commerford and his band Rage Against the Machine. As is typical of most the band's tracks, the bass has a very prominent role here.

The opening A section of this piece has a two-note motif that begins each bar during the section. Both notes should be slapped hard for a punchy sound. These notes are followed in each bar by popped double stops – for all of these, you should pop the notes with the first and second fingers together. The first double stop is a minor third interval from F♯ – this suggests a minor tonality to the piece. Note that the location of this double stop within the beat is heavily syncopated, falling on the 'e' of '1-e-and-a' vocalisation. This type of syncopation is common in funk music, which is a big part of the band's style. The double stops in the second bar are all power chords, descending chromatically from C♯ down to B. Again, these are heavily syncopated, falling on the 'e' and 'a' of the beat. The double stop in the third bar is a power chord from F♯, syncopated in the same way as the first. The fourth bar is identical to the second. These four bars are repeated.

At letter B a new riff begins, played in unison with the guitar. This is played with the fingerstyle technique, and you'll want to really dig in and play this aggressively in order to mimic Tim's hard-hitting style. When playing

this line, be sure to play the hammer-ons where indicated and ensure that the rests are indeed played as rests – doing so will help enormously with the groove. This four-bar line is also repeated.

At letter C another new groove begins, also played with the fingerstyle technique. Again, the correct use of hammer-ons and rests is crucial to the feel. Note the use of the diminished fifth interval between the F♯ and the C at the end of the first bar – this adds a menacing sound to the riff and is an interval that is commonly used by many hard rock/metal bands. There is a descending blues scale lick in the second bar: you can slide into the F♯ that begins this line. This part is followed by a repeat of the earlier groove from letter B.

At letter E a new groove begins, with the bass being featured heavily. The line here is a continuous sixteenth note part that is based on the F♯ blues scale. Again, the diminished fifth interval features heavily here. You'll need to continue to play aggressively throughout this part of the song, although the dynamic does drop downward at the beginning of the section as the rest of the band drops out. This bassline is repeated throughout this entire section, so your timing and stamina will need to be up to the task of keeping the sound and tone consistent. The line also remains the same as the drums play with a double time feel from bar 24. This part of the track

STYLE TIPS

- Pentatonic and blues scale-based unison riffs
- Aggressive tone and playing techniques
- Use of slap bass technique
- Hard-plucked power chords
- Prominent role for the bass

is reminiscent of Tim's line from the middle section of the classic Rage Against the Machine song 'Bullet in the Head'.

The final section of the piece at letter F is a recap of the main groove, heard earlier at the B section.

SOUND ADVICE

In order to get as close as possible to Tim's tone on the first Rage Against the Machine album, I recorded 'Outrage' using a 1976 Music Man StingRay. The volume and tone controls were all turned up full and the bass was strung with relatively new strings, gauge .045, .065, .085, .105. The action was set higher than I would personally like, but this meant that I was able to play quite aggressively, as Tim does. The recorded bass tone was EQ'd and compressed digitally.

Obviously, using a Music Man bass (or any bass with a single humbucking pickup) will enable you to get quite close to the recorded tone. If your bass has two pickups, I recommend using both, but favouring the neck pickup slightly. However, Tim's sound is about more than the instrument itself and the key to playing pieces of this nature is aggressive – but accurate – playing. You'll get closer to the required sound if you can really 'dig in', so a slightly higher-than-normal action will help. A little fretbuzz and string rattle is not undesirable here.

'OUTRAGE'

Written by Stuart Clayton

Drums: Jason Bowld
Guitar: Jamie Hunt
Bass: Stuart Clayton

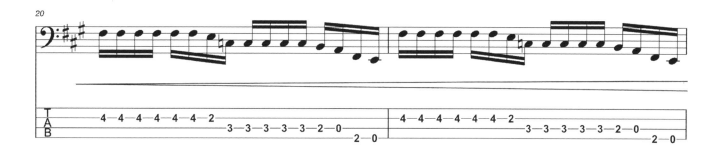

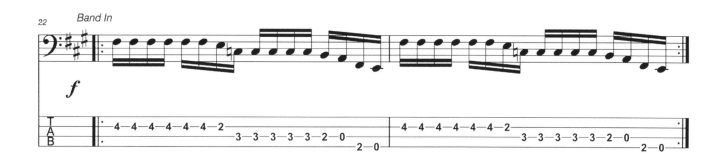

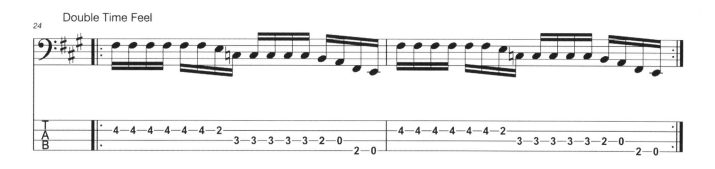

F

FLEA

As a member of funk-rock group the Red Hot Chili Peppers, Flea has been a bass icon for over thirty years. Since the release of the band's self-titled debut album in 1984, he has become one of the world's most popular bassists, winning the *Bass Player* magazine title of Best Funk Bassist for three consecutive years. In 1996 he also won the Bass Player of the Year award from the same magazine. As the Chili Peppers have evolved as a band, so too has Flea evolved as a bass player, developing his song-writing abilities and understanding of music theory as well as his formidable bass skills.

Flea – real name Michael Balzary – was born in Melbourne, Australia on October 16th, 1962. His family moved to New York when he was five years old and a few years later, his parents divorced. After his father returned to Australia, his mother married Walter Abdul Urban, a jazz bass player. Soon after, the family relocated to Los Angeles, where Michael began to develop his own interest in music. Growing up in a musical household – where jam sessions were regular occurrences – he developed a love of jazz, and at the age of ten began playing the trumpet, taking inspiration from musicians such as Miles Davis and Dizzy Gillespie. Within a couple of years, he was performing with the L.A. Junior Philharmonic and the LACC Jazz Band.

As a teen Michael attended Fairfax High School, where he met singer Anthony Kiedis and guitarist Hillel Slovak. Through his new friends, he was introduced to rock and punk music, genres he had previously had little experience of. Hillel asked Michael to join his band Anthym as the bass player, offering to teach him how to play. He agreed and was playing gigs with the group – who renamed themselves What Is This? – within a couple of weeks. Whilst working with the band,

Michael continued to check out rock acts such as Led Zeppelin and Jimi Hendrix.

Now nicknamed 'Flea', Michael drifted from band to band for a while before forming a new group with Hillel, Anthony Kiedis (vocals) and Jack Irons (drums). Known initially as Tony Flow and the Miraculous Masters of Mayhem, the band played their first gig as a support act at the Rhythm Lounge in L.A. Their initial performance consisted largely of improvised music over which Kiedis rapped poetry. Their performance was well-received however and they were asked to return. By the time they next played, they had renamed themselves the Red Hot Chili Peppers. Over the next few months the band continued playing the local club circuit, building a following and developing their original material.

By 1983 the band had begun to attract record company interest and were eventually signed by EMI on a seven album deal. Unfortunately, just prior to this Hillel Slovak and Jack Irons had signed a deal at MCA with What Is This?, with whom they had continued to work alongside the

Chili Peppers. Opting to pursue the former group, the two quit the band and were replaced by drummer Cliff Martinez and guitarist Jack Sherman.

Produced by Gang of Four guitarist Andy Gill, the band's self-titled debut album was released in August 1984 to small-scale success. Although a far less accomplished album than those that would follow later, the record is noteworthy in that it demonstrates Flea's potential – his bass playing is impressive throughout, from the chordal intro of 'True Men Don't Kill Coyotes', to his blistering slap solo on 'Out in L.A'. The band toured heavily in support of the album, but although they were able to continue building a loyal fan base, tensions between singer Kiedis and guitarist Sherman escalated to the point where Sherman was fired. He was replaced by original guitarist Hillel Slovak, who had by this point quit What Is This?.

For their next album, the band employed the production services of Parliament-Funkadelic legend George Clinton. They were able to establish a better musical connection with Clinton than they

had experienced with Gill, and the resulting album *Freaky Styley* (1985) consequently leaned more towards classic funk, with less emphasis on the guitar-driven rock that had permeated their first record. Unfortunately, upon its release the album sold poorly, despite garnering more favourable reviews than their first effort. Flea's growing fan base found plenty to enjoy on the record however, from the slap grooves of 'Jungle Man' to the funky fingerstyle lines on tracks such as 'The Brother's Cup' and a cover of Sly & The Family Stone's 'If You Want Me to Stay'.

Drummer Cliff Martinez parted ways with the group after the *Freaky Styley* tour and was replaced by original drummer Jack Irons. This meant that the band's third album, *The Uplift Mofo Party Plan* (1987) was the first (and only) official release to feature all four original members. Although the recording of the album was made difficult by Slovak and Kiedis' drug addictions, the result was the band's most successful effort at the time, charting at 148 on the Billboard 200 chart. The album is an important one in the Chili Peppers discography, featuring some of their strongest

SELECTED DISCOGRAPHY

(All with the Red Hot Chili Peppers)

Red Hot Chili Peppers
'True Men Don't Kill Coyotes', 'Baby Appeal', 'Get Up & Jump', 'Mommy Where's Daddy?', 'Out In L.A.', 'Grand Pappy Du Plenty'

The Uplift Mofo Party Plan
'Fight Like A Brave', 'Funky Crime', 'Me & My Friends', 'Backwoods', 'Special Secret Song Inside', 'Walkin' on Down the Road', 'Love Trilogy'

Mother's Milk
'Good Times', 'Higher Ground', 'Subway To Venus', 'Nobody Weird Like Me', 'Stone Cold Bush', 'Pretty Little Ditty', 'Johnny, Kick a Hole in the Sky'

Blood Sugar Sex Magik
'If You Have to Ask', 'Funky Monks', 'Suck My Kiss', 'Mellowship Slinky in B Major', 'Give It Away', 'Apache Rose Peacock', 'Sir Psycho Sexy'

One Hot Minute
'Aeroplane', 'Deep Kick', 'Coffee Shop', 'My Friends', 'One Big Mob', 'Walkabout', 'Falling Into Grace' 'Transcending', 'Stretch'

Californication
'Around The World', 'Parallel Universe', 'Scar Tissue', 'Get On Top', 'Californication', 'I Like Dirt', 'Right On Time'

Stadium Arcadium
'Dani California', 'Charlie', 'Hump De Bump', 'She's Only 18', 'Torture Me', 'Warlocks', 'C'mon Girl', 'Tell Me Baby', 'Hard to Concentrate', '21st Century'

The Getaway
'Dark Necessities', 'We Turn Red', 'Sick Love', 'Go Robot', 'Feasting on the Flowers', 'Detroit', 'Dreams of a Samurai'

Flea with his Modulus 'punk bass'

material, together with some of Flea's most impressive bass work. Tracks such as 'Fight Like a Brave', 'Backwoods', 'Skinny Sweaty Man' and 'Love Trilogy' are all excellent examples of the hard-hitting slap bass style for which he was quickly becoming renowned. The band toured after the release of the album, significantly increasing their global fan base in the process. However, the tour – although successful – was beset with problems, mostly arising from Kiedis and Slovak's ongoing battles with heroin addiction. Sadly, a few days after returning home, Slovak died suddenly from a heroin

overdose. During the ensuing turmoil, drummer Jack Irons also parted company with the group.

After much soul-searching, Kiedis and Flea decided to continue with the group and after lengthy auditions, hired guitarist John Frusciante and drummer Chad Smith. With each new member proving to be a huge asset to the band, writing and recording for their next album went smoothly. Upon its release in August 1989, *Mother's Milk* quickly became the band's most commercially successful album thus far, reaching #52 on the Billboard 200 Chart. Singles 'Knock

Me Down' and 'Higher Ground' (a cover of the Stevie Wonder classic) brought the band further recognition through extensive coverage on MTV. Thanks to slap-heavy tracks such as 'Higher Ground', 'Nobody Weird Like Me' and 'Stone Cold Bush', Flea had by this point become one of the world's most popular bass players.

After signing a new record deal with Warner Bros., the Chili Peppers opted for a different approach for their fifth album. Acclaimed producer Rick Rubin was hired, and the band rented the California mansion in which magician Henry Houdini had once lived to write and record. The resulting album, *Blood Sugar Sex Magik* was written quickly and marked an obvious shift in style for both the band and for Flea. Abandoning the punk-rock spirit that had informed a significant portion of their previous work, the songs on *Blood Sugar Sex Magik* were predominantly stripped-back funk tunes that would prove enormously popular with their ever-growing fan base. Although at this point, he was best-known for his jaw-dropping slap technique, Flea all but abandoned the style on their new material, opting instead for simple but infectious fingerstyle lines that recalled the classic funk of bands such as Parliament/Funkadelic and The Meters. Tracks such as 'If You Have to Ask', 'Mellowship Slinky', 'Apache Rose Peacock' and 'Sir Psycho Sexy' are all excellent examples of Flea's playing at this point. The album itself was extremely well-received by critics and fans alike, its popularity bolstered by the success of singles 'Give It Away' and the ballad 'Under the Bridge'. The latter track would turn out to be the song that brought the band to a mainstream audience, reaching #2 on the Billboard Hot 100 and Hot Mainstream Rock Tracks Charts, and #13 on the UK Singles Chart.

Unfortunately, mainstream popularity came with a cost: in the middle of the *Blood Sugar Sex Magik* tour, guitarist John Frusciante quit the band, having become frustrated with their newfound success. Arik Marshall was hired to enable the group to complete the tour, although he was dismissed once it was completed. In the two years that followed, the band released the greatest hits package *What Hits?*, and *Out in L.A.*, a compilation of remixes and rarities, including early demos recorded as Tony Flow and the Miraculously Majestic Masters of Mayhem.

In 1994 the Red Hot Chili Peppers held auditions to replace Frusciante, eventually hiring former Jane's Addiction guitarist Dave Navarro. After a difficult writing and recording period, *One Hot Minute* was released in September 1995. The album was a departure from the slick funk of their previous effort and had a heavier, darker sound. Although the lyrical content certainly played a

part, this largely came as a result of both Navarro's guitar style and his penchant for layering multiple guitar parts, something Frusciante had never been keen to do. Despite the presence of two hit singles – 'My Friends' and 'Aeroplane', the album received a mixed reception from critics and fans alike. Fans of Flea's bass work had little to worry about however, since the album features some of his best work: 'Aeroplane' features some of his finest slap work, whilst 'Walkabout' has a fantastic fingerstyle funk line. As a result of these and other tracks, *One Hot Minute* has remained very popular with fans of Flea's playing.

After developing drug problems of his own, Dave Navarro was dismissed from the band in 1998. John Frusciante, who had recently completed a successful drug rehabilitation program was asked to re-join and accepted. The newly reunited band spent much of 1998 writing new material and entered the studio in early 1999 to record their efforts. The resulting album, *Californication* was another stylistic departure for the band, not only recalling the funk of *Blood Sugar Sex Magik*, but pairing it with a previously unheard, more melodic side. The album was a huge success, hitting the top spot in many charts around the world. The first single 'Scar Tissue' was a huge hit worldwide, hitting the number 1 spot on both the U.S. Billboard Modern Rock Tracks and Mainstream Rock Tracks Charts. Subsequent singles 'Around the World', 'Otherside' and 'Californication' all charted well, sealing the Chili Peppers' newfound position as one of the biggest bands in the world. As he had with *Blood Sugar Sex Magik*, Flea opted for fingerstyle grooves throughout much of the new album, with tracks such as 'Around the World' and 'Californication' standing out in particular. He also used a plectrum for the first time, on the song 'Parallel Universe', which has a relentless bassline that would be very challenging to play with the fingers.

The development of the band's writing continued on their next release, 2002's *By The Way*. This time around, they largely avoided the funk rock style that had played a big part on their previously albums, now leaning towards a significantly

more melodic, softer approach. This change in direction was led by Frusciante, who wrote much of the album's melodies and harmonies, whilst also experimenting with layered guitar parts and keyboards during the recording sessions. Although the record was another global hit for the band, many of their fans were disappointed at the lack of funk-driven tunes, with only the title track and 'Can't Stop' leaning in this direction.

In 2004 the band began working on their next album, reuniting with producer Rick Rubin once again, as well as returning to the mansion where they had recorded *Blood Sugar Sex Magik*. The resulting album, *Stadium Arcadium* (2006) was the longest ever written by the band, with no less than twenty-eight songs spread across two discs. The album – which was much more collaboratively written than its predecessor – proved extremely popular with the band's fan base, who welcomed the return of the funk element in their music. In particular, the album is notable for the track 'Hump de Bump', which is a deliberate call-back to their earlier work, and which shares similarities with 'American Ghost Dance' from *Freaky Styley*. This song also arguably features Flea's finest work on the album, pairing a hard-plucked chordal riff during the verse with a biting fingerstyle groove in the chorus. Further bass highlights from the album include lead single 'Dani California', 'Tell Me Baby', 'Charlie' and 'Warlocks'. The band toured extensively throughout 2006 and 2007, for the first time

WEBSITE LINKS

www.silverlakeconservatory.org
www.redhotchilipeppers.com
www.atomsforpeace.info

hiring an additional member, Josh Klinghoffer, who played additional guitars and keyboards live. Once the tour had concluded, John Frusciante announced his departure from the band, who subsequently promoted Klinghoffer to the vacant position. Following the tour, the Chili Peppers took a two-year hiatus, during which Flea studied piano and music theory at the University of Southern California.

In October 2009 the Red Hot Chili Peppers began writing for their next album *I'm With You*, which was released in August 2011. Again produced by Rick Rubin, the album was preceded by the release of the single 'The Adventures of Rain Dance Maggie', which was well-received by fans, hitting #1 in several

U.S. and Canadian charts. The album itself was also a hit, with fans of Flea's bass work finding plenty to get their teeth into on songs such as 'Monarchy of Roses', 'Factory of Faith', 'Ethiopia', 'Look Around' and 'The Adventures of Rain Dance Maggie'. Following the release of the album the band toured throughout 2011-12.

In 2014 the Red Hot Chili Peppers began work on their next album. Seeking a change, they decided to hire producer Danger Mouse for the album, making it the first album in twenty-five years that hadn't been recorded with Rick Rubin. 'Dark Necessities', the bass-driven debut single from the album was released on May 5th, 2016, charting at #1 on the majority of the U.S. charts. The album, *The Getaway* was released to favourable reviews on June 17th with the band embarking on a world tour shortly afterwards.

Aside from his ongoing commitments with the Red Hot Chili Peppers, Flea has involved himself in several

other projects over the last decade. Following a 2001 visit to Fairfax High School (which he had attended as a teenager), Flea was dismayed to find that the majority of the music education classes had been cut from the curriculum for budgetary reasons. His response was to found the Silverlake Conservatory of Music with his old friend Keith Barry, who was now a music teacher. The new school, based in Silverlake, Los Angeles offers scholarships, workshops, summer camps and private tuition. In 2012 he released a solo EP of instrumental music entitled *Helen Burns* in order to raise money to keep the school running.

In 2009 he joined Atoms for Peace, a supergroup assembled by Radiohead frontman Thom Yorke which performed the material from his 2006 solo album *The Eraser*. In 2013 the band released their own album, entitled *Amok*. He has also collaborated with Blur frontman Damon Albarn in a side project known as Rocket Juice & the Moon.

Flea playing his sunburst Modulus on the *I'm With You* tour

BASS GUITARS

During the band's early years, Flea frequently used Music Man basses. He recorded their debut album using a Cutlass and upgraded to a StingRay for *Freaky Styley*. Although he then favoured Spector LV and NS-2 basses during the recording of *The Uplift Mofo Party Plan* and *Mother's Milk*, he continued to use his StingRay basses live.

For the recording of *Blood Sugar Sex Magik* he predominantly used a Wal Mk II bass, alongside a StingRay 5-string for the songs that required the lower register. The majority of the *One Hot Minute* album was recorded with an Alembic Epic, aside from 'Aeroplane', which he recorded with a StingRay. 'Pea' was recorded on a Sigma acoustic bass.

In the mid-nineties Flea began what would become a decade-long relationship with Modulus, developing an instrument with them that would eventually be marketed as the Modulus FB4 Flea Bass. The FB4 featured a graphite neck, Badass bridge, Lane Poor pickup and an Aguilar OBP-1 preamp. Flea used several distinctive models, most notably the 'punk bass', which was painted red, white, and blue and decorated with stickers of his favourite punk bands (see photo on page 30). The majority of the *Californication* and *By the Way* albums were recorded with his Modulus basses, aside from the song 'Cabron', which he recorded with a 60s Vox bass.

Stadium Arcadium was recorded entirely using a '61 Fender Jazz bass, which Flea received as a gift from Zach Stevens at AOL. Flea's '61 Jazz is Shell Pink, an extremely rare colour. This bass was also used for the recording of *I'm With You*. Flea now owns a second '61 Jazz Bass, a gift from artist Damien Hirst. This model is decorated with butterflies.

In 2016, Fender announced a Flea signature model, which accurately replicated the colour and playwear of his Shell Pink bass. Despite his love of Fenders, Flea has continued to tour with his Modulus basses.

Concerned that young musicians would find it hard to buy an instrument of good quality, Flea began marketing his own line of basses in 2009. Built in China, the Flea Bass was a low budget instrument that came in a variety of bright colour schemes and in two scale lengths, 30" and 34". Flea ceased selling these in 2011, after becoming frustrated with the business element of the venture.

Flea uses GHS Boomer strings, favouring a gauge of .045-.105. He has a signature string set with GHS. He favours a very low action.

EFFECTS

Flea has used a lot of effects pedals during his career with the Red Hot Chili Peppers, most notably envelope filters and fuzz pedals. He used a Mu-Tron III envelope filter on 'Sir Psycho Sexy' from *Blood Sugar Sex Magik* and an Electro-Harmonix BassBalls on 'Coffee Shop' from *One Hot Minute*. More recently he has been using an Electro-Harmonix Q-Tron in his live setup. He is also currently favouring a Malekko B:Assmaster distortion pedal and a Moogerfooger MF-103 12-stage phaser.

AMPLIFICATION

Flea is a long-time user of Gallien Kruger amps and cabinets. During the eighties and nineties, he was most often seen using the 800RB heads, with 4x10 and 1x15 cabinets. He switched to the 2001RB heads in the early 2000s. After a brief time with Acoustic 360 amplifiers and 361 cabinets in 2011, he is now using Gallien Krueger again.

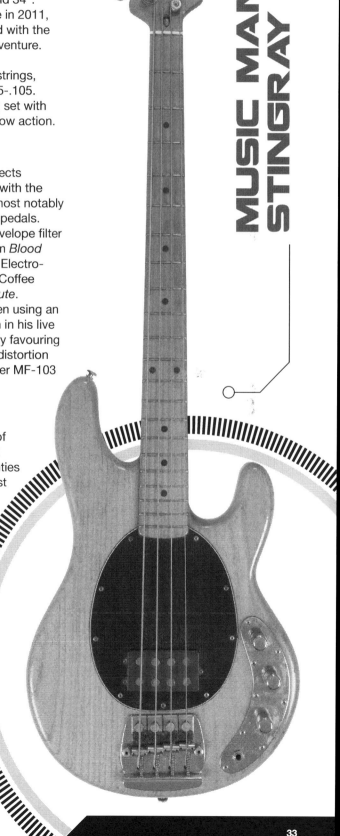

MUSIC MAN
STINGRAY BASS

PERFORMANCE NOTES

'Flea Bites' has been written to represent the fingerstyle-funk side of Flea's playing. You'll need some effects pedals to play this piece as heard on the audio track – a fuzz and an envelope filter, both of which Flea uses regularly.

This piece opens in a similar style to 'All Around the World', from *Californication*. Here, the bass plays a fast, descending E minor pentatonic riff using distortion. Note the use of a three-note grouping throughout much of the first bar of the sequence – be sure to play the hammer-ons as written here as they will help keep the line smooth. In the second bar there is a turnaround figure on the last two beats that references the E blues scale by including the B$^\flat$. This two-bar riff is played four times, although you should note the 3/4 bar on the fourth time through.

The bassline at letter B is a fingerstyle groove that is heavy on chord tones from the implied D^7 chord (D, F$^\sharp$, A and C). Note the use of a hammer-on from the minor third to the major third (F to F$^\sharp$) in the first bar – this idea reoccurs frequently throughout the line and is common in funk bass grooves. Similarly, moving from the root note (D), up to the major sixth (B) then to the minor seventh (C) is also a very common phrase. This line is relatively simple to play but be sure to focus on your timing and make sure that rests are indeed played as rests. You should also 'dig in' and play quite hard here.

At letter C a new part begins, based around G. Note that on the second beat, the minor third – major third idea is used again, although this time it is played as a bend. The second bar of this two-bar sequence is a simple, eighth note-based part on B$^\flat$ and A. This line is played four times during this section.

At letter D we revert back to the groove from letter B, although this time there are some interesting fills. The first of these occurs in the second bar of the line, at bar 27. After playing the ascending D-B-C figure, an open G is played, followed by a fast triplet on the D-string, played using two successive hammer-ons. This is followed by a C, played on the G-string, then a slide from A up to the C on the D-string. After the C, the F$^\sharp$ at the eleventh fret of the G-string is played. You can allow these two notes to ring together briefly. These are the 'most colourful' notes from the underlying D^7 chord – the third and the seventh. Using them together in this way is another very common funk move. The second fill that you should take note of occurs in bar 31. Here, a descending phrase from D-C-A is played, followed by another phrase higher up on the neck. Note that the ghost note between the two phrases is there for rhythmic interest only. The second phrase uses the minor third to major third idea that was discussed earlier. This leads us to the end of this part, which is followed by a repeat of the earlier C section, at letter E.

Letter F is the outro and features a new bass groove, played with an envelope filter. This line has a nice idea that begins each two bar phrase: after playing the A, you will play chord tones from the underlying A^7 chord, approached using double chromatic passing notes. The first of these is the C$^\sharp$ at the sixth fret of the G-string. This is the third of the chord and is approached from below by B and C. The same approach is then used for the root of the chord (A) and the fifth (E). Each time this line is played, it is followed by a different part in the next bar. You'll see that in bar 50 there is another lick that ascends to the colourful third and seventh (C$^\sharp$ and G) notes. Note that here they are played in one position (C$^\sharp$ with G above), then higher on the neck (G with C$^\sharp$ above). These notes can always be inverted in this way as they are a diminished fifth apart.

STYLE TIPS

- Use of fuzz and envelope filter effects
- Aggressive playing style
- Bassline is heavy on chord tones
- Use of classic funk moves such as the minor third moving to the major third
- Use of double chromatic approach notes

SOUND ADVICE

I recorded this track using a 1976 Music Man StingRay bass with a 2-band EQ. The instrument was strung with a set of new GHS Flea Signature Boomers gauge .045-.105. The bass was recorded direct into Logic and the EQ was tweaked to boost the mids slightly at 215Hz. Some fairly heavy compression was also applied digitally.

I played quite aggressively throughout, which resulted in a little fretbuzz and string noise, neither of which is undesirable when replicating Flea's tone. For the intro I used a Morley Fuzz Wah pedal with the fuzz almost on full (the wah was not used). During the outro section I used an MXR M82 envelope filter set as follows: Dry: 12 o'clock, FX: 3 o'clock, Decay: full, Q: 2 o'clock, Sensitivity: 3 o'clock.

Using either a Fender Jazz or a Music Man bass will get you close to Flea's sound. The important thing is to lower your action to the point where a little fretbuzz is introduced and play quite hard – Flea really digs in when playing fingerstyle lines and this is a big part of his sound.

'FLEA BITES'

Written by Stuart Clayton

Drums: Jason Bowld
Keys: Stuart Clayton
Guitar: Steve Banks
Bass: Stuart Clayton

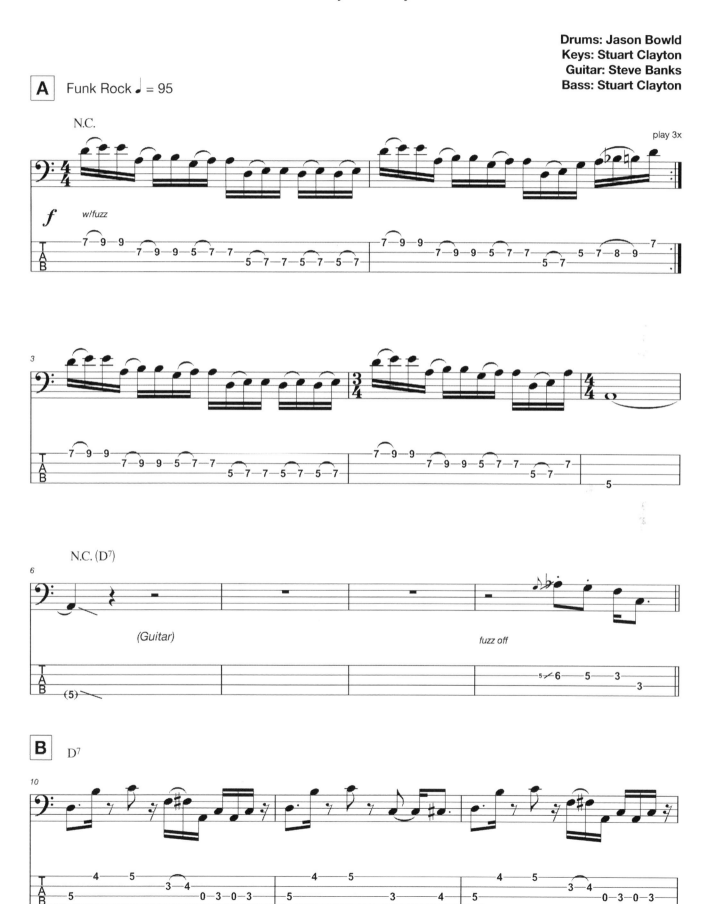

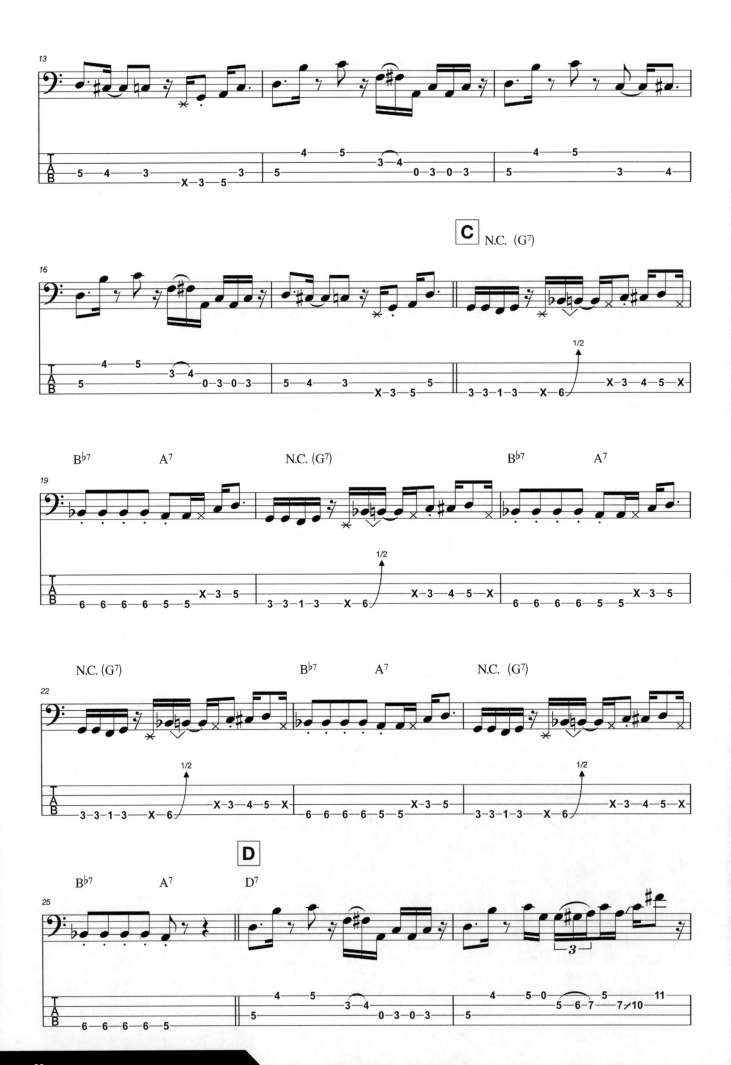

E

N.C. (G⁷)   B♭⁷   A⁷   N.C. (G⁷)

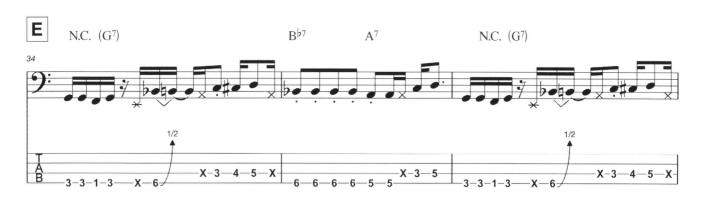

B♭⁷   A⁷   N.C. (G⁷)   B♭⁷   A⁷

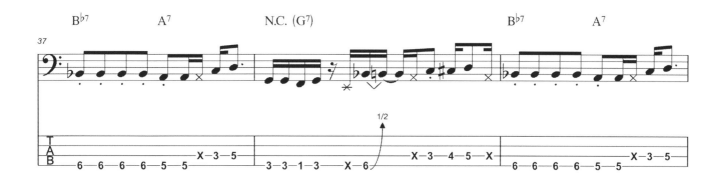

N.C. (G⁷)   B♭⁷   A⁷

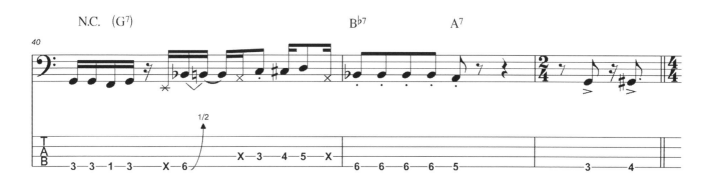

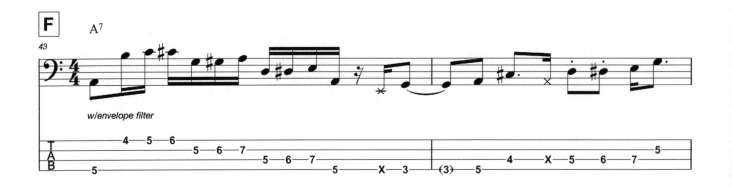

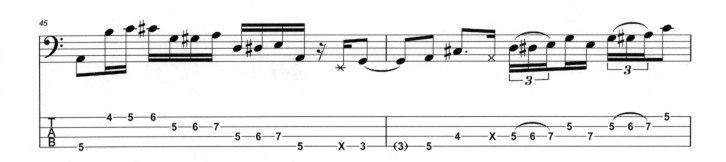

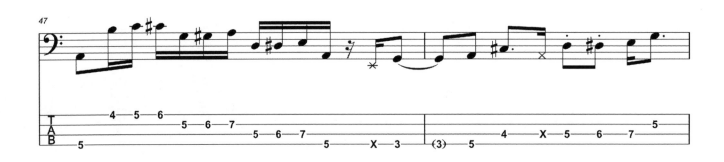

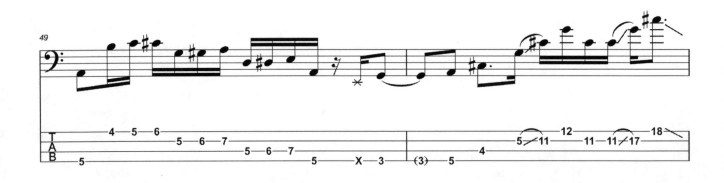

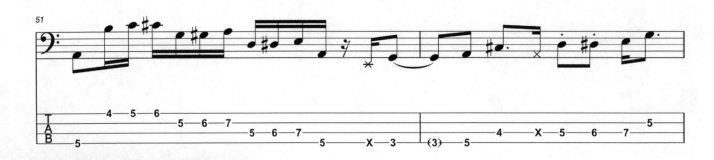

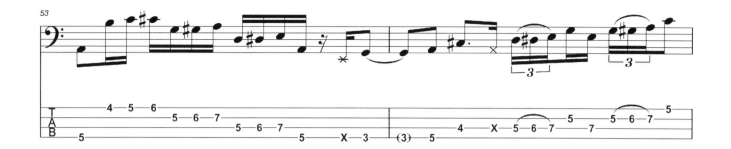

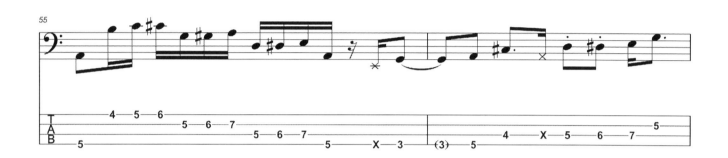

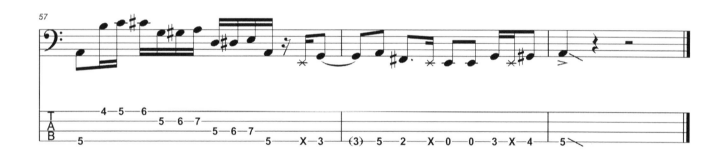

STUART HAMM

Stuart Hamm is perhaps best known as the bassist for guitar legends Steve Vai and Joe Satriani. However, for serious students of the electric bass, Hamm's influence and impact on the instrument are far more extensive. Regarded as one of the most gifted bassists to have emerged out of the jazz/rock genre in the last thirty years, Hamm has released a string of impressive solo albums, along the way becoming an ambassador for virtuoso bass playing through his mastery of the slap technique and his pioneering work with two-handed tapping and solo bass playing.

Stuart Hamm was born in New Orleans on 8th February 1960. His family were musically inclined: his father worked as a musicologist and his mother was an opera teacher. Growing up, he and his brothers listened to an eclectic mix of artists including The Mahavishnu Orchestra, Pink Floyd, Miles Davis, and Maynard Ferguson, all of which made for an ideal environment for a young musician. Stuart began his own musical journey by studying the flute and the piano as a young boy, both of which led to an appreciation of classical music. He began playing the bass in 1973 while at high school, and initially taught himself from Mel Bay tuition books. Before long he was working in the school jazz band and studying the recordings of bass legends such as Stanley Clarke, Chris Squire, Jeff Berlin and Jaco Pastorius.

In 1978 Stuart enrolled at Berklee College of Music where he began studying alongside guitarist Steve Vai. Intrigued by Vai's use of hammer-ons, it was during this time that he began experimenting with ways to play classical piano music on the bass. The result of his efforts was his development of the two handed tapping technique, which he learned to use to perform complex piano compositions such as Debussy's 'Dr. Gradus Ad Parnassum', Bach's 'Prelude in C' and Beethoven's 'Moonlight Sonata'. During this time, he also studied the work of funk bassist Larry Graham. Before long, he had mastered the slap and pop technique, and was soon able to expand on it with techniques of his own such as the 'flamenco rake', a triplet popping technique. Alongside his studies, he and Vai played together in various bands such as Axis and The Out Band before Steve decided to relocate to California. Stuart followed, forming a new group with him called The Classified and playing on his first two studio albums *Leftovers* and *Flex-able*.

In the late eighties Stuart went to Relativity Records with some demos of his music. On the strength of these he was offered a small recording contract, which enabled him to begin work on his first solo album. Released in 1988, *Radio Free Albemuth* proved to be a confident debut, with tracks such as 'Sexually Active' and 'Country Music' both demonstrating his mastery of the slap and tap techniques. The album also featured two of his arrangements of classical piano pieces, 'Dr. Gradus Ad Parnassum' and 'Moonlight Sonata'. Both are complex, fascinating examples of the kind of music that can be played on the bass using the two handed

tapping technique and did much to expand his growing reputation as a solo bassist. The album is also notable for `Flow My Tears', a slow ballad that uses the two handed tapping technique as an accompaniment device. Although Stuart had originally intended for the melody on this song to be played by a trumpet, his limited recording budget made this impossible. Instead, Relativity suggested he use one of their newly signed artists, a virtuoso guitarist named Joe Satriani. Joe played on the track in exchange for Stuart playing on his third solo album, *Flying in a Blue Dream*. He was subsequently offered the bass player position in Joe's band and toured with him in support of the album. These live shows gave Stuart ample opportunity to shine as both a supportive bassist and soloist and allowed him to showcase his abilities to a larger audience.

With an album's worth of material to now draw on, Stuart's next move was to record a tuition video for Hot Licks: *Slap, Pop and Tap for the Bass*. This video was aimed at experienced players and as the title suggests, focused on slapping and two handed tapping. Many of the pieces from his debut album were examined and dissected, as well as his popular arrangement of the *Peanuts* theme (Vincent Guaraldi's 'Linus & Lucy'). The video did much to boost Stuart's profile amongst bass players and even today it

remains one of the best resources for studying these advanced techniques.

Stuart released his second album, *Kings of Sleep* in 1989. Featuring a strong collection of bass-heavy jazz-rock tunes, as well as his arrangement of J.S Bach's 'Prelude in C', the album is essential listening for fans of virtuosic bass playing. Highlights include 'Black Ice', with its thunderous, detuned funk-rock riff, the hyperactive slap grooves of 'Call of the Wild', and the chops-busting 'Count Zero', which features his innovative flamenco rake technique. The album is also notable for the two handed tapping showcase 'Terminal Beach'.

Following *Kings of Sleep*, Stuart recorded a second Hot Licks instructional video, *Deeper Inside the Bass*. This time he focused on material from his second album, dissecting tracks such as 'Count Zero' and 'Terminal Beach' as well as his popular solo bass arrangement of 'The Star Spangled Banner', a piece which he has continued to play throughout his career.

Hamm's third solo album, *The Urge*, was released in 1991. Seeking to evolve his sound, he opted for a heavier rock approach, one inspired by his extensive touring with Satriani. This was also the first album to feature his vocals, notably on songs such as 'Who Do You Want Me to Be Today?' and the title track. It was

SELECTED DISCOGRAPHY

Stuart Hamm – *Radio Free Albemuth*
'Radio Free Albemuth', 'Flow My Tears', 'Dr. Gradus Ad Parnassum', 'Sexually Active', 'Country Music', 'Moonlight Sonata'

Stuart Hamm – *Kings of Sleep*
'Black Ice', 'Surely the Best', 'Call of the Wild', 'Terminal Beach', 'Count Zero', 'Prelude in C', 'Kings of Sleep'

Stuart Hamm – *The Urge*
'The Hammer', 'If You're Scared, Stay Home', 'Who Do You Want Me to Be Today', 'Lone Star', 'Quahogs Anyone? (119, 120, Whatever It Takes)'

Stuart Hamm – *Outbound*
'Outbound', 'The Castro Hustle', 'The Star Spangled Banner', 'The Tenacity of Genes and Dreams', 'Charlotte's Song', 'A Better World'

Stuart Hamm –
Just Outside of Normal
'The Obligatory Boogie', 'Going to California', 'The Clarinet Polka', 'Windsor Mews', 'Adagio', 'Big Roller'

Stuart Hamm – *The Book of Lies*
'The Book of Lies', 'Etude #1', 'Open Note Aria', 'Chordally Yours', Harmoni-Cali', 'Slap Happy', 'Te Extraño', 'Just a Blues'

the bass-heavy instrumental pieces that hit the hardest however, with tracks such as 'If You're Scared, Stay Home', 'Lone Star' and 'The Hammer' standing out in particular. The album also included a piece called 'Quahogs Anyone?' a live recording of his solo spot from a Satriani show, featuring excerpts from 'Surely The Best', 'Peanuts', 'Count Zero', 'Sexually Active' and 'Country Music'. Following the release of The Urge, Stuart continued to record and tour with both Vai and Satriani.

In 1998 Stuart formed jazz-fusion trio GHS with guitarist Frank Gambale and drummer Steve Smith. Their first album, Show Me What You Can Do was released in 1998 and featured incredible playing from each member. Tracks such as 'Astral Traveller' and 'Wrong & Strong' were some of Stuart's strongest compositions to date, with the latter notable for its mind-bending odd time slap grooves. A follow-up, The Light Beyond was released in 2000 and was followed by GHS3 in 2002.

In 2000, Stuart released his fourth album Outbound, which framed his virtuosic bass playing within a more contemporary sonic environment.

Tracks such as 'Outbound', 'The Castro Hustle' and 'The Tenacity of Genes and Dreams' are impressive showcases for his slap and tap techniques, whilst 'Charlotte's Song' (a solo piccolo bass piece) 'A Better World' and 'Lydian (Just Enough for the City)' demonstrated the more sensitive side of his compositional skills. Outbound also included the first recorded appearance of 'The Star Spangled Banner'.

In 2006 Stuart put together BX3, a touring bass guitar show with fellow bassists Billy Sheehan and Jeff Berlin. With backing musicians Jude Gold on guitar and John Mader on drums, BX3 was a chance for fans to see three highly regarded virtuoso bassists on one gig. Each member had their own set, with encores (including Spinal Tap's 'Big Bottom') played together. Stuart used the opportunity to play tracks from his entire career to date, including 'Radio Free Albemuth' and 'Flow My Tears' from his debut album and more recent material such as 'Nostalgia' and 'Katahdin', both of which he had recorded with GHS.

In 2007, Stuart released Live Stu x2, a live album recorded during two concerts, one with GHS, the other with his own band. Many of his best-known pieces such as 'Terminal Beach' and 'Flow My Tears' were included on the album, alongside new tracks 'Te Extraño', 'Yellow Happy' and 'A New Peace'.

Stuart's fifth studio album, Just Outside of Normal arrived in 2010. Recorded remotely using musicians from all over the world, the album was a departure from his established sound and found him tackling a far wider range of musical genres, from Dixieland jazz to polka. Naturally there was still plenty for bass players to get their teeth into: the opening track 'The Obligatory Boogie' opens with a slapped shuffle bass groove which later develops into a series of blistering solo lines, whilst 'The Clarinet Polka' features the intense fingerstyle passages and tapping runs that have made him a bass icon. Further highlights include the sliding harmonic chords found in 'Windsor Mews' and Uniformitarianism' and the cover version of the Led Zeppelin classic 'Going to California', which he continues to regularly perform as a solo piece. Compositionally, 'Big Roller', a quick-paced Dixieland tune featuring a lilting soprano sax melody and a supple swing groove, stands out as the most stylistically diverse tune on the album.

The Book of Lies, Stuart's sixth studio album – and perhaps his most ambitious to date – was released in 2015. Although there are several 'band' songs, the album is built around 'Le Petit Suite for Solo Bass', a seven song suite of solo pieces for the bass guitar. Growing up playing the flute and piano, Hamm had found no shortage of study pieces available for either instrument. Noticing a lack of similar resources for bassists (despite solo bass performance now being a popular genre for the modern player) he set out to write a suite of pieces that could be performed for auditions and at concert performances. Each piece was also written to help the student develop their technique in a specific area, whether it be chordal playing, the use of various kinds of harmonics, or slapping and tapping. The full band pieces on the album also see Stuart stretching his compositional wings: the title track is a slice of greasy Meters-esque funk, whilst 'Back to Shabalalla' has a cheerful South African Highlife vibe. A laid-back cover of The Beatles' 'Lucy in the Sky with Diamonds' closes the album. Throughout much of 2016, Stuart toured with a new band to promote the album.

Stuart playing 'Mel', his red sparkle Urge II bass

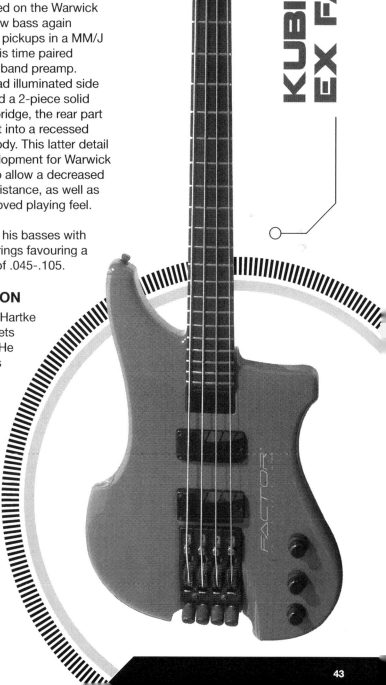

BASS GUITARS

For his first three studio albums Stuart used Kubicki Ex Factor basses. Built in California by luthier Philip Kubicki, Ex Factor basses are striking instruments that feature an innovative tuning system. With tuning pegs mounted on the bridge, the slim headstock exists only to offer an extension with two additional frets for the E-string: by flipping a lever on the headstock the user can release a capo which detunes the low E-string to D. Because of the scale extension, detuning the E-string does not alter the note positions on the fretboard.

Stuart owned several Kubicki basses: his main instrument was a blue/black model, which he still owns. He also had a red version tuned B-E-A-D and a yellow fretless.

In 1991 Stuart approached the Fender Custom Shop to discuss designing a new instrument. Much experimentation led to the development of the Fender Urge bass, a 32" scale instrument that had the appearance of a heavily updated Fender Jazz bass. The body shaping was initially based on the Fender Precision but scaled down and given deeper cutaways for improved upper register access. The neck featured a twenty-four fret fingerboard, making The Urge the first Fender bass in history to feature a full two octave board. Unusually, The Urge had three pickups in a J/P/J configuration, allowing for an enormous amount of tonal versatility. Using stacked knobs and toggle switches, it was possible to use the pickups in any configuration and in active or passive mode. With this instrument, Stuart became the first ever bass player to have a Fender signature instrument.

In 1996, The Urge II was released. This update featured a 34" scale neck and a reshaped body. Stuart's custom pickup configuration remained unchanged, although the control set was greatly simplified. Stuart owned many different versions of the Urge II bass, although he usually favoured 'Mel', the original Urge II prototype with a red sparkle finish and brass pick guard (see photo on previous page).

In 2010 Stuart moved to Washburn, with whom he had previously worked on the acoustic AB40SH bass. A new signature electric bass was developed, the Washburn SHB3 bass, nicknamed 'The Hammer'. This new bass featured EMG X pickups and unusually, had a soapbar pickup in neck position and a single coil pickup in bridge position (MM/J configuration). It also had active piezo pickups built into the bridge – each of the three pickups had an independent volume control, allowing them to be mixed together in different ratios.

In 2015 Stuart switched to Warwick, who designed him a new signature instrument. Based on the Warwick Streamer, the new bass again included EMG X pickups in a MM/J configuration, this time paired with an active 2-band preamp. The bass also had illuminated side position dots and a 2-piece solid brass Warwick bridge, the rear part of which was set into a recessed section of the body. This latter detail was a new development for Warwick and was done to allow a decreased string-to-body distance, as well as offering an improved playing feel.

Stuart strings all his basses with GHS Boomer strings favouring a medium gauge of .045-.105.

AMPLIFICATION

Stuart has used Hartke amps and cabinets for many years. He currently favours the HA5500 amplifier and HyDrive 115 and 410 cabinets.

KUBICKI EX FACTOR BASS

PERFORMANCE NOTES

'Slap and Tickle' is one of the longest and most complex pieces in this book and will require you to be comfortable with some advanced techniques such as two handed tapping and slap bass. Both are typical of Hamm's playing style and you'll find that several of his commonly used ideas – such as tapped quintuplets and the 'flamenco rake' technique – are put to use quite extensively.

The intro (at letter A) has a half time feel and is similar in style to the intro of 'Call of the Wild', a track from Stuart's *Kings of Sleep* album. When playing this part, pluck the double stop chord in bar 1 with the thumb and first finger and allow the notes to ring as you play the simple slap and pop figures that follow it. In the second bar, a descending D major pentatonic lick is played. This fast run is made possible through the use of hammer-ons and pull-offs – be sure to play these as written as they will really help with making the line sound fluid. The same techniques are used for the remainder of this section.

At letter B the main groove begins, using a slap and pop idea that allows you to repeatedly play the same note by slapping and popping it in two different positions. This only works for open string notes as you can see: by slapping the A at the fifth fret of the E-string and then alternating this with popped open A-string notes, you can create a continuous sixteenth note line. This is a technique that Stuart has used often in his playing, and you can hear examples of it in tracks such as 'Call of the Wild' and 'Country Music'. Playing this line can be quite relentless for your picking hand, so be sure to practice it slowly to begin with in order to build up the required stamina.

At letter C a contrasting line begins based around an F♯ minor tonality. The first two bars of this part use conventional slap and pop technique, so you should have no serious problems. On the final beat of the second bar (bar 16) an F♯ on the D-string is popped together with an open G-string. After popping

these with the first and second fingers, bend the F♯ upwards in pitch to a G. This resolves the conflict of hearing two notes together that are a half step apart. This is another technique that Hamm uses frequently in his playing, and it will occur again later in this piece. In the fourth bar of the riff, some triplet figures are played. The notes for these are a simple root-fifth-octave shape and are performed by slapping the lowest note with the thumb then popping the subsequent notes with the first and second fingers respectively. When doing so, your hand should 'roll' through the notes in a smooth motion (see Fig. 1). This triplet technique is another of Hamm's favourite devices, one which he refers to as the 'flamenco rake'. This technique was used as the basis for the composition 'Count Zero' from his *Kings of Sleep* album.

At letter F the bass solo begins, underpinned by a simple synth bass part. This is similar to the solo section from 'Sexually Active', a track from Stuart's *Radio Free Albemuth* album. The solo opens with a series of notes which are bent upwards in pitch, then followed with a tapped note – all of these notes are chord tones from the implied Em^7 chord. This idea of bending notes

then following them with a tapped note is also common to Hamm's solo playing and you'll hear it on 'Black Ice', as well as his solo version of the Led Zeppelin song 'Going to California'. This leads into a fingerstyle bass solo. The first phrase (bars 43-44) is a descending E Dorian lick that features a downward slide on the G-string followed by a note played on the D-string. This is a sequence and is easier to play than it sounds as only the first note on the G-string is played – the second is created by the slide.

In bar 45 a sixteenth note triplet fill is played. This lick reiterates the same note at a fast speed by playing it in two positions. This is a lick that Hamm has used in several solos – it's likely that he picked this up from studying legendary bassist Jaco Pastorius, who often used the same idea when soloing. In bar 47 there is a long phrase that uses an open string jump to move to a higher part of the fingerboard. This is a technique that upright bassists use often and it's something that Hamm explored in detail in 'Open Note Aria' from his solo bass suite on the *Book of Lies* album. The fingerstyle section of the solo closes with a series of hammer-on/pull-off licks that descend the neck.

Fig. 1: Playing triplets with the 'flamenco rake' technique

At letter G a slapped bass solo begins. This opens with some sixteenth note triplet figures that are made possible through the use of fretting hand slaps (marked 'LH' in the fingering). Using the fretting hand to perform dead notes in this way is a technique that many bass players use. This figure is followed by a double stop of F♯ and the open G – the F♯ is bent upwards to the same pitch as the G, the same technique that was used back in the C section. This idea is continued for the next three bars, each time pairing an Em⁷ chord tone with the open G-string. This leads into a slapped groove at bar 55 which culminates in some more sixteenth note triplets.

A tricky fill in bar 62 leads into the third and final part of the bass solo, which is tapped. The opening part of this section features sixteenth note triplets and tapped double stops, with each hand playing a fifth interval shape (See Fig. 2). Be sure to pay close attention to the tapping guide written between the stave when learning this line. You'll need to play these phrases slowly to begin with, ensuring that each of the notes speaks out clearly. This phrase is played several times, then leads into a simpler two handed tapping passage in bars 67-70.

Beginning in bar 71 are some tapped quintuplet arpeggios – a quintuplet is a group of five notes played in the space of four. I recommend practicing this slowly using the vocalisation 'hippopotamus' to help you play the phrase accurately.

The arpeggios themselves are basic major/minor arpeggios and there is some doubling of certain notes between the two hands. Stuart has used quintuplet arpeggios such as these many times in his playing, notably during 'Country Music', one of his best-known pieces.

There are a lot of very challenging parts in this piece, as there would be in most of Hamm's compositions. Patience and slow, methodical practice are the keys to success here. Be sure to listen carefully to the audio when learning this piece as it will be an invaluable guide.

STYLE TIPS

○ Continuous sixteenth note slap and pop grooves on the same note

○ Use of double stop pops: open G against a fretted note that is bent upwards

○ Use of the 'flamenco rake' technique

○ Use of open string jumps to reach different areas of the fingerboard

○ Tapped quintuplet arpeggios

Fig. 2: Tapping fifth intervals in two positions

SOUND ADVICE

I recorded this piece using a Kubicki Ex Factor bass – the same kind of bass that Stuart used when recording his first three albums in the late eighties/early nineties. The bass was strung with GHS Boomer strings, gauges .040, .060, .080, .100 which is a little lighter than Stuart's preferred gauge. The Kubicki has a six-way selector switch for different tone options: when recording, I set it in the third position, which puts the instrument in active mode and boosts the mid frequencies. The pan control was set in the centre position and both the treble and bass controls were turned up full. Compression was added digitally after the part had been recorded.

To get close to this tone, I recommend using an active instrument with two humbucking pickups. Set the bass and treble tones in the centre position to begin with and experiment with boosting them each a little. If you have a mid control that allows you to boost the lower mids, this can also be helpful. As with all pieces that require slapping and tapping, a healthy amount of compression will work well here.

'SLAP AND TICKLE'

Written by Stuart Clayton

Drums: Will Beavis
Keys: Stuart Clayton
Guitar: Jamie Hunt
Bass: Stuart Clayton

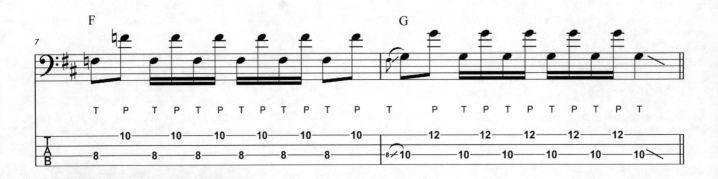

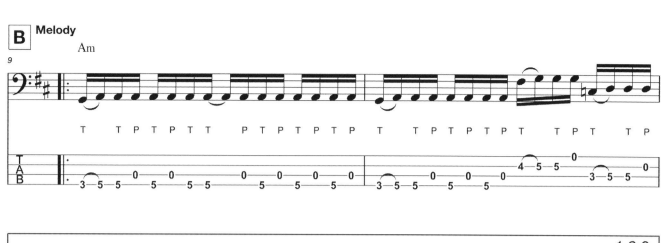

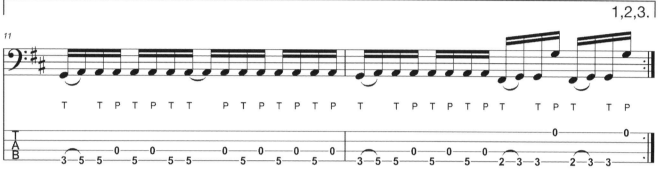

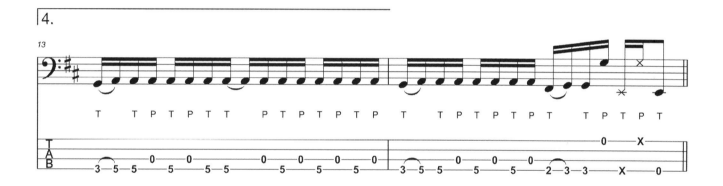

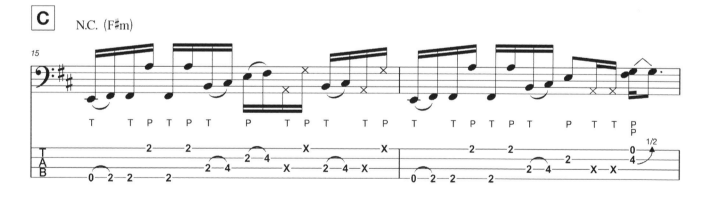

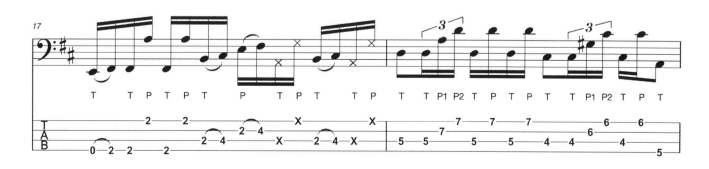

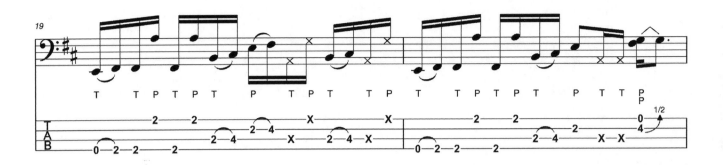

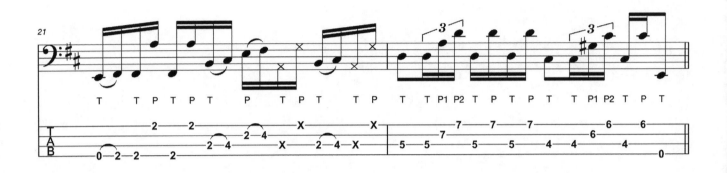

D **Melody**

Am

1.

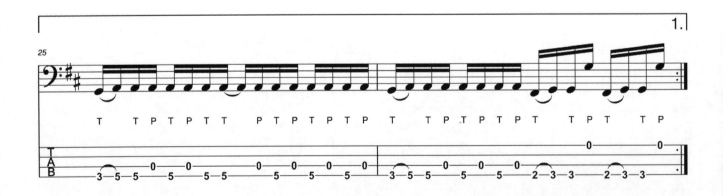

2.

Guitar Solo

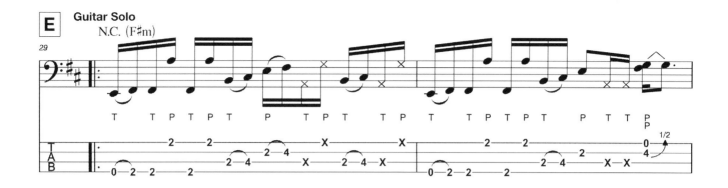

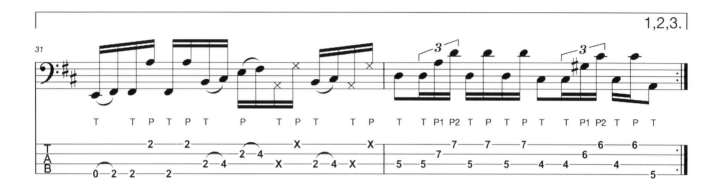

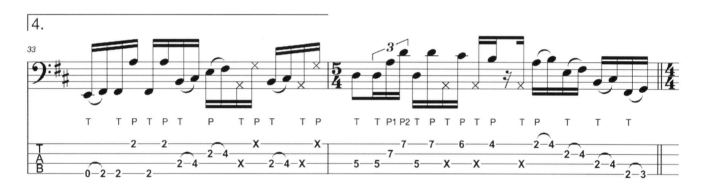

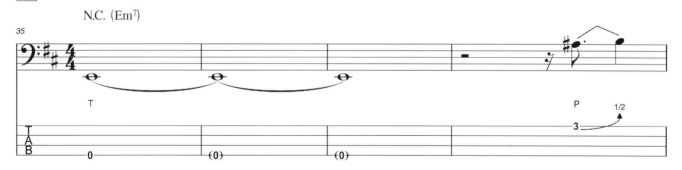

F **Fingerstyle Bass Solo**

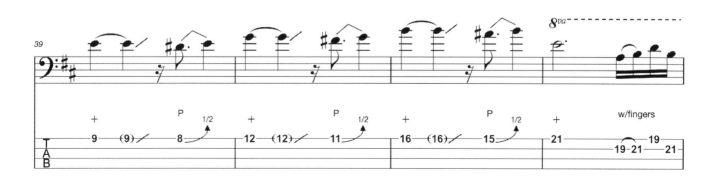

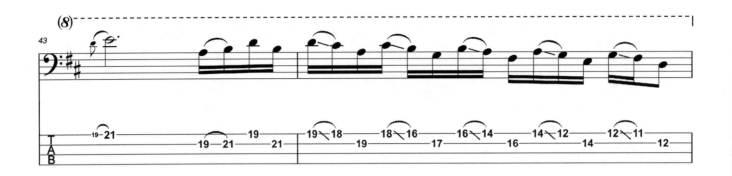

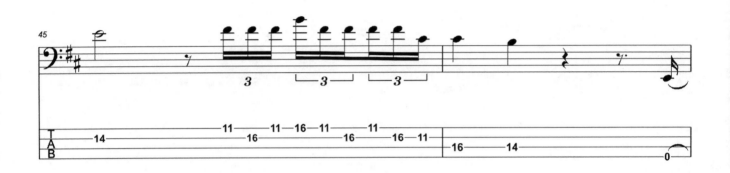

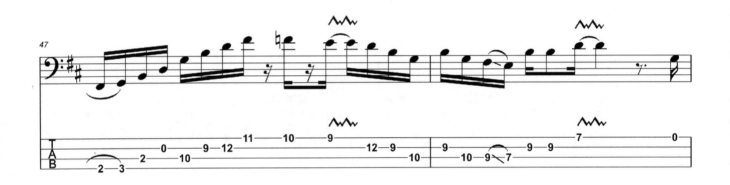

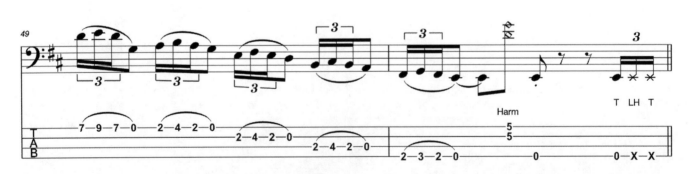

G Slap Bass Solo

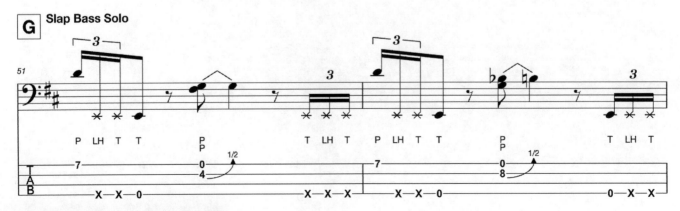

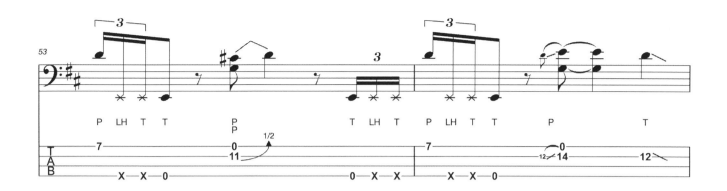

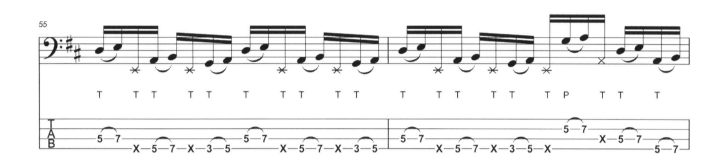

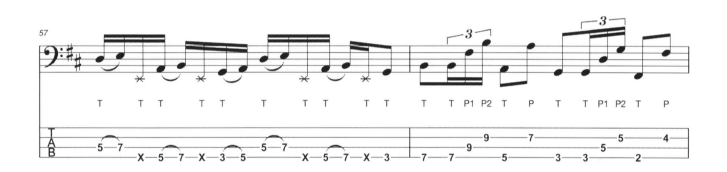

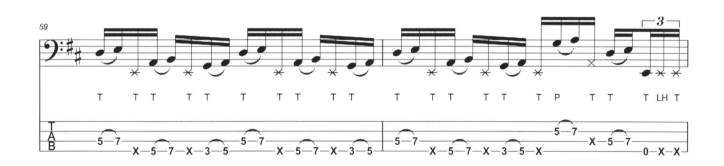

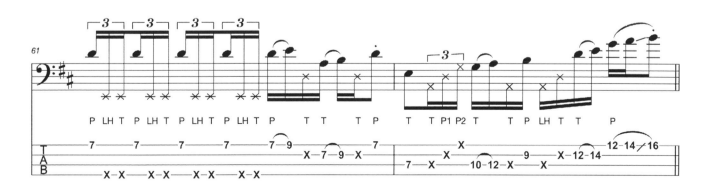

Tapped Bass Solo

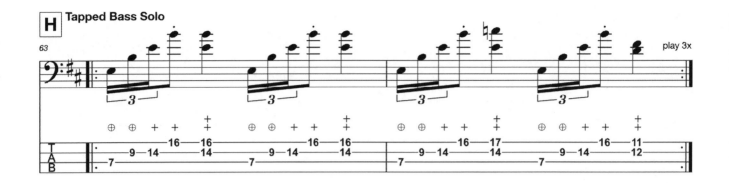

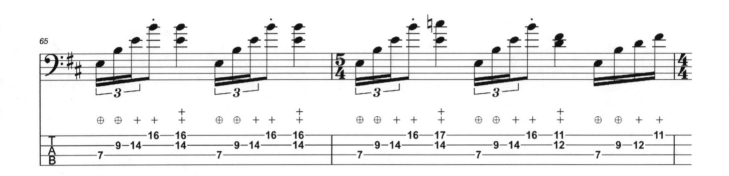

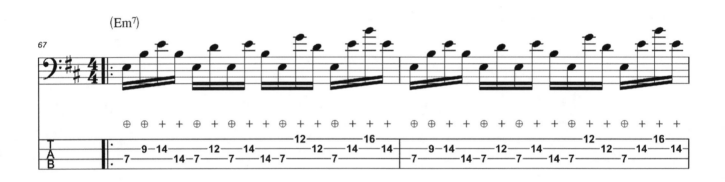

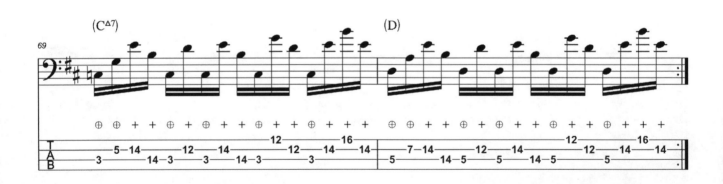

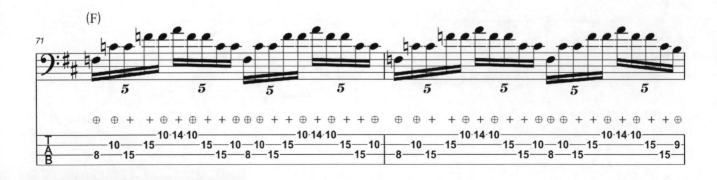

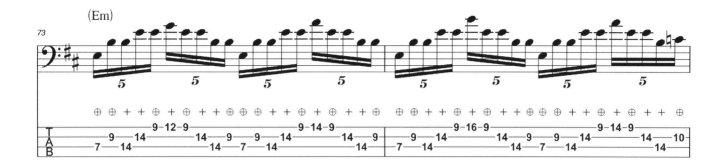

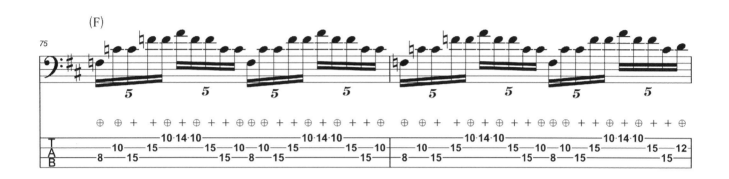

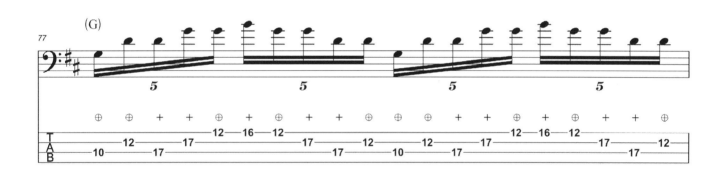

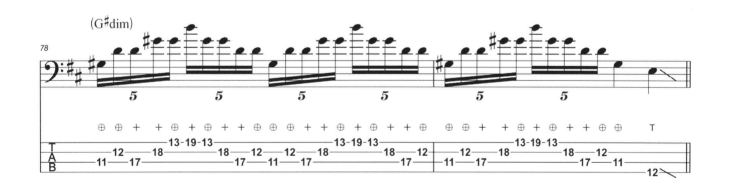

Melody

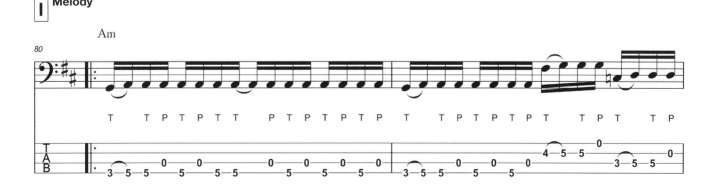

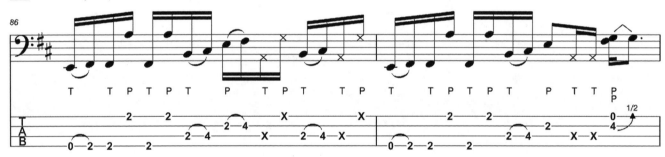
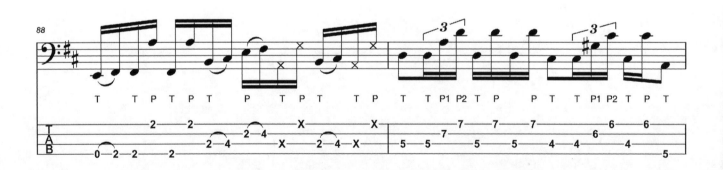
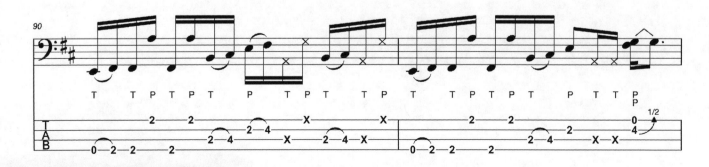

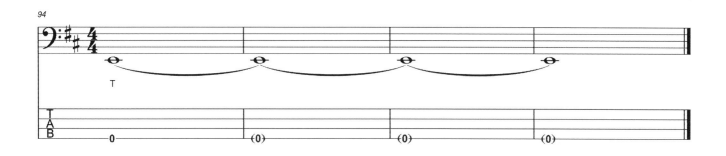

MARK KING

Mark King is one of the UK's best loved bassists and has fronted pop/funk outfit Level 42 for over thirty years. With over thirty million albums sold and twenty Top 40 hits during the course of his career, Mark has long been in the enviable position of being a highly regarded and virtuosic musician, who has also enjoyed mainstream chart success. His work with Level 42 during the eighties caused a surge of interest in the bass, largely thanks to his innovative take on the slap technique, which was considerably more complex than what had gone before.

Born on the Isle of Wight on 20th October 1958, King took an interest in music at an early age. He began playing the drums when he was 9 years old and by the age of 10 was playing in school performances. During his teens he was inspired by legendary musicians such as John McLaughlin, Chick Corea, Miles Davis and Lenny White and began studying the guitar alongside the drums. After deciding to pursue a career in music, in 1978 he moved to London where he found work as a salesman in Macari's music shop. As the shop didn't stock drums, King applied his rhythmic mind to a new instrument – the bass.

In 1980 he began jamming with fellow islanders Phil and Boon Gould and Phil's friend, percussionist/keys player Mike Lindup, who was studying at the Guildhall. As Mark had been forced to sell his drum kit during an ill-fated trip to Austria with a band called Pseudo Foot, the drum seat in the band was taken by Phil. Mark would therefore alternate with Boon on bass and guitar as they began to develop ideas through jamming. Before long, their endeavours began to take shape and they were introduced to Andy Sojka, the head of a small label, Elite Records.

Sojka took an interest in one track in particular and suggested that the band add lyrics and hire a vocalist. While Boon was happy enough to write the lyrics, the group were reluctant to bring an outside vocalist into their working unit. Mark agreed to step forward and try his hand at the lead vocals and the result was the band's first song, 'Love Meeting Love'. Sojka signed the group – who had now settled on the name Level 42 – and released the track as a single, with an instrumental version used as the b-side. As Mark had played bass on 'Love Meeting Love', he became the band's bass player.

By August of 1980, 'Love Meeting Love' had reached number 61 in the UK Singles Charts. Although by no means a smash hit, it was enough to attract the attention of the larger labels. The band were quickly signed by ATV Publishing and given an advance of £5000. Mark used his share of the money to buy his first bass, a Jaydee, which he bought because of its resemblance to the Alembic basses used by his hero Stanley Clarke.

Armed with new equipment, the band recorded the remainder of their tracks with Sojka, a collection of instrumentals and vocal songs which would later be released as *The Early Tapes*. Mark was refining his unique slap bass style by this point and tracks such as 'Sandstorm', 'Theme to Margaret', 'Mr. Pink' and '88' were all built around his powerful sixteenth note-based grooves. With Mark also now handling lead vocal duties, his position as the band's frontman meant that his bass playing was very much in the spotlight and quickly became a focal point for the group.

In 1981 Level 42 signed to Polydor and released the single 'Love Games', a fantastic showcase for Mark's playing, with its bubbling slap groove and melodic fingerstyle chorus sections. The track entered the UK Charts at #38, giving the band their first appearance on Top of the Pops and putting them squarely at the forefront of the new Brit Funk movement. Their debut album *Level 42* was released later in the same year and featured songs such as 'Almost There', 'Dune Tune', 'Starchild' and of course 'Love Games'. All of these pieces have since become classic songs in the band's catalogue, not to mention essential listening for bass players. The release of the band's debut was followed shortly after by Andy Sojka's release of *The Early Tapes*, which he had refused to sell to Polydor.

Throughout 1981 – 1984 the band toured the UK and Europe heavily, honing their song writing skills over the course of a further three albums: *The Pursuit of Accidents, Standing in the Light* and *True Colours*. With each album they edged their way closer towards mainstream pop, although their unique blend of jazz/funk and superior musicianship was always evident, particularly in their energetic live shows. As the group rose in popularity thanks to tracks such as 'The Chinese Way', 'The Sun Goes Down (Living It Up)', and 'Micro Kid', Mark King was hailed as the new hero of the bass guitar. Sales of Jaydee and Status basses – together with those of Trace Elliot amplifiers – rose in tandem with Mark's popularity and music shops across the country were soon filled with young bassists hammering out his best-known lines.

'Hot Water', from the *True Colours* album was released as a single in August 1984. Supported by what is now considered one of Mark's best-known slap grooves, the song quickly became the band's biggest single to date, reaching #18 in the

SELECTED DISCOGRAPHY

Level 42 – *Level 42*
'43', 'Almost There', 'Love Games', 'Dune Tune', 'Starchild', 'Foundation & Empire', 'Forty Two'

Level 42 – *The Early Tapes*
'Sandstorm', 'Love Meeting Love', 'Theme to Margaret', 'Autumn (Paradise is Free)', 'Mr. Pink', '88'

Level 42 – *The Pursuit of Accidents*
'Weave Your Spell', 'The Pursuit of Accidents', 'You Can't Blame Louis', 'Eyes Waterfalling', 'The Chinese Way', 'Return of the Handsome Rugged Man'

Level 42 – *A Physical Presence*
'Almost There', 'Mr. Pink', 'Kansas City Milkman', 'Follow Me', 'Foundation & Empire', 'Hot Water', 'Bass Solo', 'Love Games', '88'

Level 42 – *World Machine*
'A Physical Presence', 'Something About You', 'I Sleep On My Heart', 'Dream Crazy', 'Good Man in a Storm', 'Lying Still'

Level 42 – *Guaranteed*
'Guaranteed', 'Overtime', 'Her Big Day', 'Seven Years', 'Lasso The Moon', 'If You Were Mine', 'At This Great Distance', 'As Years Go By'

Mark King – *Influences*
'The Essential', 'Clocks Go Forward', 'I Feel Free', 'Picture on the Wall', 'There is a Dog'

Mark King – *Trash (Volume 1)*
'Just Like That', 'Outstanding', 'Throwing Sevens', 'Keep Climbing', 'Don't Think I Don't', 'Sooner Or Later', 'Hell's Bells'

UK Charts. That same year, Mark was able to convince Polydor that his popularity as a bassist was sufficient enough to warrant his own solo record. The resulting album, *Influences*, was a mind-blowing journey through all of the musical genres that had influenced Mark up until that point. The first track – an eighteen minute epic entitled 'The Essential' – features some superb bass work from Mark, showcasing all aspects of his playing, from funky slap grooves and tight fingerstyle lines to harmonic-based lines and chordal passages. The album also included a cover of Cream's 'I Feel Free', which Mark recorded as a tribute to bassist Jack Bruce, one of his biggest influences. Although the material from this album was never performed live at the time, Mark played the majority of the pieces during his week-long residency at Ronnie Scott's in 2012. A live album, *Mark King & Friends Somewhere in Soho* was released soon after.

In order to further build on their growing popularity, in 1985 Level 42 made a conscious effort to steer their song writing in a more commercial direction. The resulting album – *World Machine* – quickly became

their biggest hit thus far, sporting the hit singles 'Something About You' (#6 in the charts) and 'Leaving Me Now' (#15). Despite being a more 'mainstream pop' record, fans of Mark's bass playing nevertheless found plenty to marvel at, from the slick fingerstyle grooves of 'A Physical Presence' and 'Good Man in a Storm' to the slapped funk of tracks such as 'I Sleep on My Heart' and 'Dream Crazy'. However, while the band was now establishing itself as one of the UK's premier pop acts, the decision to move away from their original jazz/funk roots had sown seeds of disquiet within the group.

Riding high on their newfound success, the band toured the U.S. in support of acts such as Steve Winwood, Tina Turner, and Madonna in an effort to establish a connection to the American market. Back in the UK, record company requests for another single led to the band recording three new songs – 'Lessons in Love', 'Children Say' and 'Freedom Someday'. All three tracks would appear on their next album, the hugely successful *Running In The Family*, while 'Lessons in Love' would bring the band their highest UK chart position – #3. Released in

March 1987, *Running in the Family* quickly became the band's biggest selling album and boasted no less than five hit singles: 'Lessons in Love', 'Running In The Family', 'Children Say', 'To Be With You Again' and 'It's Over'. During this peak period of their career, Level 42 also worked as the house band for the Prince's Trust charity concerts in which they played alongside many legendary musicians such as Eric Clapton, Paul McCartney, George Martin, Phil Collins, Elton John, and Mark Knopfler. However, exhausted by the continuous touring, combined with dissatisfaction over the band's change of direction, the Gould brothers both decided to leave in late 1987. They were eventually replaced by drummer Gary Husband and guitarist Alan Murphy.

Level 42's next album, *Staring at the Sun* was released in September 1988 and featured the hit singles 'Heaven in My Hands', 'Take a Look' and 'Tracie'. The ensuing tour was a huge success, but the band were dealt a devastating blow when guitarist Alan Murphy suddenly died in late 1989. Level 42 subsequently took an extended hiatus that gave Mark time to finish building his home studio and

Mark King in 1985, playing one of his Jaydee basses

Mark King playing one of his Status Paramatrix Kingbasses

for keys player Mike Lindup to record his solo album *Changes*.

Level 42 returned in 1991 with *Guaranteed*, an album that had ended their record contract with Polydor and gained them a new one with RCA. The album was noticeably different in style to their previous efforts and saw the band investigating alternative musical genres. Mark also began to stretch his wings as a bass player on this album, using a fretless bass for the first time on 'Seven Years', a 5-string on 'If You Were Mine' (which was written by drummer Gary Husband) and a MIDI bass on Mike Lindup's song 'Lasso the Moon'. As the band had not replaced Alan Murphy at this point, guitar duties for the album were split between Dominic Miller (who was known for his work with Sting, but who had also rehearsed with the band in their early days) and the legendary jazz-fusion guitarist Allan Holdsworth, who also toured with the group during a lengthy and successful run of shows at the Hammersmith Odeon. Several singles were released from the album: the title track, which charted at #17, 'Overtime', which reached #62 and 'My Father's Shoes', which reached number #55.

In 1994 Mark King and Mike Lindup decided to reunite with original drummer Phil Gould for their next album. The result was *Forever Now*, a slick pop record that is regarded by many to be one of the band's finest. As with all Level 42 albums, there were many highlights for bass players, such as the fingerstyle lines on tracks such as 'The Bends', 'Romance' and 'Past Lives' and the slap grooves from 'Model Friend', 'All Over You' and 'Tired of Waiting'. The first single, 'Forever Now' charted at #19 and was followed by 'All Over You', charting at #26 and 'Love in a Peaceful World' which reached number #31. When Phil Gould decided not to tour in support of the record, drummer Gavin Harrison was hired, and the band toured in late 1994. It would however be the band's final tour in their original incarnation.

After a four-year break, Mark King returned in 1998 with his second solo album, entitled *One Man*. Written with former Level 42 guitarist and lyricist Boon Gould, the album focused more on Mark's vocals and song writing skills than his bass playing. It contained one single, 'Bitter Moon', which failed to chart in the UK. Mark toured with a new band (featuring his younger brother Nathan

King on guitar) to promote the album, playing a combination of new songs and old Level 42 classics.

In 1999 Mark released an out-takes album entitled *Trash* through his website. The album – which consisted mainly of material that he had written after the break-up of Level 42 – featured Mark not only playing bass, but drums, guitars, and keys as well. Full of his trademark bass pyrotechnics, this small-scale mail order album quickly became popular among Level 42 fans, hungry for new material. Songs such as

YOU MIGHT ALSO LIKE...

If you're a fan of Mark King, be sure to check out the following bassists:

— ○ **Stanley Clarke**
   (Giants of Bass: 60s - 70s)

— ○ **Jack Bruce**
   (Giants of Bass: 60s - 70s)

— ○ **Larry Graham**
   (Giants of Bass: 60s - 70s)

'Just Like That', 'Outstanding', 'Throwing Sevens' and 'Keep Climbing' all featured superb bass work from Mark and were all played live when he toured with a new band in 2000/2001. A mail-order CD-ROM of a show filmed at the Ryde Theater on the Isle of Wight was released later in 2001.

In 2002, Mark came to an agreement with Mike Lindup to acquire the sole rights to the Level 42 name, enabling him to tour with his new band under the name. Over the next few years he played several Greatest Hits tours with his new line-up, releasing live albums after each tour. Mike Lindup

re-joined in 2005 and a new studio album was recorded. Written entirely by Mark and original guitarist Boon Gould, *Retroglide* was released in September 2006. Bass players were in for a particular treat with the song 'Sleep Talking', which featured a punchy slap groove throughout much of the song, followed by a busy, Jaco-esque fingerstyle groove for the outro section (Interestingly, Mark recorded this fingerstyle line using his original Jaydee bass, the first time it had been heard on a Level 42 record since the mid-eighties).

In 2010 Level 42 toured to celebrate their thirtieth anniversary, playing a setlist that featured all of their biggest hits, together with early favourites such as 'Almost There' and '43'. The band toured again in

2012 for the twenty-fifth anniversary of *Running in the Family*, on this occasion playing several songs from the classic album that had never been heard live before. During these shows, the band also played a short acoustic set, featuring songs such as 'Out of Sight, Out of Mind' and 'Guaranteed'.

In late 2013 Level 42 released *Sirens*, an EP featuring six new tracks, all mixed by noted American DJ John Morales. The new material was heavily inspired by the old school funk/dance scene that had been so important to the group in their early days, with Mark's lines on 'Sirens', 'Too Much Time' and 'Where's Yo' Head At' proving to be undeniable bass highlights. Level 42 toured throughout 2014 and again in 2016 to promote the album.

BASS GUITARS

During the very earliest days of Level 42, Mark used a Gibson EB-2 bass that he had borrowed from the manager of Macari's Music Shop, where he worked. After the band had signed their publishing deal, he purchased a Jaydee Supernatural bass from Sounds music shop in Shaftesbury Avenue, London. This bass – which would be the first of many Jaydees owned by Mark – was finished in cherry red and featured a five-piece laminated neck and Brazilian mahogany wings. It also boasted all of the Jaydee trademarks: Saturn neck inlays, rosewood controls, striped wooden pickup covers and large circular string anchors. Mark used this bass extensively in the early eighties, recording the band's first few albums with it. He still owns it and most recently used it on the second half of the song 'Sleep Talking' from the band's 2006 album *Retroglide*.

During the eighties, Mark acquired several further Jaydee basses. The most notable of these was the 'Starchild', a white model with angels inlaid into the fingerboard. Mark later had a Kahler tremolo arm fitted to this bass. He also owned several Jaydees with a pearlescent finish and can be seen using the pink model on the *Level 42 Live at Wembley* DVD.

In the mid-eighties Mark was introduced to Status Graphite basses, which featured moulded graphite necks, with a headless design. Before long, Mark owned several of these instruments, including an all-graphite Series 2000 and Series I models in several colours including pale blue, pale green, white and FPPR (F**king Postman Pat Red). He recorded all of the tracks on the *True Colours* album (1984) with Status basses – the tone is noticeably different to that of a Jaydee.

In 1985, Mark was approached by Alembic (who made basses for his hero Stanley Clarke), who offered to build him some basses. His initial pair of instruments took over a year to build: the first had a cocobolo top and back, semi-hollow mahogany body, maple accents and a 7-piece maple/purple heart neck. The second had the same specifications but with an AAAAA quilted maple top. Both had ebony fingerboards, fretboard LEDs, a DS5 external power supply and gold hardware. These basses had a 34" scale and a consistent neck width. Mark began using them for live shows and ordered two more instruments that were the exact same spec, but with 32" scale necks. Mark sold some of his Alembic basses to the Bass Centre in the mid-nineties, but still owns his 32" scale models.

During the recording sessions for *Guaranteed* in early 1991, Mark used a wide selection of basses. Alongside his Alembics, he also used a Wal bass that was fitted with an MB4 MIDI interface (as heard on 'Lasso the Moon'), a Moon bass that he removed the frets from (as heard on 'Seven Years') and a Status Empathy 5-string bass for the tracks 'If You Were Mine' and 'With a Little Love'. The Status Empathy bass was one of the first Status basses with a headstock and this and a 4-string model were used by Mark during the band's record-breaking run of gigs at the Hammersmith Odeon during December 1990.

While recording *Forever Now* in 1993, Mark used 4 and 5-string Music Man StingRay basses. During the tour that followed the album's release, he used his Alembic basses again, although the video for their final single 'Love in a Peaceful World' features him with a new Status Empathy 4-string. During the tour Mark was also presented with a new Jaydee which John Diggins built for him

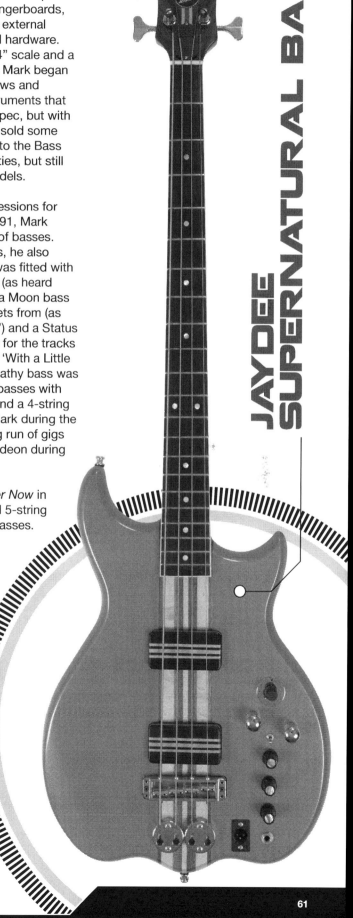

JAYDEE SUPERNATURAL BASS

Mark King in 2010, playing one of his Status KingBasses

as a birthday present. Based on the Calibas model, the Mark King Birthday Bass features a book-matched quilted Maple front and back and is double stained black and cherry red.

In 1998, Mark combined his new musical direction on *One Man* with a new bass, a modernised Fender Jazz American Deluxe model. This bass had a flat fingerboard profile and was retrofitted with SIM's LED fretboard markers. Fender released the bass as the Mark King Signature model, of which just 42 were made. However, Mark found that they did not suit his playing style when used live and before long was using a selection of basses built by UK luthier Bernie Goodfellow. Mark had four GB's built for him: two were Fender-style 'Spitfire' instruments, while the other two were through-neck 'Rumour' models. All featured LED fretboard position markers, a feature which by now had become synonymous with Mark's instruments. Unfortunately, Mark experienced problems while using these basses on tour, and switched back to his Alembic basses.

In 1999 Mark met with Status founder Rob Green to discuss

building a signature bass. The result was the Status KingBass, a completely new headless instrument that featured a consistent width 32" scale neck, narrow string spacing and fretboard LED's. Addressing Mark's concern over losing one of his favourite phrasing tools – the ability to bend the string behind the nut to manipulate the pitch – a 'Bendwell' was added. This was a large, scalloped area behind the first fret which allowed Mark to press down on the strings after playing harmonics and bend them accordingly. Mark began using the KingBass live in 2001 and initially had two instruments made that were identical in specifications, but with different body woods: one had a rosewood top over a walnut back with blue LEDs, the other had a quilted maple top over an alder body and green LEDs. Both basses can be seen on the *Level 42 Live at Reading 2001* DVD.

Over the next few years, Rob Green built additional KingBasses for Mark, the first of which was the 'Princess' bass, an ivory white model decorated with the princess artwork from the first Level 42 album. Further KingBasses included the 'Black Beauty', a black lacquered model

with exposed body binding and red LEDs, and the Retroglide KingBass, which featured an unusual 'woven chrome' finish.

In 2007, Mark and Rob reconvened to collaborate on a new version of the KingBass. The KingBass MKII – a 34" scale headed instrument with a larger body – was a clear progression from the original design, with similar body shaping, a graphite neck and fingerboard LEDs. This instrument also had single coil pickups and had a Bendwell incorporated into the headstock. Mark initially had two of these basses built: one with an alder body topped with quilted maple and green LEDs, the other with a walnut body, a cocobolo top and white LEDs. Rob Green also built him a 5-string model fitted with the pickups and circuitry from his old Trace Elliot T-bass, which had been built by Rob for Trace Elliot back in the nineties.

By 2010 Mark had returned to the headless KingBass model and began using a new pair of instruments built to mark the thirtieth anniversary of Level 42. These new instruments also featured the J-Bass pickups from the second KingBass model. Mark had two of these new instruments built: the first with a mahogany body, bird's eye maple veneer and Vintage Amber Sunburst, the second with a flamed maple top and a Cherry Amber Sunburst finish. Each bass had custom 'star' LEDs on the front face and Mark's name at the twelfth fret, backlit with LEDs.

The new KingBasses were developed further in 2012 with the release of the KingBass Paramatrix, which features a radical new EQ design with dual parametric circuits and new Tri-Max pickups. Mark later had one of his initial Paramatrix basses heavily modified by Crystal Rocked to include over 1,680 Swarovski stones on the front face. He continues to use this instrument, along with newer chrome and gold faced models built for the band's 2014 *Sirens* tour. In 2015, an additional Indigo coloured bass was built for the band's show at the IndigO2 venue. Mark continued using this instrument – which can be seen in the photograph below during the band's 2016 *Sirens II* tour.

EFFECTS

With regard to effects, Mark is known for using chorus in his slap tone. When the band began, he used the chorus effect that was built into the Roland JC-200 amplifier that he was using. He later began using Yamaha E1010 analog delay units and had two in his rack – one for chorus, the other for delay. Level 42 tracks with chordal fingerstyle bass parts such as 'I Want Eyes' and 'Hours By the Window' are good examples of his work with the E1010 delay unit. Mark kept the E1010's in his rack until the nineties, when they were joined by an Eventide H3000 Harmonizer.

When Mark began touring with Level 42 again in 2001, he used TC Electronic's TC 2290 effects processor, as heard on the *Level 42 Live in Reading 2001* DVD. In more recent years, Mark has favoured individual pedals and currently has TC Electronic's Corona Chorus, Hall of Fame Reverb, Vortex Flanger, Helix Phaser, Shaker Vibrato and Flashback Delay. He has several 'toneprints' available for download through the TC Electronic website.

AMPLIFICATION

When Level 42 started out Mark was using a Roland JC-200 amplifier with a Marshall 8x10 guitar cabinet. After a year of touring with this setup he went looking for something more suitable and discovered Trace Elliot, a new company who were building bass amplifiers and cabinets. After seeing Mark play at a Level 42 gig, the company offered to supply him with equipment, beginning what would become a long-standing professional relationship between the two. Throughout the eighties Mark used the company's GP11 amplifier and two 4x10 cabinets, upgrading to the GP12 preamps in in the nineties. His GP12s were powered by Trace Elliot RA500X power amps and fed a series of 2x10 cabinets.

When Mark returned to live playing in 1998, he began using Ashdown amplifiers, initially opting to pair his new Fender signature bass with an 8x10 combo which Ashdown marketed as 'The King Combo'. After a brief flirtation with Eden amplifiers and cabinets (as seen on the *Level 42 Live at Ryde Theatre 2001* DVD), he was back with Ashdown, using a new signature model amplifier, the Ashdown AL-MK500 amp.

In 2010 Mark switched to TC Electronic and began using their lightweight RH450 amplifier with two RS410 cabinets. He upgraded to the more powerful RH750 amplifier in 2012, then to the Blacksmith, their most powerful amp, which he continues to use.

PERFORMANCE NOTES

'King for a Day' has been written to represent the early work of legendary Level 42 bassist Mark King and is a jazz-funk tune with a busy slap bass groove. Similar to classic tracks such as 'Mr. Pink', '43' and 'Sandstorm', this piece features complex sixteenth note-based slap lines, the use of tenths to imply harmony, funky fingerstyle grooves and a bass solo that features Mark's trademark 'machine gun triplets'.

The opening A section of this piece establishes the four-bar slap groove that is used for several parts of the track. This line requires you to use the fretting hand (marked 'LH' in the slap guides) to 'fill in the gaps' in the line with percussive ghost notes. Fretting hand slaps are performed in a similar way to how you would use the hand to mute an open string, by bringing it to rest gently on the string. In this case, the action is performed more aggressively, with enough force to produce a 'dead' note (See Fig. 1). This is a technique that Mark uses frequently in his playing and is the contribution to the slap bass style that he is probably best known for. Fretting hand slaps are usually followed by either a thumb slap or a finger pop: using both hands in this way is the key to playing complex, continuous sixteenth note lines such as this one. As an example, to play the opening beat of bar one, you would slap the open E with the thumb, perform a ghost note with the fretting hand, slap another ghost note with the thumb, then pop the D at the seventh fret of the G-string. Because the work is being split between the two hands (as well as the thumb and fingers) it's possible to work parts like this up to considerable speeds. Using this explanation, it should be possible for you to learn the remainder of the part yourself. You should also note that ghost notes are written on the string where it is considered easiest to play them. You don't have to stick to this too rigidly – a ghost note is, after all, a ghost note, whichever string you play it on. Take care to play hammer-ons where written as these will help with the groove. On the third beat of the fourth bar of this riff there is a long group of notes played in one

stroke. To play this, I recommend fretting the A at the seventh fret of the D-string with your fourth finger, sliding quickly up to the B♭ and back again, then pulling-off to the G at the fifth fret of the D-string, which should already be fretted with the first finger. The fourth finger of the fretting hand can then hammer-on to the E at the seventh fret of the A-string. When playing this phrase, the trick is to keep all of the notes at a consistent volume. After this riff has been played twice there is a pause, where the bass plays a trill (bar 5). To play this, pluck the open E-string with your thumb and the D at the seventh fret with your first finger. The trill is performed by rapidly hammering-on and pulling-off to the E at the ninth fret of the G-string.

At letter B the same bassline is used to underpin the main melody. At letter C, a different part begins. Here, the bass plays a much simpler line using conventional slap and pop technique. Tenth chords (major and minor third intervals separated by more than an octave) are used to support the harmony here. For example, for the G△9 chord in bar 11, the bass plays a G on the E-string and a B a tenth higher, on the G-string. These notes should be allowed to ring together to create a

chordal effect. Using tenths in this way illustrates the tonality of the chord progression, meaning that even without another instrument playing the chords, you should be able to hear whether the chords are major or minor. This section of the track closes with a strummed power chord in bar 18, followed by a unison figure played with the fingerstyle technique in bar 19 – this is doubled by the piano and guitar. When playing this, I recommend playing with your picking hand close to the end of the neck so that you can really dig in.

After a repeat of the melody section at letter D, a new part begins at E. The bassline here is played with the fingerstyle technique and I recommend plucking with your picking hand closer to the bridge in order to achieve a tighter, funkier sound. When playing the pull-off and hammer-on phrases in the second bar of the riff (bar 25 for example), you can afford to allow the open A-string to ring beneath them.

At F, a new slap groove begins, although this is much simpler than the previous slapped parts. This line is based around A and requires only conventional slap technique. This leads into a repeat of the earlier,

Fig. 1: Using the fretting hand to perform ghost note slaps

tenth-based groove at letter G. This is played in the same manner as before, this time leading into the Breakdown section at letter H.

During letter H the bass is absent aside from a single harmonic which is manipulated in pitch by pressing down on the string behind the nut – a phrasing technique that Mark uses often. To do this, play the harmonic, then lift your finger off – the harmonic will continue ringing. Now, press down on the string behind the nut, raising the pitch a full tone, then releasing (see Fig. 2). You will need to have light strings on your bass

in order to bend the note up a full tone – Mark uses .030 as his lightest string for this very reason.

An eight-bar bass solo begins at letter I. Several of the bars in this solo open with a fast trill. This is played in the same way as the trill earlier in the piece: pluck the open E-string with the thumb and the D at the seventh fret of the G-string with your first finger. Note that this time the trill is a specific number of notes, with a notated rhythm. This is followed by a series of notes on the E-string, which in turn is followed by a descending string of notes which

Fig. 2: Bending a harmonic by pressing down on the string behind the nut

imply an Em7 chord. To play these, pop the D on the G-string, slap the G at the fifth fret of the D-string, then hammer-on to the E at the seventh fret of the A-string with your fretting hand. These notes are followed by an open E-string, slapped with the thumb. Because each of these notes is performed with a different digit/hand, it's possible to play this very rapidly. The remainder of this bar and all of the next is performed using the slap techniques discussed earlier.

A string of sixteenth note triplets is played in the climax of this solo, in bar 60. This is another Mark King trademark and is simpler to play than it might seem. Each triplet is played by popping a note on the G-string, performing a ghost note with the fretting hand, then slapping a ghost note with the thumb. Again, because each note is played with a different finger/hand, this can easily be done at very high speeds.

SOUND ADVICE

I recorded this piece using a Jaydee Supernatural Series III Mark King Signature bass. The bass was strung with light gauge Rotosound stainless steel strings, .030, .050, .070 and .090, the same set favoured by Mark. The pickup selector was centred, and the passive tone controls were set on full. The active treble and bass tone controls were also set to full, and the mid control was centred. I added compression and chorus digitally in order to more closely mimic Mark's early eighties tone.

In order to get close to this sound, I recommend using an instrument with two humbucking pickups if possible – single coil pickups as found on jazz and precision-style instruments are not as appropriate for this kind of tone, although you may prefer the sound they offer. A 'scooped' EQ setting will work well here: boosting the bass and treble frequencies, resulting in the 'smiley face' graphic EQ shape. Adding just a touch of chorus to the sound will also help you get close to Mark's early slap tone.

'KING FOR A DAY'

Written by Stuart Clayton

Drums: Mark Whitlam
Keys: Dan Moore
Guitar: Steve Banks
Bass: Stuart Clayton

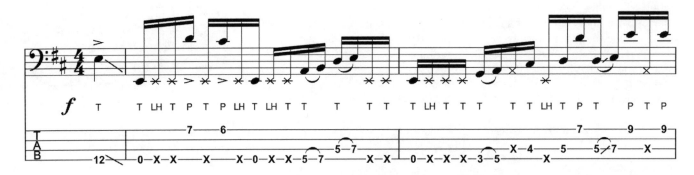

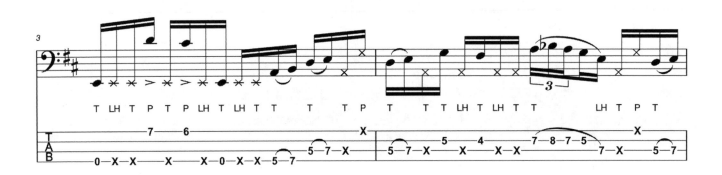

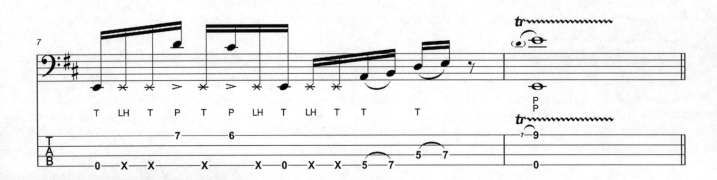

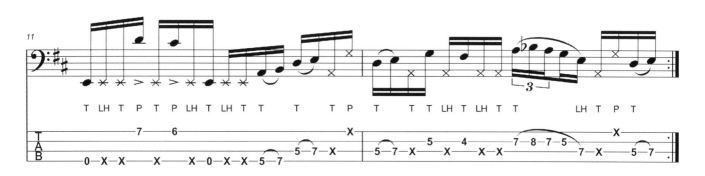

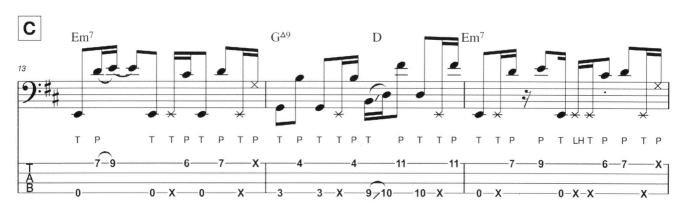

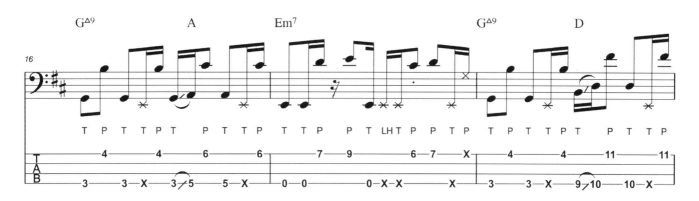

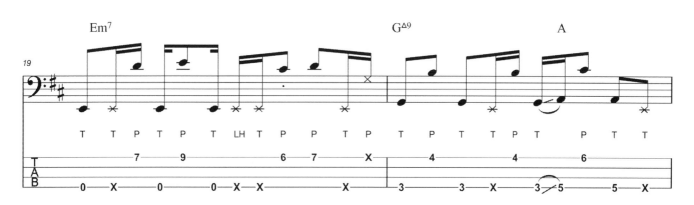

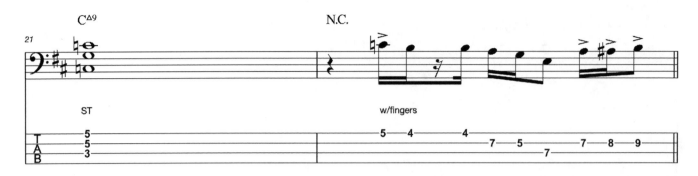

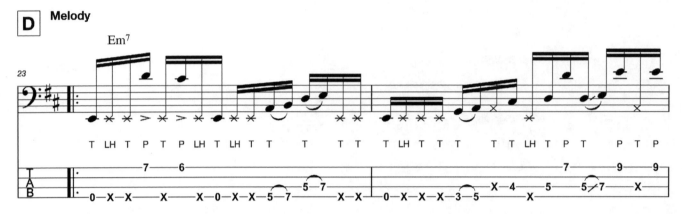

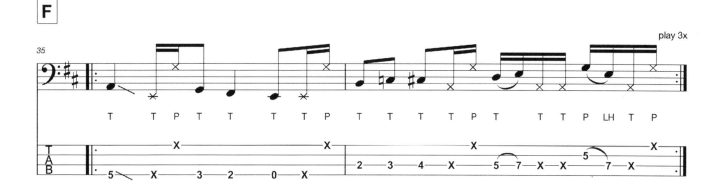

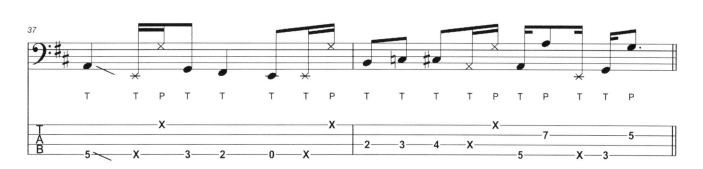

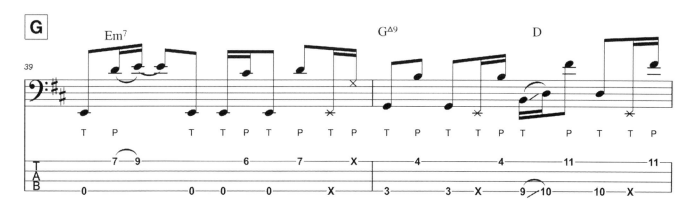

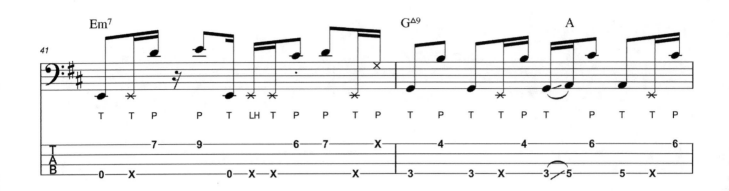

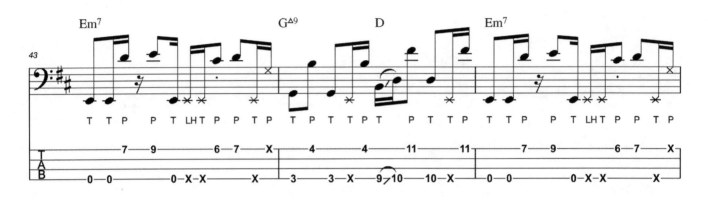

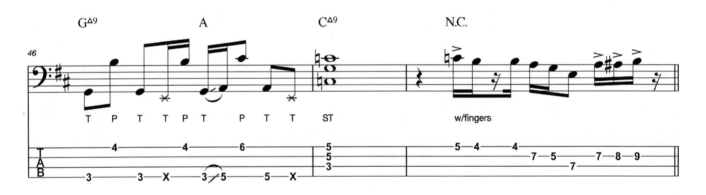

H **Breakdown**

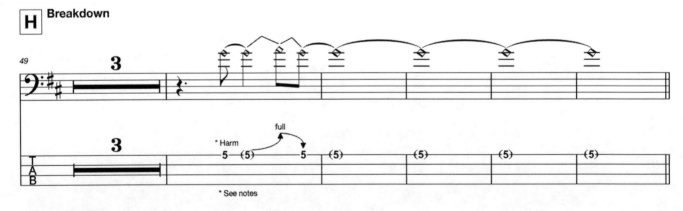

I **Bass Solo**

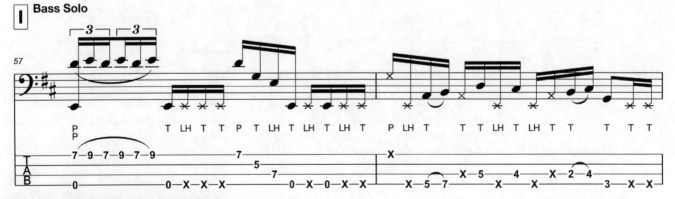

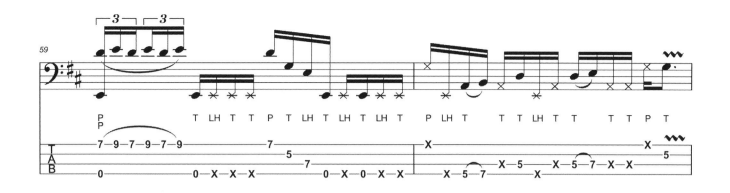

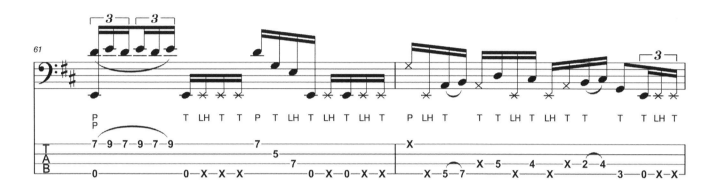

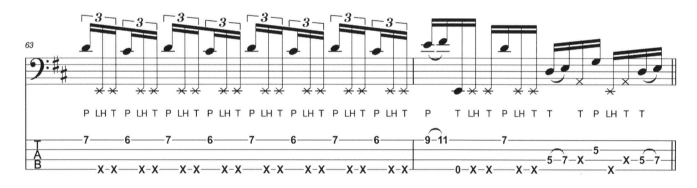

J **Melody**

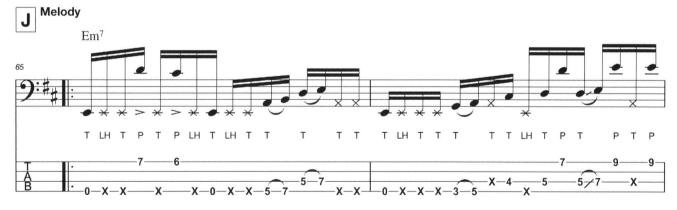

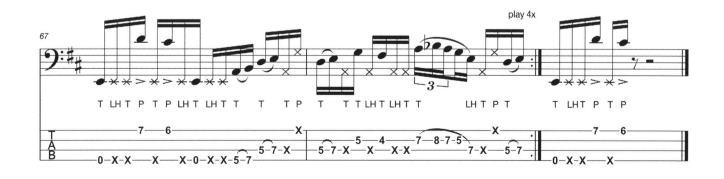

MICHAEL MANRING

Michael Manring is unquestionably one of the world's most gifted solo bass players. During his long tenure as the house bassist with independent label Windham Hill, and later through his work as a solo artist, Manring has worked tirelessly to help establish the bass guitar as a viable medium for solo instrumental performance. His 2005 release *Soliloquy* was his first solo bass album, an incredible achievement that stands as a testament not only to his incredible virtuosity and mastery of alternate tunings, but also to his unique compositional voice.

Michael Manring was born on 27th June 1960 and is the youngest of four brothers. He was brought up in a very musical environment and was inspired to take up the bass after hearing one on a television show. Although he initially thought what he heard was a piano, he later discovered it was a bass guitar and so persuaded his parents to buy one for him for his tenth birthday. 'Ever since I started playing the bass, I liked hearing it played by itself' he recalls. 'I composed little pieces for myself right from the very beginning.'

Michael went on to study both the electric and upright bass at high school and in the late seventies attended the prestigious Berklee College of Music. Despite his interest in solo performance, he left the college after a year to tour with a Top 40 band. 'When I talked to my friends about it, they suggested it was unlikely anyone would ever want to listen to solo bass music, so I concentrated on ensemble playing instead'.

After just a few months, he discovered that life on the road playing pop music was not going to satisfy his creativity. He therefore returned home and began working with fusion group Natural Bridge, and guitarist Michael Hedges, a similarly ambitious musician who had been exploring the sonic possibilities of the guitar through the use of altered tunings. Michael played with Hedges on an album called *Breakfast in the Field*, which was recorded for a small independent record label named Windham Hill. Both Hedges and Windham Hill would prove to be enormously important to Michael's development as a musician.

Despite these promising developments in his career, in 1983 Michael decided to move to New York, where he was able to study with renowned jazz bassist Jaco Pastorius. He began to find work on the thriving New York jazz scene but left the city after a year when more appealing musical opportunities began to present themselves on the West Coast. He relocated to San Francisco in 1984 and began working on his first solo album, *Unusual Weather*. Released two years later, this record would be the first to feature his growing interest in the unlikely genre of solo bass performance, a field which he found was being influenced from multiple sources. 'There are several traditions I refer to as a soloist, including chamber music, solo jazz guitar and piano and fingerstyle guitar' he notes. 'But I've drawn inspiration from so many sources it's always hard to try to come up with a list. I would like to mention one person, however. When I was about 23, I saw a solo saxophone performance by the great Ned Rothenberg, and it was a pivotal experience for me. Although the fact that he was playing what may be an even more unlikely solo performance instrument than the bass was certainly encouraging, it was the depth of what he was able to do that really got to me. The combination of virtuosity, openness, creativity, and relevance in his music helped open my eyes to the possibilities of the solo context and after that there was no turning back!'

Over the next few years Michael continued to work as the house bassist at Windham Hill and continued to release his own solo records. The follow-up to *Unusual Weather* was 1989's *Towards the Center of the Night* and was followed by *Drastic Measures* in 1991. The latter album – which was produced by Pat Metheny bassist Steve

Rodby – was Michael's finest work thus far, and to this day stands as a testament to his vision of the bass guitar as a solo instrument. Combining astonishing virtuosity with thoughtful arrangements and compositions, *Drastic Measures* features ensemble pieces and four solo bass pieces. Two of the latter are covers: '500 Miles High' by Chick Corea and 'Purple Haze' by Jimi Hendrix. The remaining two are 'Red Right Returning' and 'Watson & Crick', which is played on two basses simultaneously.

Michael's next album was 1994's *Thonk* and was something of a departure from his established sound. Alongside solo bass compositions, Michael recorded heavy rock/fusion ensemble pieces featuring guest artists such as guitarists Steve Morse and Alex Skolnick and Primus drummer Tim 'Herb' Alexander. The solo compositions on *Thonk* feature his Zon Hyperbass (see Gear Analysis on page 75) in myriad tunings: 'Monkey Businessman' is played in C-F-B♭-E♭, while 'The Enormous Room' features over twelve basic tunings and more than a hundred tuning alterations throughout. But surely with so many tuning possibilities on offer it must be next to impossible to retain any kind of fretboard knowledge? 'I'm more fluent in some tunings than others, but I don't think it's as hard as it may seem' says Michael. 'It's just a matter of keeping track of the intervals between the strings. If you're used to working with various tonalities in standard tuning, it's not an unfamiliar process'.

In 2005 Michael finally realised a childhood dream by releasing *Soliloquy*, an album containing only solo bass compositions. 'I always wanted to do an all-solo recording' Michael explains. 'It's my feeling that the bass has so much expressive range it's capable of creating deeply engaging music on its own. Whilst I was signed to a major label from 1984-1997, they understandably weren't willing to take a risk on it, but that may have been a good thing because it gave me a chance to develop my ideas a bit'. The album opens with 'Helios', named after the Greek god of the sun. This piece, together with its sister piece 'Selene' (goddess of the moon), was written

to explore the possibilities of the Hyperbass and is a showcase for Michael's outstanding use of highly rhythmic right hand techniques. 'My perception of the bass is that it has enormous expressive potential in virtually all aspects of music, certainly in the world of rhythm. I often think of it as a kind of percussion instrument, and I've studied as much percussion music as I can for inspiration. Over the last few years I've had a lot of fun borrowing ideas from Carnatic and Hindustani music and I'd have to say the tradition of Indian percussion music has been another major influence on my solo performance. Recently I've been developing a kind of system for studying and practicing various rhythmic ideas on the bass and I'm having a great time with it!'

The sister composition 'Selene' is another of the album's many highlights and features multiple tuning alterations on the Hyperbass. '"Selene" was the first piece I wrote on the Hyperbass, and I had actually put a lot of it together in my head before the bass was completed. A lot of the impetus came from the awareness that I'd be able to do contrary motion re-tuning on the

TOP TRACKS

'Spirits in the Material World'
Drastic Measures

'Red Right Returning'
Drastic Measures

'Purple Haze'
Drastic Measures

'Watson & Crick'
Drastic Measures

'500 Miles High'
Drastic Measures

'The Enormous Room'
Thonk

'Helios'
Soliloquy

'Excuse Me, Mr. Manring'
Soliloquy

'I Left America'
Soliloquy

'Selene'
Soliloquy

instrument – to move some strings move up in pitch while others are moving down. That idea provided some of the initial thematic material for the composition and other than that it was just about trying to form a complete and expressive musical statement'.

Further album highlights come in the shape of 'I Left America' a beautiful, harmonic-laden ballad performed on a Larrivée 5-String acoustic and 'Excuse Me Mr. Manring', a funky chordal piece that once again showcases Manring's highly developed sense of rhythm. The album is not without some decidedly strange moments either, one of which comes in the form of 'Solipsism', a composition that while performed on the bass guitar, sounds little like anything ever before heard on Earth! 'That's a prepared bass piece' offers Michael. 'Preparing an instrument is an idea that was invented by the great American composer John Cage in the 30's as a way of extending the timbral palette of an instrument. For "Solipsism" I put binder clips at strategic points on the strings to give it a kind of metallic sound. The primary theme of *Soliloquy* is solitude and I wanted to dedicate a piece to the epistemological concept of solipsism. This seemed like the best way to do it!'

Michael Manring has done more than most to further the development of the bass guitar as an unaccompanied solo instrument and has seen the genre develop and grow considerably over the past two decades. 'I'm not sure I have much objective perspective on this as I tend to be kind of obsessed with my own vision of where I'd like to take the concept, but it is very inspiring to see all the cool things people are doing with solo bass these days. It's hard to say where things will go in the future, but it seems to me there are folks making some great music on unaccompanied bass. I'd love to feel I've been able to pass on some of the inspiration I've received from my heroes and to be part of a thread of continuity, but my focus is on just trying to make good music. I'd like to say thanks to everyone who supports creative music of all kinds. It may be idealistic, but I believe music really is a positive force in the world.'

Michael Manring with his Zon Hyperbass

BASS GUITARS

The instrument that Michael Manring is most commonly associated with is the Zon Hyperbass, a unique bass guitar which allows for a staggering number of different tuning possibilities, all at the flick of a lever. The instrument was conceived as Michael began to develop more solo pieces in altered tunings, some of which required on-the-fly tuning adjustments. Initially, Michael was able to achieve this by memorising the positions of the tuning pegs but realising that this was far from the ideal solution, he went in search of a luthier who could build him a revolutionary new instrument designed for this very purpose. Although several luthiers dismissed the idea, Manring struck gold with Joe Zon of Zon Guitars who was keen to take on the challenge. After a year in development, the result was the Zon Hyperbass, a fretless instrument with a full three octave composite neck and a heel-less, extended cutaway that allows for complete access to the upper register. The headstock of the Hyperbass features four custom-made Hipshot de-tuners (one per string) meaning that multiple altered tunings are quickly available. These retuning possibilities are augmented further through the addition of a custom-built bridge, which features levers for raising and lowering the string saddles either together or individually, allowing for further tuning alterations.

The Hyperbass has quadrophonic electronics consisting of a single Bartolini magnetic pickup and four Fishman piezoelectric transducers which are built into the body and neck of the instrument. The bass can be used in either regular mono mode – where the combined pickup/transducer signal is routed through the on-board Zon circuit to the ¼" jack – or in full quadrophonic mode, where each output is routed to an 8-pin connector. In quadrophonic mode, the signal from each string can be processed separately.

Michael took delivery of the first Hyperbass in 1991, shortly before the recording of his *Drastic Measures* album. The bass can be heard on every album he has released since, but perhaps his most notable recording on the instrument is 'Selene', from his 2005 album *Soliloquy*. This extraordinary piece features almost continuous manipulation of the instrument's tuning, and even features sections in which the tuning levers are used to create 'contrary motion', where two melodic parts move in alternate directions.

Michael regularly uses the first prototype Hyperbass as well as a custom Sonus/Hyperbass hybrid. He also often uses 'Vinny', a Zon VB4 headless bass which he can be seen using on his performance of Stanley Turrentine's 'Sugar' from the *Bass Day '98* DVD.

Prior to using Zon basses, Michael regularly used instruments by Paul Reed Smith, Steinberger and Music Man. He also uses Larrivée acoustic basses, one of which can be heard on 'I Left America', from *Soliloquy*.

Michael uses D'Addario strings, usually preferring EXL220's. Because of the demands placed on the strings by retuning, he strings his Hyperbass with very light strings, gauges .020, .032, .042 and .052.

AMPLIFICATION

During the nineties Michael used SWR amplification, usually favouring an Electric Blue head and a Baby Blue 2x8 cabinet. He is currently a Markbass endorsee and uses the Little Mark II amplifier, which he runs into two Markaudio AS602 cabs and an AS121S cabinet. He also uses the Markbass Traveler 121H cabinet, the Multiamp and the MoMark amplifier.

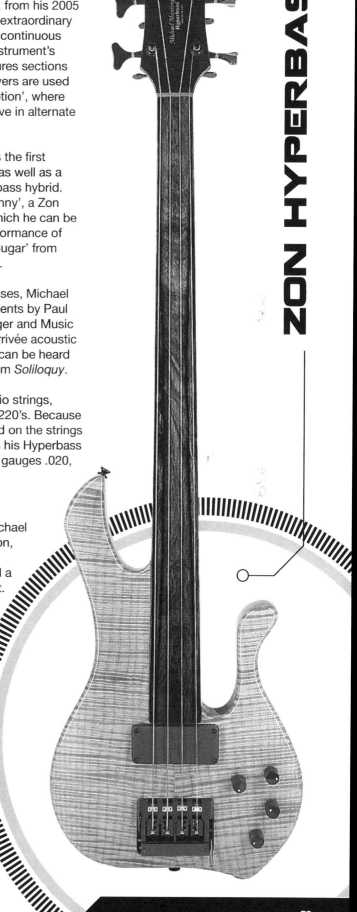

ZON HYPERBASS

PERFORMANCE NOTES

'You're Excused...' is a challenging solo bass composition that has been written in the style of Michael Manring, a bassist who has been very successful in combining multiple techniques into one seamless performance. Although Manring's penchant for utilising multiple tunings is not reflected here (very difficult without a Hyperbass...), this piece nevertheless covers many of the techniques that he frequently uses in his playing, including slapping, strumming, two handed tapping and palm muting.

The opening A section of this study is performed with palm muting. To use this technique, you'll need to rest the edge of your picking hand across the strings near the bridge (See Fig. 1). Doing so will mute the strings, but you'll probably need to experiment with the amount of pressure that you apply. With the strings muted, the notes are plucked with the thumb (not slapped) and the index and middle fingers. The majority of this line can be performed with the thumb in conjunction with the index finger, although there are a couple of places where the middle finger will be required. The first of these is the opening bar, which features a quick series of ghost notes played across the four strings after the initial open E. I recommend playing this phrase as follows: play the open E with the thumb, then immediately use the thumb again to play the ghost note on the A-string. The two ghost notes on the D and G-strings can then be plucked with the index and middle fingers. The second ghost note on the D-string should be played with the index finger.

The second part that requires clarification is in bar 4. After the open A-string is played with the thumb during the third beat, the fretting hand should hammer-on a D at the fifth fret of the A-string. This is then followed by ghost notes on the D and G-strings, played with the index and middle fingers respectively. This sequence is then repeated twice more, without the open A-string: the fretting hand hammers a pitched note and is followed by two ghost note plucks. All ghost notes here

are played as thirty-second notes, meaning that they will go by quite quickly. As the notes are ghost notes, this figure is purely a rhythmic decoration.

At letter B, the main theme of the piece is introduced – this section was inspired by Michael's composition 'Excuse Me, Mr. Manring', hence the title of the piece. The main idea behind this part is a slapped E on the first beat, followed by a series of ghost notes and a second low E, all on the second beat and all of which are performed using the double thumbing technique. When playing this group of four notes, slap the E-string with the upper part of the thumb and allow it to come to rest on the A-string – don't bounce the thumb away as you would with conventional slap technique. You can then bring the thumb back upwards, playing the string on the way. This is essentially like using your thumb as a pick and is known as 'double thumbing.' You can see a photograph illustrating the double thumbing technique on page 150.

The second half of the bar features a descending sequence of harmonics. These are played using conventional

fingerstyle technique and should be allowed to ring into one another in order to create a chordal effect. In the following bar this sequence is replaced with two major ninth chords played as a combination of fretted notes and harmonics. These chords are very much a tip-of-the-hat to legendary bassist Jaco Pastorius, who used similar chords in his composition 'Portrait of Tracy'.

The C section of this piece is performed using slapping and strumming techniques and is a little more aggressive. Slap guides have been written between the staves for guidance, although you'll need to ensure that you are comfortable strumming upwards and downwards to play this part. Many of the chords in this riff are played in conjunction with open strings – you should allow all of the notes to ring into one another when playing this line. After this section the main theme returns (at letter D) but is developed slightly: an $F^{\triangle 13}$ chord is added in place of the $G^{\triangle 9}$ in bar 19 and the section closes with a longer turnaround that features four different chords played as a combination of fretted notes and harmonics (bars 23 and 24).

Fig. 1: Picking hand position for the palm muting technique

At letter E a new part begins. Here, an F^13 chord is played using the same voicing that was used back in bar 19. You should use the chordal fingerstyle technique to play this chord, switching to slap technique for the final F of the first beat. This F is followed by a fretting hand ghost note slap, after which another F is slapped. This is immediately followed by a double stop, tapped with the picking hand (See Fig. 2). The double stop is then repeated and pulled-off to sound the open D and G-strings. The fretting hand then hammers-on another double stop at the tenth fret. This is followed by a final double stop tapped by the picking hand. This is pulled off to sound the open A and D-strings, after which the fretting hand hammers-onto the G at the tenth fret of the A-string. The majority of the note choices in this part reflect the overall F^9 tonality.

The second bar of this sequence is extended by two beats to be 6/4. The principles of performing it are exactly the same as the previous bar, but with added double stop taps and pull-off figures. After several repeats, this line segues nicely back into the main theme for one final time.

The final section of this piece (at letter G) is another slapped and strummed line, based on the earlier part from letter C. This time the line is extended into a four-bar part, with added chords that turn it around. As before, this section can be played louder and more aggressively than the previous part. Note that there is also a slight acceleration here.

Have fun with this piece – there's a lot to digest and it will require a lot from you in terms of technical skill. Whilst this piece is a great opportunity for you to put all of your techniques to the test, try to make the end result sound musical. Dynamics, phrasing, and timing are all just as crucial to creating a captivating performance as the techniques are.

Fig. 2: Tapping double stops

SOUND ADVICE

I recorded this piece on a Zon Sonus 4-string bass. This instrument worked well as I have a 'ramp' installed between the two pickups, which makes using the palm muting and double thumbing techniques easier. This is because the ramp reduces the string-to-body distance and there is therefore less room for your fingers or thumb to snag on the strings as you play. You don't need to install a ramp on your bass to play this piece and indeed, there are many amazing bassists who don't bother with them.

In order to bring out the harmonics effectively, I favoured the bridge pickup slightly and boosted the midrange – you'll find it difficult to get the harmonics at the second the third frets to speak out effectively without doing this. Whatever instrument you use to perform this piece, try to do the same. If you don't have a mid control on your bass, boost the midrange on your amp if you can. Some compression and reverb were added digitally – both of which are important when playing solo pieces of this nature.

'YOU'RE EXCUSED...'

Written by Stuart Clayton

Bass: Stuart Clayton

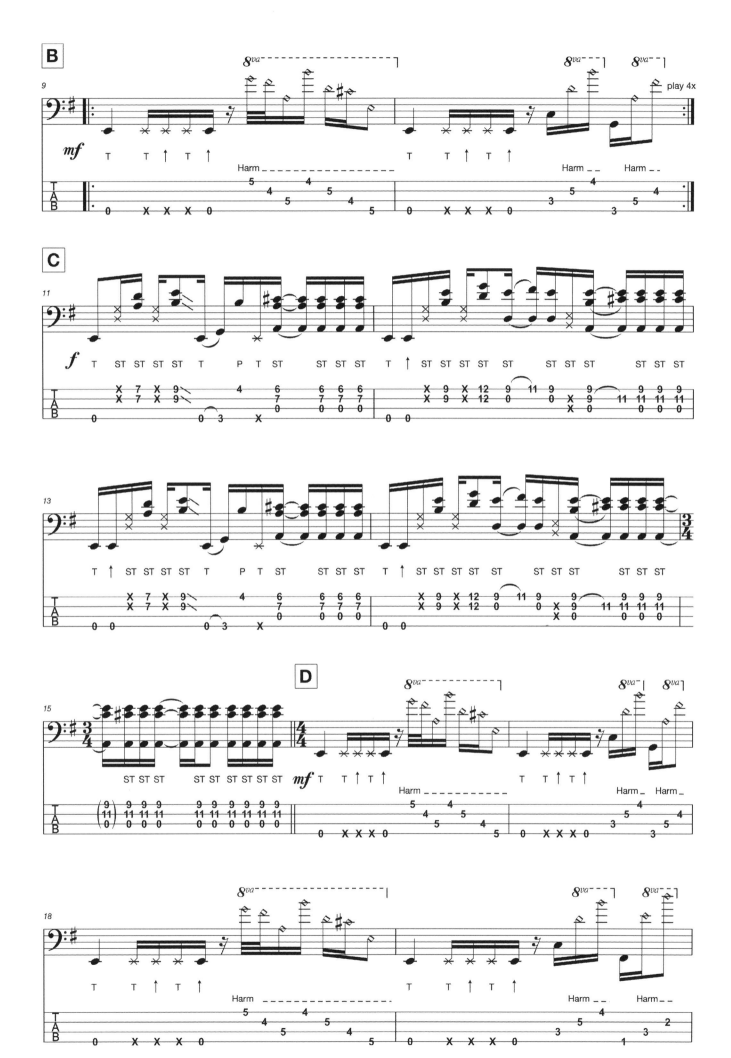

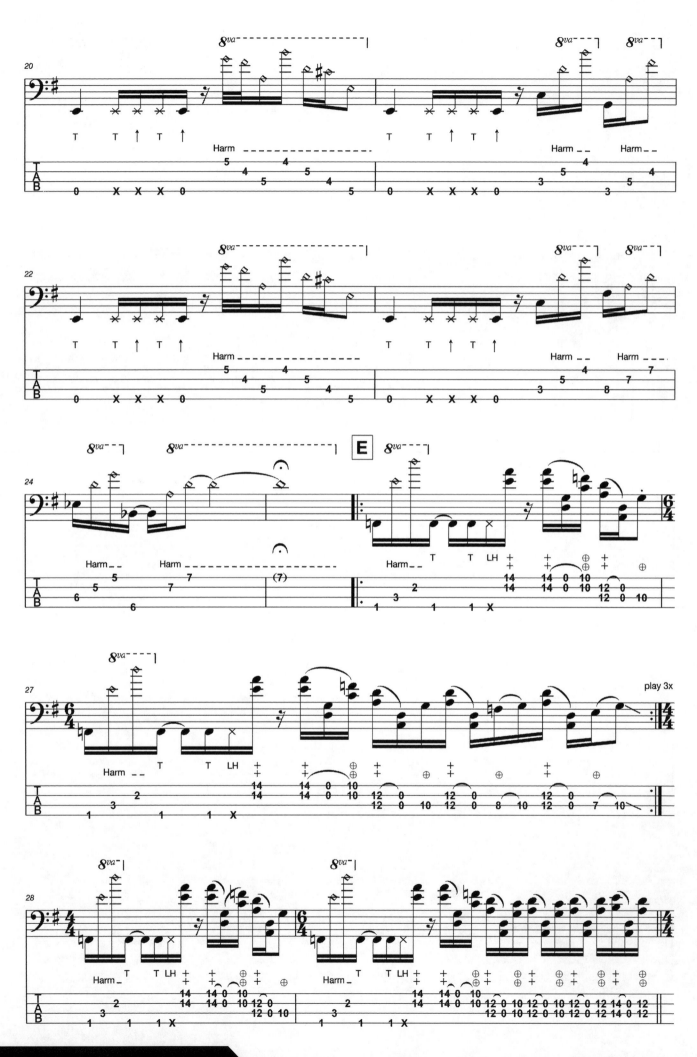

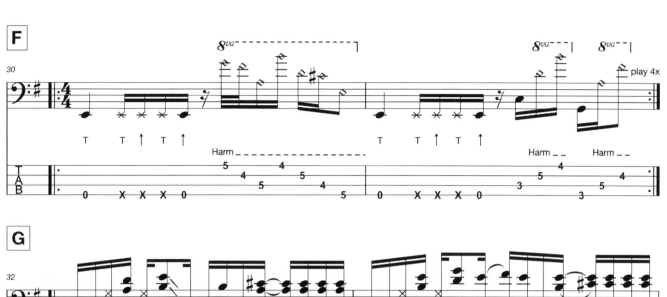

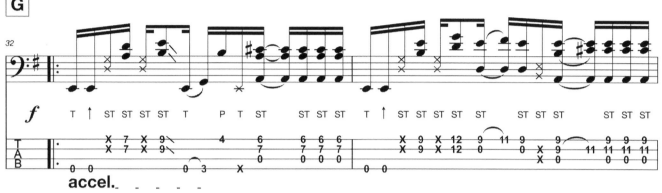

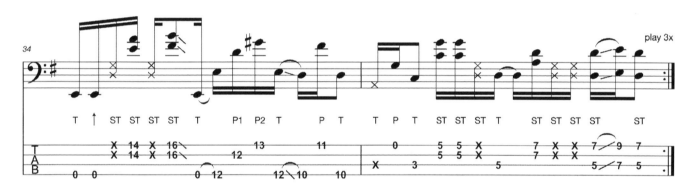

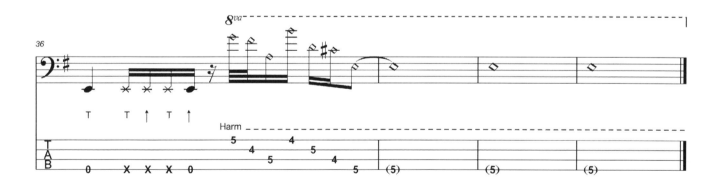

MARCUS MILLER

Diversity is one of the keys to success for a musician, and it's certainly a concept that Marcus Miller has embraced throughout his career. Segueing effortlessly from the thriving seventies New York studio scene into high-profile work with artists such as Miles Davis, Luther Vandross, and David Sanborn, somehow Miller also found the time to forge a solo career that has made him one of the world's most respected bass players. His popularity amongst bassists remains as high as ever, resulting in him having one of the most recognisable and widely imitated voices on the instrument.

Marcus Miller was born in Brooklyn, New York on 14th June 1959 and brought up in the Jamaica district of Queens. Not only was he born into a musical family (his father was an organist and jazz pianist Wynton Kelly was his second cousin) but he also found himself surrounded by musicians in his local neighbourhood. Captivated by R&B acts such as The Jackson 5, Stevie Wonder and Kool & The Gang, he began his musical endeavours first by playing the piano and singing, then at the age of 10 learning to play the clarinet. Realising that the clarinet was unlikely to land him a place in any of the local R&B groups, he went in search of a new instrument under the guidance of his music teacher Mr. Guarino. After first trying his hand at the saxophone, he finally found his instrument when his best friend was given a bass guitar. Realising that the bass was the foundation of the music that he loved, Miller now knew where he must focus his efforts and before long had his own bass, a semi hollow bodied Univox.

Alongside his bass guitar studies, Marcus continued to hone his clarinet skills and was eventually awarded a place at the prestigious New York High School of Music & Art. From there he progressed to Queens College on a clarinet scholarship, supplementing his studies with bass gigs in the evenings. Studying the instrument during one of its most fertile periods, he had no shortage of inspiration, with bassists such as James Jamerson, Robert Bell, Wilton Felder, Jaco Pastorius, Stanley Clarke and Larry Graham all exerting a strong influence on his playing. His school friend Kenny Washington also encouraged him to study jazz, introducing him to the work of Paul Chambers, Eddie Gomez, and Ron Carter. Miller's jazz studies allowed him to significantly advance his understanding of harmony and composition.

Marcus's earliest professional gigs were with keys player Lonnie Liston Smith and Harlem River Drive, a band which also included his cousin Ronnie Miller and drummer Omar Hakim. In 1977, Ronnie began working with renowned jazz flutist Bobbi Humphrey and was quick to mention Marcus's name when she needed a new bass player. Soon after joining Bobbi's band, Marcus wrote a song for her called 'Love When I'm in Your Arms'. Humphrey liked it and asked to record it on her next album, convincing producer

Ralph MacDonald to use Marcus on the session. Impressed with Marcus's playing and reading skills, MacDonald began employing and recommending the young bassist for studio work around New York. Starting with TV commercials and radio jingles, Marcus soon found himself working around the clock at studios all over the city. During this period, he also began playing with fellow Jamaica district resident Lenny White, who was well-known for his work with Chick Corea and Return to Forever. Marcus initially toured with White and subsequently played on his solo albums *Big City* (1977) and *Streamline* (1978).

In 1978 Marcus began playing for the *Saturday Night Live* TV show. It was here that he met saxophonist David Sanborn, with whom he became friends and began writing and recording. Miller played on Sanborn's 1981 album *Voyeur* as well as writing and co-writing a number of tracks. The slap bass driven 'Run for Cover' in particular quickly became popular with bassists and has since become one of Miller's best-known compositions. This early recording of the track finds Miller on fine form and features a powerful slap

groove and a tasteful solo. Long-time fans of Marcus will notice that his heavily chorused bass sound on this version of the song is somewhat different to the famous tone that he later developed on his Sadowsky-modified '77 Fender Jazz bass.

During this key period of his career, Marcus also began working with jazz vocalist Roberta Flack, becoming friends with backing vocalist Luther Vandross in the process. Miller and Vandross began writing and demoing material together, beginning a collaboration that would not only make a superstar out of Vandross, but would also see them writing material for Aretha Franklin's early eighties comeback. The Queen of Soul's Grammy-nominated song 'Jump to It' (from the 1982 album of the same name) was written by the pair and produced by Vandross.

In 1981 Marcus received a phone call from legendary jazz trumpeter Miles Davis asking if he could be at his studio in two hours. Miller agreed and found himself being auditioned to play on Davis's 1981 album *The Man with the Horn*, his first release in six years. The success of this album led to Marcus working extensively

SELECTED DISCOGRAPHY

Marcus Miller – *The Sun Don't Lie*
'Panther', 'Rampage', 'Scoop', 'Mr. Pastorius', 'Moons', 'Teen Town', 'The King is Gone (For Miles)'

Marcus Miller – *M²*
'Power', 'Lonnie's Lament', 'Nikki's Groove', 'Goodbye Pork Pie Hat', 'Cousin John', '3 Deuces', 'Red Baron'

Marcus Miller – *Free*
'Blast', 'Funk Joint', 'Free', 'Strum', 'Jean Pierre', 'Higher Ground', 'What is Hip?'

Marcus Miller – *Renaissance*
'Detroit', 'Redemption', 'Slippin' Into Darkness', 'Setembro', 'Jekyll & Hyde', 'Revelation', 'Mr. Clean', 'Gorée', 'Cee-Tee-Eye'

Marcus Miller – *Tales*
'Tales', 'Eric', 'True Geminis', 'Rush Over', 'Running Through My Dreams', 'Ethiopia', 'Brazilian Rhyme', 'Infatuation', 'Come Together'

Marcus Miller – *Silver Rain*
'Bruce Lee', 'La Villette', 'Frankenstein', 'Boogie On Reggae Woman', 'Girls and Boys'

Marcus Miller – *Tutu Revisited*
'Tomaas', 'Backyard Ritual', 'Splatch', 'Portia', 'Jean Pierre', 'Hannibal', 'Tutu'

Marcus Miller – *Afrodeezia*
'Hylife', 'B's River', 'We Were There', 'Papa Was a Rolling Stone', 'I Still Believe I Hear', 'Son of Macbeth', 'Water Dancer'

with Miles over the next few years, appearing on the live album *We Want Miles* in 1982, *Star People* in 1983 and *Tutu* in 1986. *Tutu* was significant for both Davis and Miller: Davis received the 1987 Best Jazz Instrumental Performance, Soloist Grammy for the album, while Miller wrote the majority of the material, played many of the instruments himself and co-produced the record alongside Tommy LiPuma.

Having now garnered an enviable reputation for himself as a first-call session bassist – not to mention as a writer, multi-instrumentalist, and producer – Miller began to take steps to establish his own solo career. His first two albums, *Suddenly* (1983) and *Marcus Miller* (1984) were commercial R&B records with a focus on his song-writing and vocal skills. Both albums were under-promoted and therefore unsuccessful, despite containing strong material and an impressive cast of musicians. Although these records are not essential listening in the same vein of much of Marcus's later work, several gems can still be found on them: the slapped intro of 'Superspy' and the slap/synth grooves of 'Juice' in particular

stand out, as does his fretless work on 'Nadine'. Following the lack of commercial success with these albums, Miller began working with Lenny White in The Jamaica Boys and continued to focus on his studio career. He also branched out into film music in the late eighties – his first score was for the popular comedy *House Party* (1990), after which he worked on the Eddie Murphy comedy *Boomerang* (1992).

In 1993, nine years after his previous solo effort, Marcus wrote and recorded a third album, *The Sun Don't Lie*. Featuring a sophisticated collection of jazz and funk-influenced instrumentals, the album met with critical acclaim both amongst the bass community and a wider jazz audience, reaching #9 on the Billboard Contemporary Jazz Chart. Dedicated to the memory of Miles Davis (who had passed away shortly before its release), the album featured guest appearances from highly regarded musicians including Wayne Shorter (Weather Report), Vernon Reid (Living Colour), Joe Sample (The Crusaders) and Tony Williams (Miles Davis Band). Unsurprisingly, *The Sun Don't Lie* album gave bass players plenty

to get their teeth into: from the opening solo phrases of 'Panther', to the infectious slap grooves of 'Rampage', and the stellar fretless work on 'Moons' it was clear that Miller was not just a first rate studio musician, but was also fast becoming one of the most exciting new voices on the instrument. However, it was his slapped cover version of the Weather Report classic 'Teen Town' that drew the most admirers: Miller had been playing the bass-led tune as a lead-in to the commercial breaks on *Saturday Night Live* for some time and it had generated a considerable buzz amongst bass players. Traditionally a piece that would be played fingerstyle, Miller's highly developed slap technique allowed him to navigate the intricate, meandering melody with ease, and without sacrificing the groove. Unsurprisingly, this piece has since become a favourite amongst his fan base.

Marcus followed the success of *The Sun Don't Lie* with *Tales* in 1995. Seeking to focus specifically on his solo career for an extended period of time, Marcus took three months off from other commitments to write and record the album. Inspired to

A promo shot for Marcus's signature bass with Sire

Marcus playing his signature Sadowsky-modified Fender Jazz bass

include elements of rap and hip-hop in his music, Marcus decided to build the album around the history of black music, using samples of renowned musicians speaking about their experiences. *Tales* also featured collaborations with fellow bassist Me'Shell NdegéOcello on 'Rush Over' and vocalist Lalah Hathaway on 'Infatuation'.

Marcus remained busy throughout the remainder of the nineties: he produced saxophonist Wayne Shorter's 1996 album *High Life,* and formed the Legends band with Eric Clapton, David Sanborn, Joe Sample and Steve Gadd. He also released a live album, *Live and More* (1998).

His next album, *M²*, arrived in 2001. Dedicated to the memory of Grover Washington Jr., the record again featured a stellar cast of musicians including Herbie Hancock, Wayne Shorter, Chaka Khan, Raphael Saadiq, Branford Marsalis, Maceo Parker, and Fred Wesley. Again inspired by hip-hop and rap, many of the pieces utilised slower tempos,

allowing Marcus greater rhythmic flexibility in his playing – this is particularly evident in the album opener 'Power' where Marcus not only uses quick-fire double thumbed passages, but also adds rhythmic 'ghosting' between notes and phrases in the same way that a jazz drummer might play ghost notes on the snare drum. Inspired by the way artists such as Miles Davis and John Coltrane would play cover versions of their favourite songs, Miller began to do the same with this album, hoping to introduce a new generation to classics such as 'Red Baron' (Billy Cobham), 'Goodbye Pork Pie Hat' (Charles Mingus) and 'Lonnie's Lament' (John Coltrane). *M²* was also reflective of his movie scoring career: a string section was used on several songs, whilst 'Boomerang' was a development of a short piece that he had written for the Eddie Murphy movie of the same name, and which had become popular with his fans. Of course, there was plenty for bass players to marvel at throughout the album, including the infectious bass riff of 'Power', the palm-muted funk

of '3 Deuces', and his astonishing hard-plucked solo on 'Red Baron'.

In 2005 Marcus collaborated with operatic tenor Kenn Hicks on Avanti, an album of famous arias set against a jazz/gospel background. The project had its roots in the late eighties when Hicks had been recommended to Marcus as a vocal

YOU MIGHT ALSO LIKE...

If you're a fan of Marcus's work, be sure to check out the following bassists:

○ **Stanley Clarke**
Giants of Bass: 60s - 70s

○ **Jaco Pastorius**
Giants of Bass: 60s - 70s

○ **Larry Graham**
Giants of Bass: 60s - 70s

coach. After hearing Hicks singing an aria, Marcus told him he wanted to record it in a jazz setting, setting in motion a project that would come to fruition over fifteen years later. Also in 2005, Marcus released a new studio album, *Silver Rain*. The title track featured Eric Clapton, who had written the song with Marcus whilst they were playing together in the Legends band. *Silver Rain* is notable for bass-driven tracks such as 'Bruce Lee' and 'La Villette' and cover versions of Edgar Winter's 'Frankenstein', Stevie Wonder's 'Boogie On Reggae Woman' and Beethoven's 'Moonlight Sonata'.

In the latter part of the decade, Marcus began seeking out new challenges. This resulted in the formation of SMV, a bass guitar super-group with fellow low-enders Stanley Clarke and Victor Wooten. The seeds for this particular venture had been sown at *Bass Player* Live back in 2006 when Miller and Wooten had joined Clarke on stage after presenting him with the magazine's Lifetime Achievement Award. An album – *Thunder* – was released in 2008, featuring new compositions alongside cover versions from the back catalogues of the three bassists. The group, backed by a full band, toured successfully following the album's release.

In 2010, Marcus toured to celebrate the twenty-fifth anniversary of Miles Davis' acclaimed album, *Tutu*. Recalling Davis' preference not to look to the past, Marcus decided to approach the project in a way that was respectful to Davis' habit of seeking out young musicians who would benefit from his experience. Recruiting a brand new band, Miller reworked and updated the tunes appropriately, the results of which can be heard on the stunning live album *Tutu Revisited* (2011).

Revitalised by the *Tutu Revisited* tour, Marcus decided to write his next album around his new group. The result was *Renaissance* (2012), arguably one of his best and most complete statements as a solo artist.

Largely eschewing cover versions this time around – aside from hard-hitting versions of Weldon Irvine's 'Mr. Clean' and War's 'Slippin' Into Darkness' – the album featured a wide variety of music, from the slick funk of 'Detroit', the jazz-tinged ballad 'Setembro (Brazilian Wedding Song)', to the CTI record label-inspired 'Cee-Tee-Eye'. Marcus is on top form throughout the album, soloing effortlessly with his highly developed slap technique on 'Detroit' and 'Mr. Clean', playing upright bass on 'February' and boasting flawless fretless and bass clarinet work on 'Gorée'. This particular song was written following a visit to the island of Gorée, a former slave camp off of the coast of Senegal. Miller performed this piece during the *Renaissance* tour and after a show in Paris, was approached by the director of UNESCO, who was impressed with the story behind the song. This meeting led to Miller taking on the role of Artist for Peace for UNESCO and becoming a spokesperson for their Slave Route Project.

Marcus's new role resulted in *Afrodeezia (2015),* a new album written in part to help raise awareness in young people about the history of slavery. Recorded at a variety of studios around the world, Marcus collaborated with musicians from West Africa, South America and the Caribbean. The result was an album of songs that celebrated the music of African slaves who had, in his words, 'figured out a way to turn their pain and suffering into amazing sounds: spirituals, blues, jazz, R&B.' *Afrodeezia* is notable for both Miller's bass work and the adaptation of traditional African musical styles and instruments into his own style: album opener 'Hylife' references West African highlife music, under-pinned by Marcus's inimitable slap grooves, while on 'B's River' he plays the melody on a gimbri, an African instrument considered to be a distant ancestor of the bass guitar. Following the release of *Afrodeezia*, Marcus embarked on a global tour to promote the album.

BASS GUITARS

Marcus Miller has spent the majority of his career playing one key instrument – his modified 1977 Fender Jazz. This bass, which was purchased for $265 in 1977, has an ash body and a maple fingerboard. It was heavily modified in the late seventies by Roger Sadowsky: as well as installing a Leo Quan Badass II bridge, he added a modified Bartolini TCT preamp and fitted a new, extended scratchplate to cover the additional routing for the preamp. The resulting tone proved to be exactly what Marcus was looking for and was soon being sought-after by bass players everywhere.

Fender released a Marcus Miller Signature bass in the late nineties, sporting most of the same features as Marcus's original: ash body, maple neck and fingerboard, mother-of-pearl block inlays and a Badass II bridge. In place of the modified Bartolini circuit was a custom-made Fender FMEQ active preamp with the same control set as the Bartolini. A 5-string edition of the instrument was released in 2003.

Throughout his career, Marcus has used several other Jazz basses, including a mid-sixties sunburst model which has been converted to a lined fretless. He also regularly uses a Fodera Emperor 5-string and a Modulus Graphite 6-string fretless. On *Afrodeezia* (2015) he also used a Music Man Sterling Fretless with a piezo pickup.

In 2015, Marcus began working with Sire, a Korean company who were becoming known for their ability to build high-quality instruments at an affordable price. Keen to promote an instrument that would be both affordable and beneficial to young musicians, Marcus ended his long relationship with Fender to begin working on a signature model with Sire. Two models were released: the V7 and the M3. The V7 is a Jazz-style instrument, available in two configurations: swamp ash with a maple neck and fingerboard, or North American alder with a maple neck and rosewood fingerboard. The M3 is a more modern-looking

instrument with two Music Man-style soapbar pickups with exposed pole pieces. Both instruments feature the same electronics – the Marcus Heritage 3-band preamp with sweepable mid control.

Throughout the nineties, Marcus used DR Hi Beam strings, gauges .045-.105. DR manufactured a popular Marcus Miller signature string set for many years. In 2015, Marcus began using Dunlop Super Bright strings and now has a signature set with the company.

EFFECTS

Marcus did not use effects pedals to a significant degree until his 2012 *Renaissance* album. During this time, he began using an MXR Bass Octave Deluxe and a Fulltone OCD Overdrive, both of which can be heard on 'Detroit'. During the sessions for *Afrodeezia*, he also used a Sanford and Sonny BlueBeard fuzz/distortion.

AMPLIFICATION

Over the years Marcus has used a few different setups. He favoured SWR throughout the nineties and early 2000's, often pairing an Interstellar Overdrive Preamp into two SM-900 power amps. For cabinets, he used SWR Goliath III cabs. In 2006 SWR built a Marcus Miller signature 2-channel preamp.

During the early 2000's Marcus began using EBS equipment, which he continues to use. He favours either the HD350 or HD650 amps paired with two ProLine 4x10 cabinets.

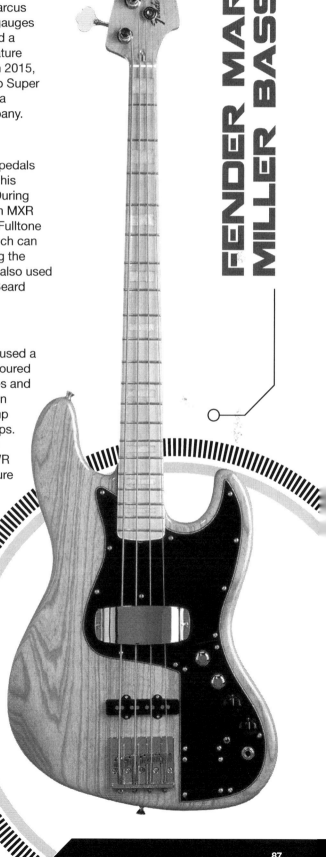

FENDER MARCUS MILLER BASS

PERFORMANCE NOTES

This piece is one of the more challenging in this book and references Marcus's more recent work on albums such as *Silver Rain, Renaissance* and *Afrodeezia*. The bass part is slapped throughout and will require you to be comfortable using more advanced techniques such as double thumbing and slapping/popping fast sixteenth note runs. In short, there's plenty here for you to get your teeth into.

The track opens with a short phrase played by the bass. This bluesy lick requires several hammer-ons and pull-offs from the fretting hand and you'll need to work on playing this cleanly and with all notes at a consistent volume. This line leads into the main groove at letter A, which is similar in style to 'Detroit' from Marcus's 2012 album *Renaissance*. This line is based around G minor pentatonic and blues scales and is challenging to play because of the slow funk tempo: playing busy parts such as this and maintaining a strong groove is a huge part of Marcus's style and it's where you should focus your efforts when learning this line. Watch out

for the trill figure in bars 3-4 and the descending blues scale run in bar 8. When playing this you'll find you have to play three notes on the D-string in quick succession using the slap and pop technique. It can be difficult to do this cleanly and ensure that all notes speak out at an equal volume, but this another important part of Marcus's style.

At letter B there is a key change to E minor and a new part begins. Here, you'll be playing simple hammer-on/pull-off phrases on the G-string whilst supporting them with bass notes on the E-string. You'll need to be careful of the fingerings you use here. For example, when playing the second half of bar 11, you should fret the D on the E-string with the second finger. This will allow you to place your first finger on the E at the ninth fret of the G-string and your third or fourth on the F# to perform the pull-off (see Fig.1). Using this fingering will enable you to keep the low bass note ringing under the top notes. Again, for this riff you'll need to be comfortable popping and slapping on the same string. In this case you'll be doing so on the G-string, and

you'll need to focus closely on your slapping technique here in order to get the right attack. The same idea is used for the next three bars.

At bar 15, the top part becomes a little more complex, requiring you to slide downwards to an additional melody note at the end of each phrase. Doing this and releasing the lower bass note at just the right moment is tricky and will require practice. Note that the line hangs on the B$^{\flat\triangle 7}$ chord before the anacrusis phrase from the intro reintroduces the main theme.

At letter D the main theme leads into a new section, another sixteenth note-based line. Note that tenth intervals are used in the first bar of the riff to support the chords, while a descending A minor pentatonic lick is played in the second bar. Playing this riff with the slap technique is difficult, as you'll need to maintain the same level of attack from string to string and with slaps and pops. I recommend that you closely follow the slap guides written between the staves when learning this since they illustrate the best way to play it.

Fig. 1: Recommended fingering for the bass/melody parts in the B section

STYLE TIPS

- ◯ Slow, funky slap grooves
- ◯ Use of slapped and popped notes on the same string – sometimes on the same note
- ◯ Use of minor pentatonic and blues scales
- ◯ Bass solo evolves out of the main riff of the piece
- ◯ Use of the double thumbing technique

At letter E the bass solo begins. Marcus's bass solos often grow organically out of his basslines (see 'Frankenstein' and 'Detroit') and I wanted that to be the case here. This solo starts with a part closely based on the main theme of this piece, which then ascends the neck following the G blues scale. This is played with conventional slap and pop technique and is then repeated. The next line (bars 38-41) is based on a sliding octave idea which is similar to way that Marcus opens his solo on his cover of the Edgar Winter classic 'Frankenstein'. When playing this, leave the lower note ringing whilst popping the notes on the G-string as this will really thicken up the sound. The second and fourth bars of this section feature simple blues scale and pentatonic-based fills. Watch out for the two successive popped notes at the end of the third beat of bar 39 – you'll need to use both your first and second fingers to pop these as indicated in the slap guides.

Bars 42-45 each open with a burst of C's. These are played using a rapid slap-pop sequence that is tough to execute cleanly. Be sure to follow the slap guides and practice this slowly.

The final section of the solo (bars 46-49) requires some double thumbing. The main phrase is a descending blues scale, four notes of which are played on the D-string. These are played with a down-up-down-up motion. If you've never used the double thumbing technique before, it is essentially treating the thumb as

a plectrum. You'll need to slap a little closer to the top of the thumb, on the corner of the nail. When playing the down stroke, allow the thumb to pass through the string, ready to come up again, plucking the string on the way (See Fig. 2). Marcus uses this technique often in his playing and you'll hear great examples in 'Power' and 'Detroit'. You can also find out more about this technique in *Ultimate Slap Bass*, also available from Bassline Publishing.

Fig. 2: Performing an upstroke with the thumb

SOUND ADVICE

I recorded this track using a Fender Marcus Miller Signature Jazz Bass, strung with Dunlop Super Bright strings. All of the controls on the bass were turned up full and I recorded direct into Logic. Once recorded I tweaked the EQ slightly, boosting the low mids at around 158Hz in order to add a little more punch. A healthy dose of compression was also added.

The key to playing this piece – or indeed any of Marcus's tracks – is a solid slap technique that you can control at slower tempos. It's one thing playing slap bass fast, but quite another to make it groove at slow tempos. This is probably the key thing I would encourage you to focus on when learning this piece.

Following the above advice regarding technique will be the biggest part in capturing Marcus's sound. Using an active Fender Jazz-style instrument will obviously also be a big help. Marcus's new signature bass with Sire is an excellent – and very affordable – active Jazz-style instrument.

'MILLER TIME!'

Written by Stuart Clayton

Drums: Mark Whitlam
Keys: Dan Moore
Guitar: Steve Banks
Bass: Stuart Clayton

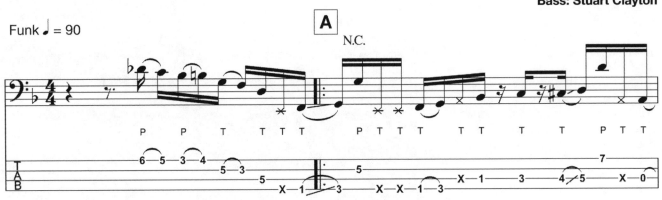

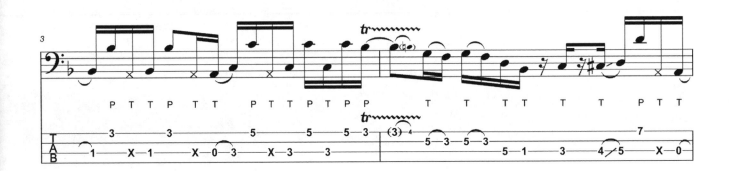

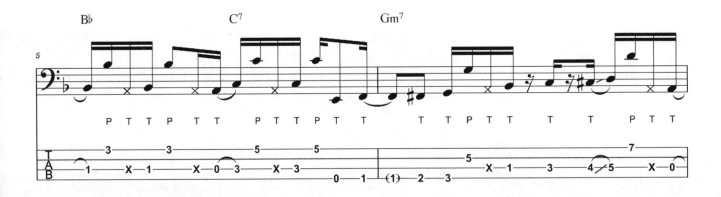

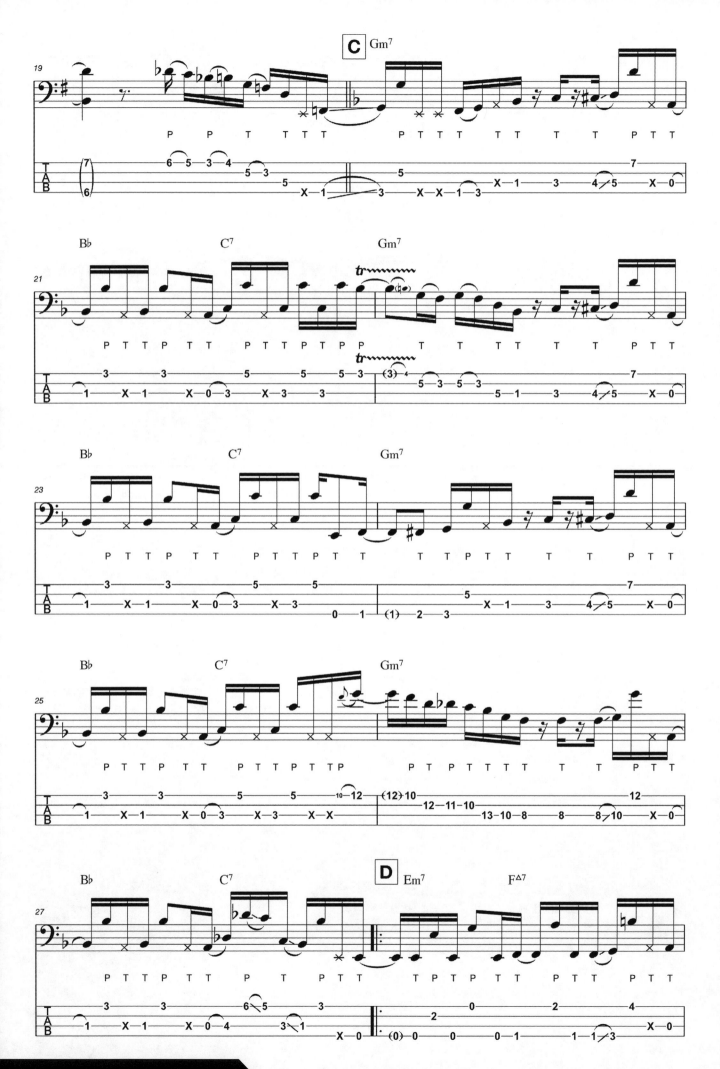

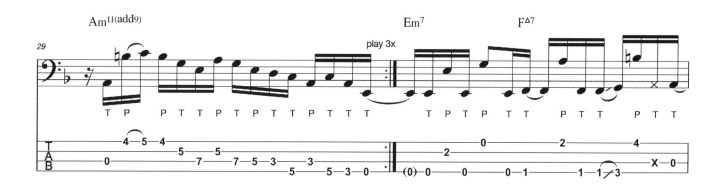

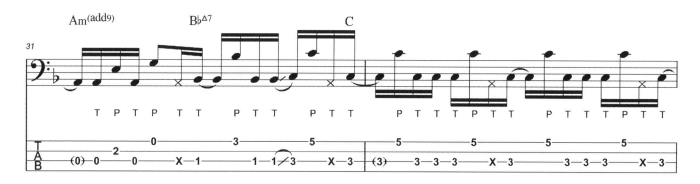

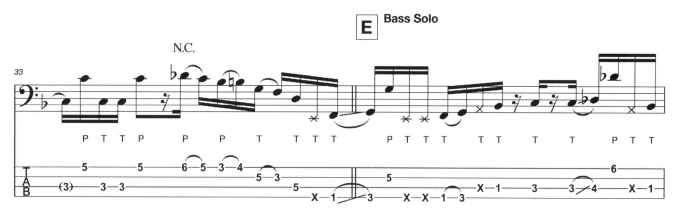

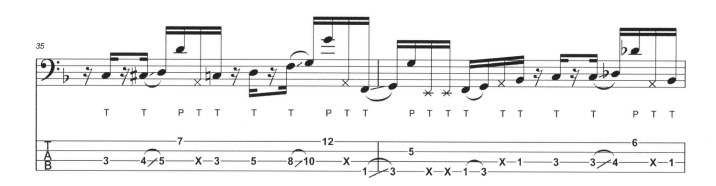

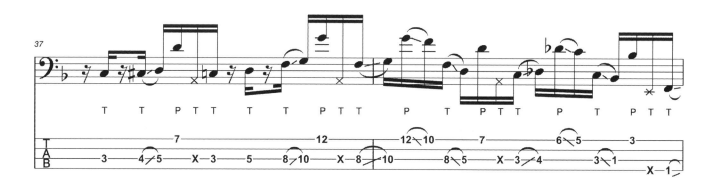

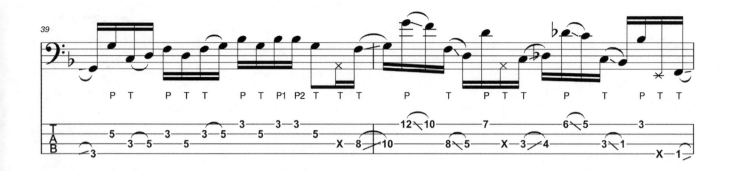

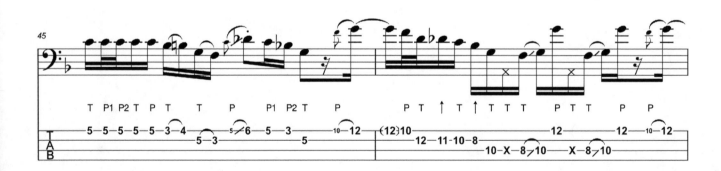

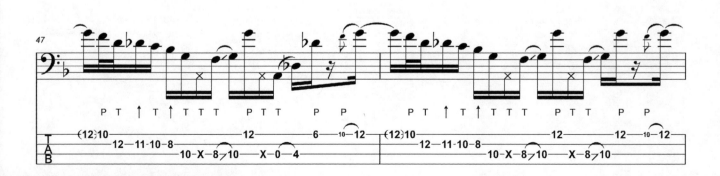

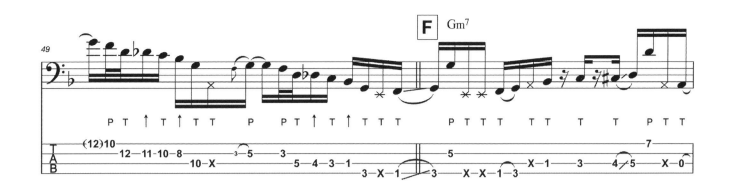

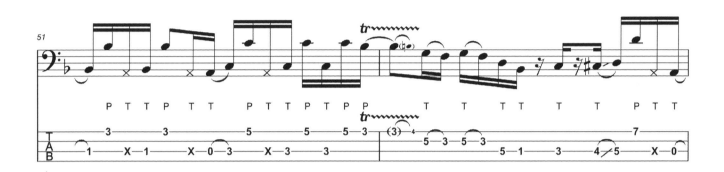

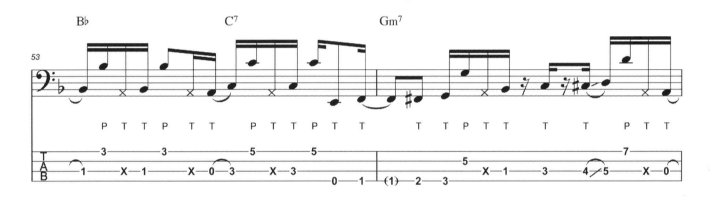

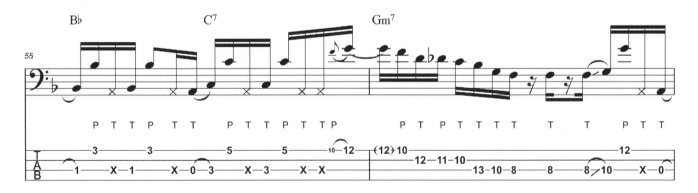

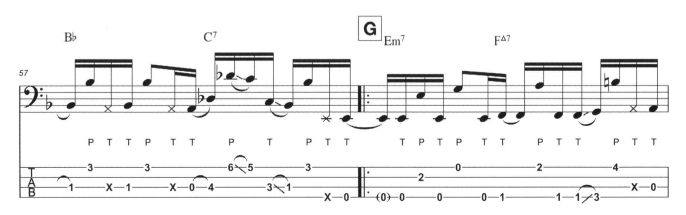

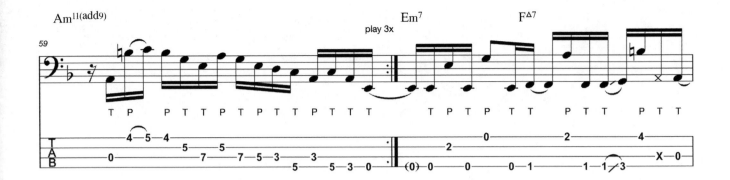

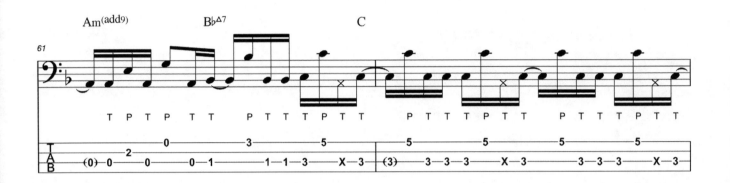

JOHN MYUNG

John Myung is a founding member of progressive metal titans Dream Theater and is arguably one of the genre's most gifted bassists. Throughout the band's thirty year career, Myung has anchored their complex, progressive music, navigating complex unison runs, extended song forms and multiple time signature changes with ease. Despite his reputation as the most reclusive and private member of the band, Myung has topped bass player polls the world over, and has undoubtedly earned his reputation as one of the giants of the bass guitar.

John Myung was born on January 24th, 1967 in Chicago, Illinois. His family later moved to New York, and he grew up in the Kings Park area of Long Island. Although his parents were not musicians themselves, they listened to a lot of classical music at home and at the age of five, John's mother insisted that he take up the violin. His violin lessons continued for the next ten years until as a teenager, he discovered metal bands such as Iron Maiden and Black Sabbath, and progressive rock groups such as Rush, Jethro Tull, Yes and Genesis. After realising that he played the violin, one of his friends asked him to join his band as their bassist, reasoning that a bass guitar also had four strings and John should therefore be able to adapt to it easily enough.

After buying himself a bass, John took to the instrument with enthusiasm, finding inspiration in the work of bassists such as Steve Harris, Geddy Lee, Chris Squire, and Billy Sheehan. During this time, he became friends with fellow Long Island resident John Petrucci, who played the guitar and shared similar musical tastes. The pair would frequently get together to practice, working through Iron Maiden and Rush albums, each practicing for over six hours a day.

Upon graduating from high school, Myung and Petrucci had set their sights on attending the prestigious Berklee College of Music in Boston, where many of their musical heroes had learnt their craft. Fortunately, their parents were supportive of their choice and in September 1985, they were enrolled at the college. It was here that they met drummer Mike Portnoy, with whom they forged an instant musical connection. The three began playing together frequently, initially working on cover versions of their favourite songs, then writing and demoing their own original material. They christened themselves Majesty, a suitably pompous name for a fledgling progressive rock band, arrived at after hearing a friend describe the guitar solo on the Rush song 'Bastille Day' as 'majestic'.

Majesty knew that in order to fulfil their potential, they would need to find a keyboard player and vocalist. After failing to find a suitable keyboard player at Berklee, they recruited Kevin Moore, another Long Island resident who had grown up with Myung and Petrucci, but who had instead gone to the State University of New York. A suitable vocalist was found in the form of Chris Collins, another Long Island friend who in the time Myung and Petrucci had been at Berklee, had developed an incredible singing voice. After completing their first year at Berklee, Myung, Portnoy and Petrucci realised that they would not be able to properly immerse themselves in their studies and pursue the band at the same time. They therefore decided not to return for their second year, convincing their parents to support them whilst they pursued the band.

Majesty began playing live in the summer of 1986 and after only a handful of shows it became clear that Collins was not the right fit for the group. He was replaced by Charlie Dominici and before long the band had caught the attention of Mechanic Records, a small New York-based record company. The band signed with the label in 1988 and immediately began recording their first album. However, upon discovering the existence of another group named Majesty – who had trademarked the name – the band were forced to find a new identity.

They eventually settled on Dream Theater, named after a small, art deco cinema that Mike Portnoy and his father had often attended.

The debut Dream Theater album *When Dream and Day Unite* was released in March 1989. Although commercially unsuccessful due to Mechanic's lack of promotion, it was well-received by critics and enabled them to continue building a loyal fan base. Of all the tracks from the album, 'The Ytse Jam' was the standout. This instrumental piece is an astonishing showcase for all members of the group and features complex unison passages, odd time signatures and a blazing, distorted bass solo from Myung.

With one album under their belt but having made no real progress, the band were forced to carefully consider their next move. They decided that Dominici – who was considerably older than the rest of the band – was not the right front man for the group and so the search was on for a replacement singer. Numerous vocalists were auditioned over the next year and at one point the band became so frustrated with their search that they considered becoming a purely instrumental group. Fortunately, in 1990 they met Canadian vocalist James Labrie, a talented singer with an incredible range and who fit perfectly with the band's look. With their new singer on board, the band negotiated a release from their contract with Mechanic, signed a new record deal with ATCO and immediately began demoing material for their second album.

Images and Words was released in 1992 to critical acclaim. Although confident in their material, the band knew that as it was released, they were fighting against the popular grunge movement, which eschewed technical skill in favour of much simpler song writing. They were therefore stunned when the low-budget promo video they had shot for 'Pull Me Under' went into heavy rotation on MTV, resulting in the song becoming a considerable hit. As a consequence, *Images and Words* went on to sell over half a million copies, wildly outstripping both the band and their record label's expectations. Still regarded by many of the band's fans as their finest

work, the album features incredible bass work from Myung throughout: tracks such as 'Take the Time' and 'Learning to Live' showcase his ability to play long, fast unison passages and navigate complex time signatures, while 'Metropolis – Pt. 1: "The Miracle and the Sleeper"' features a tapped bass solo that soon had Myung's fans tying their fingers in knots trying to play it.

The surprise success of their second album enabled Dream Theater to expand their audience and led to them playing much larger venues. Keen to capitalise on their investment, ATCO were eager for new material, and so the band entered the studio in May 1994 to begin recording their third album. The result – *Awake* – was released in October that year and charted at #32 on the U.S. Billboard 100 Chart and #65 in the UK Charts. Despite featuring some undeniably strong material, the band were unable to replicate the huge success of 'Pull Me Under', partly due to a shift in the musical landscape which was by now heavily favouring grunge and alternative rock groups. Nevertheless, there was plenty

TOP TRACKS

(with Dream Theater)

'The Ytse Jam'
When Dream and Day Unite

'Metropolis – Pt.1'
Images & Words

'Caught in a Web'
Awake

'Lifting Shadows Off a Dream'
Awake

'New Millennium'
Falling into Infinity

'Trial of Tears'
Falling into Infinity

'The Dance of Eternity'
Scenes from a Memory

'Panic Attack'
Octavarium

'Breaking All Illusions'
A Dramatic Turn of Events

'Enigma Machine'
Dream Theater

for bass players to get their teeth into on *Awake*, from the complex unison passages on tracks such as '6:00' and 'Caught in a Web', to the chords and harmonics intro to 'Lifting Shadows Off a Dream'. Unfortunately, shortly after the release of the album, keyboard player Kevin Moore announced his departure. He was quickly replaced by Derek Sherinian for the tour.

Following *Awake's* lack of commercial success, Dream Theater found themselves under pressure to write a more accessible album in the hopes of them reaching a wider audience. The result was 1997's *Falling into Infinity*, which was promoted with the single 'You Not Me', a more commercial rock song which was accompanied by a suitably moody promo video. Fortunately, although the album was a focused attempt to reach a larger audience, the band were able to retain significant progressive elements in the music, ensuring that they retained their existing fan base. Myung was able to develop his role in some new directions on the album, using a Chapman Stick on the opening track 'New Millennium' and playing fretless for the first time on 'Peruvian Skies'. However, despite the band's best efforts, *Falling into Infinity* did little to broaden their appeal and was considered by their label to be another commercial disappointment.

For their next album Dream Theater insisted on complete creative control. After dismissing Derek Sherinian, they hired new keyboard player Jordan Rudess and began work on their fifth studio record, a concept album which was a 'sequel' to the track 'Metropolis – Pt.1' from *Images and Words*. The result, 1999's *Scenes from a Memory*, was released to rave reviews from critics and fans alike, charting at #73 on the Billboard 200 Chart and #2 on the Billboard Top Internet Albums Chart. In 2012 it would be voted #1 in *Rolling Stone* magazine's poll 'Your Favourite Prog Rock Albums of All Time'. The album, which is now considered by many fans to be their best,

features some stunning bass work from Myung, notably on the lengthy instrumental piece 'The Dance of Eternity', a track which features all of the progressive elements expected from the band, as well as another blistering bass solo. The band toured to promote the album, playing it in its entirety along with a handful of other popular songs from their back catalogue. A live DVD, *Scenes from New York* was released in 2000 and is an excellent chance to see Myung and the band in action during this key period in their career.

Having now established a loyal fan base, Dream Theater continued to record new albums and tour with regularity. In 2002 they released the critically praised *Six Degrees of Inner Turbulence*, which featured the longest piece the band had written to date, the 42-minute-long title track. *Train of Thought* followed in 2003, an attempt by the band to write a much heavier, darker album. Another live DVD was recorded in 2004, this time filmed at the legendary Budokan arena in Tokyo, Japan. This show is notable for 'Instrumedley', a 12-minute medley of many of the instrumental pieces Dream Theater had recorded up to this point. The DVD extras allowed the viewer to watch this track through single camera angles, meaning that it was possible to watch each member in isolation.

After releasing *Octavarium* in 2005, the band celebrated their twentieth anniversary in 2006 with a show at Radio City Music Hall in New York. During the show, the band played with a full symphony orchestra on songs such as 'Sacrificed Sons', 'Six Degrees of Inner Turbulence' and the 24-minute 'Octavarium'. *Score*, a DVD of the show was released later in 2006 and again, is highly recommended viewing.

Dream Theater continued releasing albums and touring until in 2010 founding drummer Mike Portnoy announced his shock departure from the group. Stunned by this development, the remaining members subsequently began the search for a new drummer, holding auditions with seven of the world's top players. They eventually hired virtuoso Mike Mangini, who had previously worked with Extreme, Steve Vai and Annihilator. The

audition process was documented in a three-part YouTube series *The Spirit Carries On*.

Despite this setback, Dream Theater's 2011 album, *A Dramatic Turn of Events* was their most successful yet, reaching #8 on the U.S. Billboard 200 Chart and earning the band its first Grammy nomination for the song 'On the Backs of Angels'. Along with this track, the album is notable for 'Breaking All Illusions', a song which recalls the band's *Images and Words* era, and which has proven extremely popular with their fans.

The band's twelfth album, simply titled *Dream Theater* was released in 2013. It was another huge success, earning positive reviews, charting well, and resulting in a second Grammy nomination, for the song 'The Enemy Inside'. John Myung's bass enjoys a particularly good place in the mix on this album, with his aggressive, distorted tone shining through on the bass breaks of instrumental 'The Enigma Machine' as well as 'Behind the Veil' and the stunning album closer 'Illumination Theory'.

In 2016, Dream Theater released *The Astonishing,* a well-received double concept album set in a dystopian future where music has been abolished. The band embarked on a lengthy world tour in February 2016, playing the album in its entirety and hiring a production company to create suitable visuals and staging. During the tour the band made it clear that they would not be playing any other material from their back catalogue during the show.

Alongside his work with Dream Theater, John Myung has worked with progressive/fusion side projects Platypus and The Jelly Jam. Platypus, which features Myung alongside King's X guitarist and vocalist Ty Tabor, keyboard player Derek Sherinian and Dixie Dregs drummer Rod Morgenstein, were formed in 1997 and released *When Pus Comes to Shove* in 1998. *Ice Cycles* followed in 2000, although the group disbanded in the same year. In 2002, Myung, Morgenstein and Tabor formed The Jelly Jam, who have to date released three albums, with a fourth due in late 2016.

BASS GUITARS

John's first bass was a Memphis branded copy of a Fender Precision, which he quickly upgraded to a Fender Jazz bass. Whilst recording Dream Theater's debut album he used a combination of his Jazz bass and a Music Man StingRay, which had been modified to include an additional neck position pickup.

For the recording of the *Images and Words* album in 1992 John used a Spector NS-2 bass, although on tour, he played a Tobias 6-string. By the time of the *Awake* album in 1994 he had begun endorsing Tung basses, built by ex-Tobias luthier Nicolas Tung. He can be seen using these instruments in his 1996 tuition video *Progressive Bass Concepts*.

John switched to Yamaha basses in 1996, initially using TRB and John Patitucci signature models. However, after finding these unsuitable to his playing style, he then worked with Yamaha to design a signature bass. The RBX6JM was based on the company's RBX range and featured an alder body with a flame maple veneer. The instrument was available in two colours (Ruby Red and Turquoise Blue) and had an 'infinity' dot inlay on the ebony fingerboard. John used these basses when recording the *Falling into Infinity* and *Scenes from a Memory* albums and can be seen using them on the *Scenes from New York* DVD.

In 2002 a second iteration of John's Yamaha signature bass was released. This updated instrument reflected Yamaha's changes to the RBX line and featured a shorter, 34" scale and a single Seymour Duncan SMBa humbucker. John used these basses for the *Train of Thought* and *Octavarium* albums.

John switched to Music Man basses in 2006 when recording *Systematic Chaos*. Although he initially used a Bongo HS 5-string, he later developed a custom bass with Music Man. This instrument had the body from a 6-string Bongo, fitted with the neck from a 5-string, but accommodating six strings with tighter spacing. By 2013 he was still using these basses, but now had two

models: an HS (humbucker/single coil) and a HH (dual humbucker). On the HS he had no controls other than master volume, while on the HH he had just volume and a 4-way switch that changed the polarity of the pickups. These instruments are unique to John and have not been released as a signature instrument.

John strings his basses with Ernie Ball stainless steel strings with gauges .032, .045, .065, .085, .105, .130. He typically records with his basses set with a lower action, raising it up slightly when on tour.

EFFECTS

John's main effect is distortion. In the past this has been provided by Pearce BC-1 preamps (with the Billy Sheehan modifications) and MXR Double Shot distortion pedals. He currently uses a Mesa Boogie Grid Slammer and a Fractal Audio Axe-FX, which has been used to model his old Pearce preamps. This unit also supplies all chorus and flanger effects as needed.

AMPLIFICATION

During the early part of his career John used Mesa Boogie equipment, usually Bass 400+ and M2000 amps and Strategy 400 and 500 power amps. He also used a Mesa Boogie Triaxis guitar preamp, which was modified to work for bass. Throughout the 2000s he used various combinations of Demeter, SWR and Ashdown amps and power amps, favouring Demeter optical compressors, preamps, and power amps as of 2011. As the band now uses in-ear monitoring, John no longer has any speaker cabinets onstage.

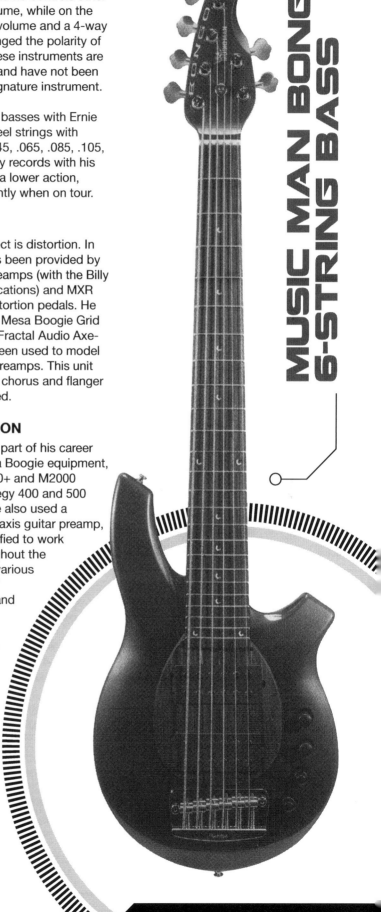

MUSIC MAN BONGO 6-STRING BASS

'A Nightmare… for the Fingers'
is one of the longest pieces in this
book, which seems appropriate for
a progressive metal composition!
**This track combines many of the
elements that are typical to both
Dream Theater's music and bassist
John Myung's playing: upper
register melodies, aggressive rock
riffs, odd time signatures, metric
modulations and a fast, distorted
bass solo.**

The piece opens with a melody that
is played by the bass in the upper
register – you'll need to listen for the
hi-hat count-in when playing this with
the backing track as the piece starts
with thunder and lightning sound
effects. You'll be able to play the first
three bars of the melody using the
finger-per-fret technique: put your
first finger on the E at the fourteenth
fret of the D-string. Technically, you
could play the first four bars using
this technique by playing the G and
F♯ notes on the D-string. However,
when recording this piece, I felt
that the line flowed better using a
slide down to these notes on the
G-string. You'll also need to move
out of position again for the D at the
nineteenth fret in bar 5. This melody
is simple to play, but it's the details
that bring it to life: note length,
slides, etc. Whilst this melody is
being played, the guitar and drums
play a series of rhythmic figures –
try not to be distracted by these
when playing the melody. This idea
is similar to the intro of the Dream
Theater song 'The Glass Prison'.

At letter B the bass begins playing
a meaty riff in the lower register.
This line is built from the E blues
scale and is simple to play. As the
chords change in the fourth bar, the
bass plays root notes. There is a
rallentando the fourth time through,
bringing this opening section of the
song to a close.

At letter C a new riff begins, at a
much faster tempo of 210bpm. This
part is initially played only by the
bass, and you can afford to play
quite aggressively here. This riff is
again based on the E blues scale,
with the F♯ in the fourth bar hinting
at the E natural minor scale. You can
play this riff with condensed fingering

for the most part (four fingers
covering three frets), with the first
finger covering the D on the A-string
and the fourth playing the E two frets
higher. You should shift to finger-per-
fret fingering at the end of the riff: put
your second finger on the G on beat
three of bar 20 in order to play the
tail of the phrase smoothly. Note the
groupings of three notes at the end
of the second time through this riff
(bars 23-24). When playing this part,
the first note of each group of three
should be accented slightly. After the
initial eight bars of the bass playing
the riff alone, the guitar enters, and
both play the riff together a further
two times.

At letter D, the same riff continues,
but this time there are some bars of
3/4 added in to alter the part slightly.
Although this will likely be confusing
initially, it's simpler to play than it
sounds. This time, the tail of the
riff is marked by some arpeggiated
root-fifth-ninth chords (bars 40 and
41). These arpeggios are very tough
to play due to the string crossing
required, so you'll need to work on
this part slowly. I recommend fretting
these arpeggios with the first finger
on the root, the third finger on the
fifth and the fourth finger on the ninth
– this is shown in Fig. 1 below.

At letter E a new riff begins. When
playing this, I recommend fretting
the F♯ on the E-string with the first
finger and the C♯ on the A-string with
the third. The only notes that change
throughout this line are those on
the A-string and you'll find that the
finger-per-fret technique works well
here. You'll need to 'barre' across
the second fret with the first finger
to play the B in bar 43 if you use this
technique. Note the use of a simple
phrase in 3/4 at the end of this riff.
This is played twice the first three
times through and three times on the
fourth time.

At letter F, a guitar solo section
begins using the riff that was
introduced back at letter B. Again
a new phrase in 3/4 is added in the
seventh and eighth bars (bars 57 and
58). This time the phrase is arpeggio-
based and is a similar idea to parts
heard in tracks such as 'Erotomania'
and 'The Enigma Machine'. Both
phrases can be played with the
finger-per-fret technique, starting
with the first finger.

At bar 65 a complex, syncopated
line begins. This is played in unison
with the guitar and is simple to play,
although the rhythm used is quite
challenging. This phrase is used to

Fig. 1: Fretting the root-fifth-ninth figures in bars 40-41

set up a metric modulation: note that rhythmically, each note in the phrase adds up to the value of a dotted eighth note. This rhythm is repeated over and over (hence the unpleasant syncopations) and becomes the new quarter note tempo (280bpm) for the next section. This is shown above the score, indicating that the dotted eighth note now become the quarter note pulse. This is a fairly simple metric modulation – Dream Theater have used this technique in far more complex ways. Check out the intro to 'The Mirror' from the *Awake* album for a several great examples of metric modulation.

With the tempo now at a very brisk 280bpm, there is an eight-bar piano solo at letter G. This has a 'ragtime' feel, something that the band have used several times in their music, notably in 'The Dance of Eternity' and some live versions of 'A Change of Seasons'. This is followed by an eight-bar bass solo. This solo is based on the opening melody of the piece and is very challenging to play at this tempo. The best advice here is to practice it slowly to begin with, figuring out all of your preferred fingerings first – all of the first four bars can be played in one position using the finger-per-fret technique (see Fig.2). In the second half of the solo you'll need to shift through different positions in order to play the descending pull-off figures. This solo – like John Myung's solos on tracks such as 'The Ytse Jam' and 'The Dance of Eternity' should be played with distortion, as this will really help it to stand out. The bass

then switches very quickly back into a walking bassline beneath a reprise of the piano solo, so you'll need to quickly switch off the distortion for this section.

At letter H, the final section of the song begins with an abrupt downshift in tempo to a much slower 90bpm. The bass plays supportive root-based parts for the first eight bars before switching to a more melodic line from 101 onwards. In comparison to some of the earlier parts of this piece, this is a very simple line to play.

Fig. 2: Fretting position for the opening four bars of the bass solo

SOUND ADVICE

This track was recorded using a Music Man Bongo HH 5-string bass. Both pickups were used and the tone controls on the instrument were set flat. The bass was strung with D'Addario stainless steel strings, gauge .045-.135. These were played in for a few days to take the edge off of the brightness of new strings. The main (clean) bass part was recorded direct into Logic. Having listened closely to some of John's isolated bass parts, I decided to play quite aggressively and used a reasonably low action. This resulted in some of the string noise and fretbuzz that can often be heard in his sound. The resulting tone was then EQ'd and compressed digitally. As John is a known admirer of the distorted tone that Billy Sheehan achieved through his Pearce BC-1 preamp, I decided to use the EBS Billy Sheehan signature drive pedal (second edition) for the bass solo. This has a distorted tone which is similar to the Pearce.

Using a bass with two humbucking pickups is obviously desirable when playing this piece, but playing the instrument hard enough to cause a little fretbuzz and string rattle is also a big part of the tone!

'A NIGHTMARE...
FOR THE FINGERS'

Written by Stuart Clayton

Drums: Jason Bowld
Keys: Fjokra
Guitar: Charlie Griffiths
Bass: Stuart Clayton

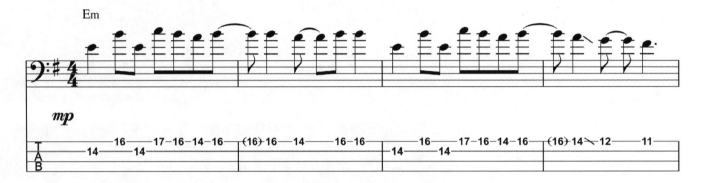

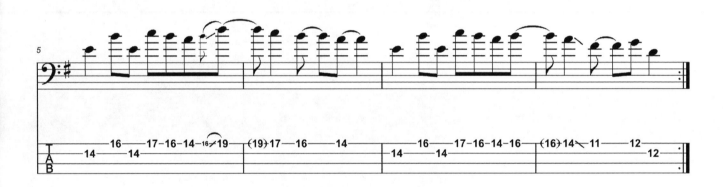

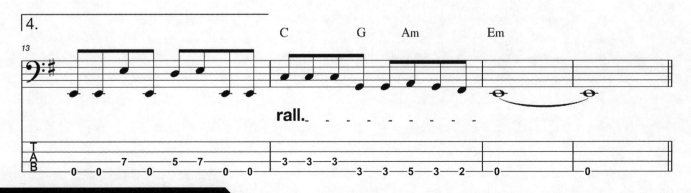

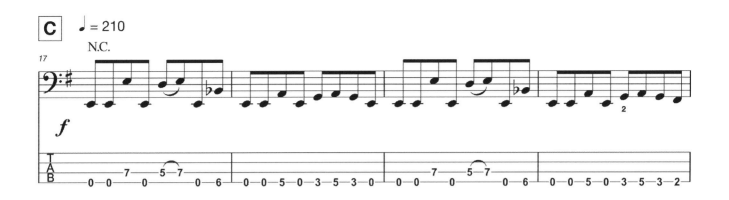

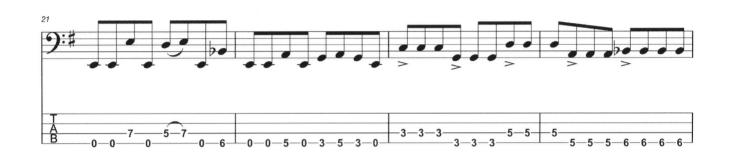

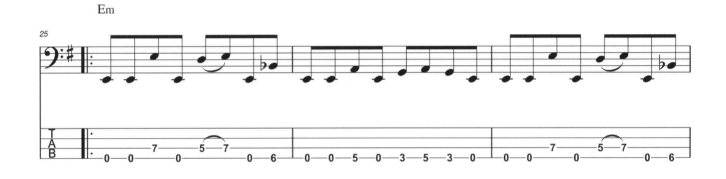

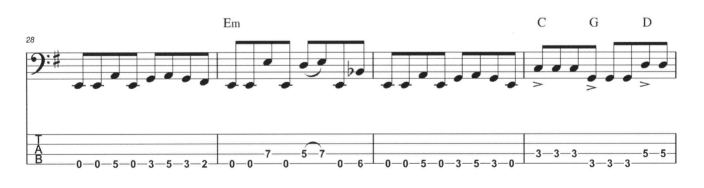

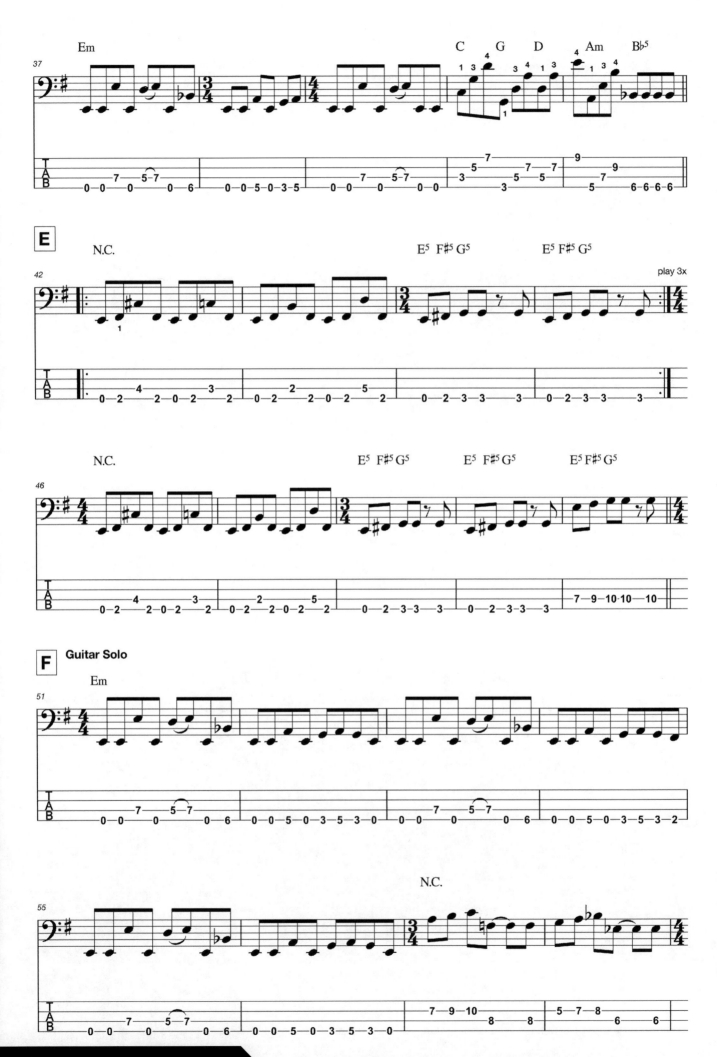

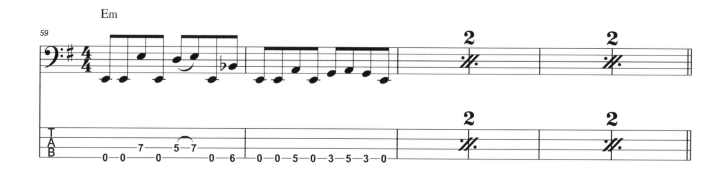

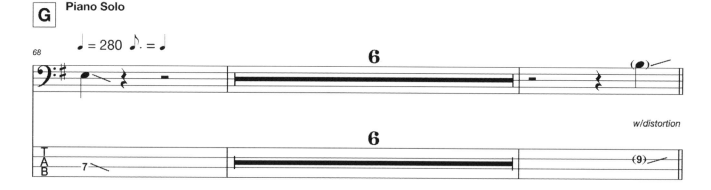

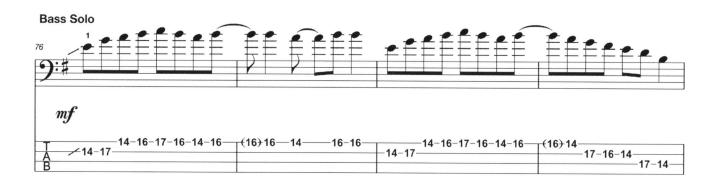

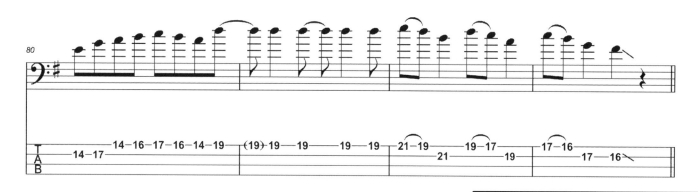

Piano Solo

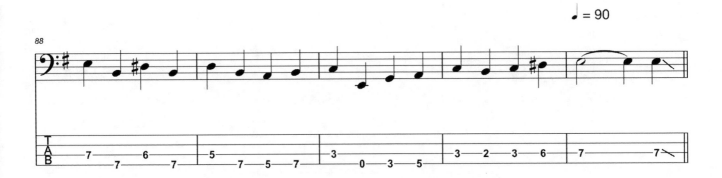

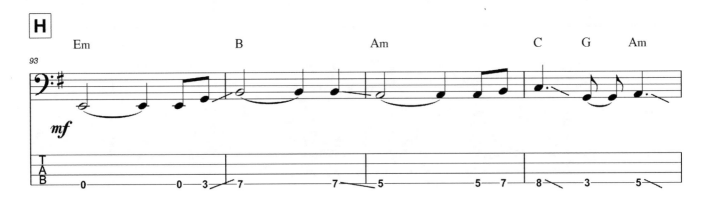

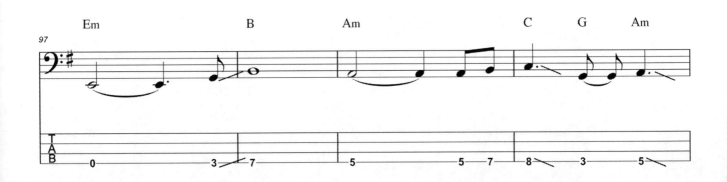

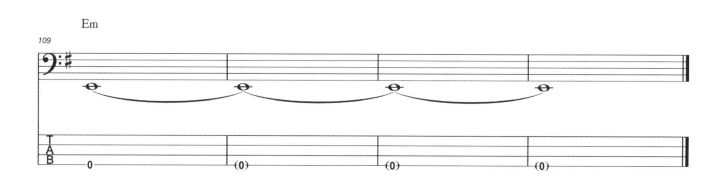

PINO PALLADINO

Pino Palladino is a musical chameleon. After stunning the bass world with his unique fretless work on hits by Paul Young and Gary Numan during the eighties, he segued effortlessly into funk-filled grooves with D'Angelo and a host of other R&B/hip-hop acts during the nineties. In more recent years, Pino has toured and recorded with legendary rockers the Who following John Entwistle's tragic passing, and in 2003 he performed with folk/pop duo Simon & Garfunkel on their long-awaited reunion tour. Able to blend into any musical situation, Pino remains one of the world's busiest bass players.

Pino Palladino was born on October 17th, 1957 in Cardiff, Wales. After seeing a priest playing the guitar at his Catholic school, Pino was inspired to begin playing the instrument himself, initially using his sister's acoustic. He had classical guitar lessons for a while, before discovering rock bands such as Led Zeppelin and Yes in his teens. By the time he was 16, he was playing electric guitar in a rock cover band, but found his true calling when he one day picked up the bass player's Rickenbacker. Feeling instantly at home on the instrument, he decided to make the switch to bass.

Taking inspiration from James Jamerson, Jaco Pastorius, Anthony Jackson, Rocco Prestia, Bootsy Collins and Stevie Wonder's synth bass work, Pino began to develop his own bass skills by playing along with his favourite records. In 1978 he landed a gig working at a Cardiff TV station, where he remained until in 1980 a friend suggested that he audition for the new band that ex-Squeeze keyboard player Jools Holland was putting together.

After successfully auditioning for Holland, Pino played on his first album *Jools Holland and the Millionaires* and joined the band on a tour of the U.S. and Europe. Whilst touring in the UK, the band were supported by The Q-Tips, a new group fronted by talented singer Paul Young. He and Pino became good friends during the tour, a relationship that would prove to be greatly beneficial to Pino's career in the coming years. Another pivotal event occurred whilst the band were touring in the states: upon visiting Sam Ash Music in New York, Pino found a fretless Music Man StingRay bass, which he immediately fell in love with. Little did he know, his discovery of this instrument would soon have a huge impact on his career as a bassist.

Upon his return to the UK, Pino received a call to audition for synth pop artist Gary Numan, who was seeking a fretless bass player for his new studio album. After impressing Numan with his playing, Pino was hired and his unconventional bass work quickly came to play a prominent role on the subsequent album *I, Assassin*. This recording is an excellent starting point for fans of Pino's fretless playing: 'Music for Chameleons' features a beautifully slippery bassline that is one of the song's most memorable hooks, whilst 'White Boys and Heroes' features a fantastic double-tracked, slapped fretless groove.

Having now found his voice with his Music Man fretless bass, in 1983 Pino appeared on *No Parlez*, the debut album by Paul Young. Asked to play a simple melodic intro for the song 'Wherever I Lay My Hat (That's My Home)' Pino was happy to oblige but was later stunned to hear the song on the radio, with his bass enjoying an extremely dominant role in the mix. When the song reached #1 in the UK charts in the summer of 1983 (and remained there for three weeks), it made a star of Young and led to Pino being called to add his fretless magic to recordings by artists such as Dave Gilmour, Elton John, Nick Heyward and Don Henley. From this period, 'Murder' (David Gilmour) and 'New York Minute' (Don Henley) stand out as superb examples, not only of his fretless playing, but his skill at finding just the right part for the song.

Pino worked with Paul Young again on the singer's 1985 album *The Secret of Association*. By this point,

he had begun to develop his fretless voice further still, now often using a Boss OC-2 pedal to enable him to create more synth-like basslines. This new development in his playing had originally occurred during a recording session for Jackie Brooks: producer Laurie Latham suggested that Pino double parts of his line an octave higher in order to have them better stand out in the mix. In the end, Pino ended up doubling his entire part and was so taken with the sound, he immediately began seeking out a pedal that could help him achieve the same results in one take. He quickly discovered that the Boss OC-2 enabled this, although it meant that he had to reverse his approach and play the line in the upper octave, allowing the pedal to generate the lower part. Combined with chorus and compression, this sound enabled Pino to get closer to the expressive synth lines that Stevie Wonder had often played on his Moog, and which had been an important early inspiration. Pino used this new technique to superb effect on 'I'm Gonna Tear Your Playhouse Down' from Young's second album.

Throughout the eighties, Pino continued to be called to add his unique fretless playing to recordings with Phil Collins, Chris de Burgh, Joan Armatrading, Tears for Fears, Go West and many more.

As the nineties arrived, Pino tired of playing melodic fretless lines and began favouring a fretted '63 Fender Precision bass for recording work. Sessions with blues guitarist B.B. King for his album *Deuces Wild* led to Pino's first meeting with neo soul singer/songwriter D'Angelo, who was featured with King on the song 'Ain't Nobody Home'. Liking what he heard, D'Angelo immediately hired Pino to play on the sessions for what would become his Grammy-winning album *Voodoo* (2000). Pino's sparse, relaxed funk grooves on tracks such as 'Chicken Grease' and 'Send It On' are a world away from the fretless melodic lines he became known for during the eighties but are no less infectious.

Pino's work with D'Angelo led to him recording with other notable hip-hop/neo soul artists including

TOP TRACKS

'White Boys and Heroes'
Gary Numan

'Music for Chameleons'
Gary Numan

'Wherever I Lay My Hat (That's My Home)'
Paul Young

'I'm Gonna Tear Your Playhouse Down'
Paul Young

'Everytime You Go Away'
Paul Young

'Hot Fun'
Paul Young

'Don't Dream It's Over'
Paul Young

'Stop On By'
Paul Young

'New York Minute'
Don Henley

'Shoot Down the Moon'
Elton John

'I Wish It Would Rain Down'
Phil Collins

'Murder'
Dave Gilmour

'Give Blood'
Pete Townshend

'Send It On'
D'Angelo

'Chicken Grease'
D'Angelo

'Penitentiary Philosophy'
Eryka Badu

'Who Did You Think I Was'
John Mayer Trio

'Good Love is on the Way'
John Mayer Trio

'Monday Afternoon'
PSP

'Various Methods of Escape'
Nine Inch Nails

Eryka Badu, Musiq Soulchild and De La Soul. He also joined with fellow D'Angelo band members James Poyser (keyboards) and Ahmir Thompson (drums) to form a writing partnership that later crafted songs for Eryka Badu, Roy Hargrove and Earth Wind and Fire.

2002 was a busy year for Pino. After working with singer Edie Brickell on her album *Volcano*, he was contacted by her husband Paul Simon, who was interested in using him for his forthcoming album, *Surprise*. Pino recorded several tracks with Simon and would go on to work with him again the following year, on the hugely anticipated Simon & Garfunkel reunion tour.

In late June 2002, Pino was stunned to hear of the sudden death of John Entwistle, bassist with legendary rockers the Who. Just as he was

digesting this shocking news, he was contacted by remaining band members Roger Daltrey and Pete Townshend, who asked him to step into the band on short notice to enable them to meet their impending touring commitments. With just a few days to prepare, Pino quickly learnt the set and joined the band on stage at the beginning of July for their U.S tour. He would later go on to record on the Who's 2006 album *Endless Wire* and tour with the band several times over the next few years.

In 2005 Pino joined with guitarist John Mayer and drummer Steve Jordan – with whom he had worked several times – to play a short gig for NBC's Telethon in aid of the 2004 tsunami disaster. The well-received show inspired the trio to continue working together, releasing the live album *Try!* in late 2005. Pino's inventive playing on tracks

such as 'Who Did You Think I Was' and 'Good Love is On the Way' are excellent examples of his busier playing style within a trio setting. Pino continued to work with Mayer afterwards, playing on his studio albums *Continuum* (2006) and *Battle Studies* (2009).

In recent years Pino has remained as busy as ever. Alongside sessions for hit albums with Cee Lo Green and Adele, he has worked with keyboardist Philippe Saisse and drummer Simon Phillips in the trio PSP, a group which saw him begin using his fretless Music Man bass again. He recorded with Nine Inch Nails in 2013 for their album *Hesitation Marks* and subsequently joined the band on tour. In 2016 he toured again with the Who for their 50th anniversary tour, *The Who Hits 50!*.

Pino Palladino with his '63 Fender Precision Bass

BASS GUITARS

Pino's first bass was a Fender Precision, which his father bought for him after he decided to switch from guitar to bass. He used this instrument through his early playing career at the Cardiff TV station and on the first Jools Holland album *Jools Holland and the Millionaires*.

The instrument that Pino is best-known for however is his fretless '79 Music Man StingRay. Purchased in 1981 from Sam Ash Music in New York, this bass is a stock 2-band model with a sunburst finish. Over the years that Pino has owned it, the fingerboard has been replaced several times. This was the instrument that he used throughout the eighties, on sessions with Paul Young, Gary Numan, Dave Gilmour, Chris de Burgh and many more.

Since switching to fretted basses in the nineties, Pino has often been seen with a '61 Fender Precision bass in Fiesta Red. This instrument was used throughout the 2003 Simon & Garfunkel Reunion tour and was later used as the template for the Fender Custom Shop Pino Palladino Signature Precision Bass. Pino also has a '63 Precision bass which he often tunes a whole step lower (D-G-C-F).

Whilst touring with the Who, Pino used Fender Jaguar basses. He also used a Moon Larry Graham Signature Jazz Bass for a brief time with the band, although it was stolen from the stage at a gig in Leeds.

Other basses that Pino has used over the years include a '96 Lakland 55-64 Deluxe 5-string, a Lakland Joe Osborn Signature Jazz Bass, a Warwick Thumb Bass 5-string, a Status headless 6-string, a '67 Ampeg fretless AUB and an 80s Reissue Fender Jazz which was usually used in conjunction with the Roland V-Bass modelling system.

Pino usually strings his basses with La Bella heavy gauge flatwounds, although he prefers roundwound strings when playing with the Who. His fretless Music Man StingRay is usually strung with Rotosound Swing Bass roundwound strings.

EFFECTS

Pino became well-known during the eighties for his use of a fretless bass combined with the Boss OC-2 octave pedal.

AMPLIFICATION

Pino used Trace Elliot AH500X amplifiers and 2x10 and 2x15 cabinets whilst touring with Paul Young during the eighties. He switched to Ashdown in the early 2000s, initially favouring an ABM 900 head, which he used on his first tour with the Who in 2002. By 2004 he was pairing his Ashdown amp with Epifani T-212 2x12 cabinets for many gigs, but when touring with the Who in 2006 he used Ampeg SVT-VR Vintage Reissue amps with SVT 810AV cabinets.

For studio work Pino often uses a Phil Jones PJB Briefcase amp and has also been seen using a Phil Jones M-300 head with an 8T/16B cabinet when playing live in recent years.

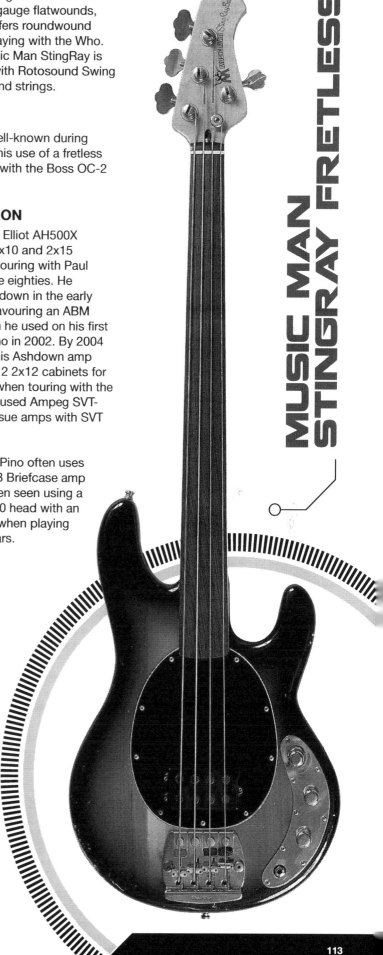

MUSIC MAN STINGRAY FRETLESS

PERFORMANCE NOTES

'Don't Fret...' is a piece written in the style of the music Pino made with Paul Young during the eighties. In a nod to the unique style that Pino became known for, the majority of this line is played in the upper register of the instrument, with the lower part supplied by an octave pedal.

The opening A section of this piece features a simple, repeating four-bar chord progression. The bassline here is very melodic, but also features plenty of space, which allows the part to breathe. In the first bar, note the descending phrase from Db to C to Bb: The Db does not belong to the underlying Gm chord, but is taken from the blues scale. In fact, it is the 'blue note' in the G blues scale and sounds great when used quickly as it is here. This note slides downwards to C, then to Bb, the minor third of the chord. On the second beat, the seventh (F) is played, followed by the root note (G) on the second half of the beat. This is a strong melodic phrase, and it is used several times during this section. At the end of the bar a simpler phrase leads into the Cm chord in the second bar. After the first note, the bass remains silent for this bar. In the third bar a phrase similar to that heard in the first bar is played. Note that this time the line begins on D rather than Db – this is because the chord is now D minor, and the Db would not sound correct against it. A simple phrase at the end of this bar returns us to a Gm chord for the fourth bar, during which the bass is mostly silent. This four-bar

line is now repeated several times with one variation, the upper register fill in bar 12. As this section of the track draws to a close, a complex sixteenth note fill is played in bar 16. This fill uses the G minor scale and I recommend starting it with the third finger of the fretting hand on the G at the twelfth fret of the G-string – this will enable you to play the entire fill in one hand position. Be sure to play the pull-offs as written here as they will help keep the line sounding fluid.

At letter B a 'pre-chorus' section begins. The bassline makes extensive use of chord tones here and is relatively simple to play. That said, you'll need to watch out for the complex fill in the final bar (bar 24). To play this accurately, fret the F and C on the first two beats with the first and third fingers respectively, then shift position to put your first finger on the G at the twelfth fret – this will enable you to play the phrase without shifting position.

At letter C, the 'chorus' part of the piece begins. The bass is the main melodic instrument here. When playing the opening phrase of bar 25, I recommend that you fret the G with the first finger, then shift that same finger to the D at the twelfth fret. This will enable you to perform the G to A hammer-on with the first and third fingers, with the fourth free to reach the Bb.

At letter D we return to the original 'verse' bassline, which is the same as before, but with some additional

fills, such as the Jaco Pastorius-like part in bar 33. The bluesy fill in bar 40 is classic Pino and uses a repeated descending phrase, which is played with a syncopated rhythm. I recommend listening closely to the audio when working on this line. Pino played parts similar to both of these fills in the Paul Young track 'I'm Gonna Tear Your Playhouse Down'.

The remaining sections of this track are repeats of earlier parts, with some small variations. When working on this piece overall, you should ensure that you play all slides, hammer-ons, pull-offs and staccato dots as written, particularly if you are using a fretless bass – doing so will be a big help in achieving the required sound/feel.

STYLE TIPS

- ○ Extremely melodic bassline
- ○ Use of space
- ○ Use of slurs, slides, vibrato
- ○ Synth-like bass tone created by playing in the upper register and using an octave pedal to supply the lower register
- ○ Use of a fretless bass with chorus effect

SOUND ADVICE

I recorded this track using a fretless Squier Jazz Bass. All controls on the bass were set to full and the part was recorded through a Boss OC-2 Octave pedal. The controls on the pedal were set as follows: Oct 2 – OFF, Direct Level – 2 o'clock, Oct 1 – 2 o'clock. Setting the pedal in this way meant that notes an octave below where they were played were heard but notes two octaves below were not. Once the part was recorded, chorus and compression were added digitally, and some minor EQ tweaks were made in order to bring out the upper mids a little.

The key to mastering Pino's eighties tone lies in using a fretless bass with an octave pedal. The fretless that I used was a relatively inexpensive model, but it allowed me to a achieve a similar tone because of the way it was played. When performing lines such as this one on a fretless instrument, a significant part of the desired sound is achieved through expression: the use of vibrato, slurs, slides, all of the little details. Concentrating on these elements will be a big help to you in replicating Pino's tone.

'DON'T FRET...'

Written by Stuart Clayton

Drums: Will Beavis
Keys: Stuart Clayton
Guitar: Stuart Ryan
Bass: Stuart Clayton

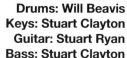

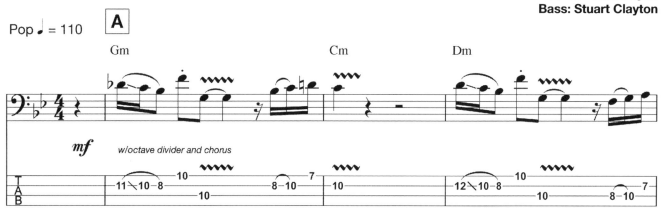

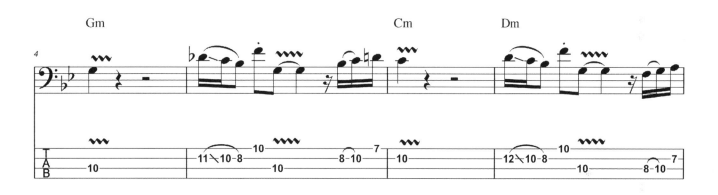

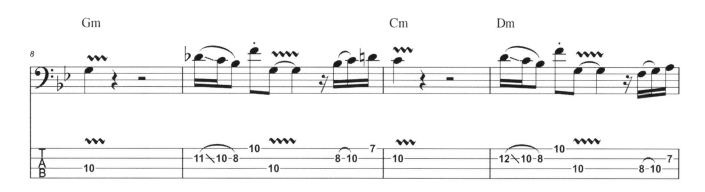

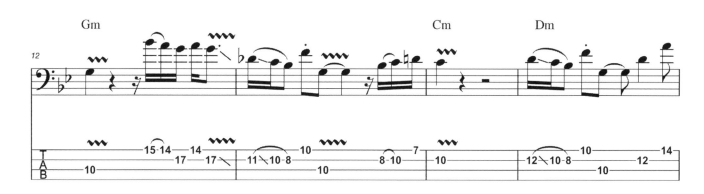

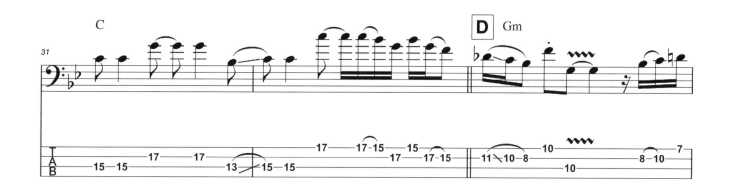

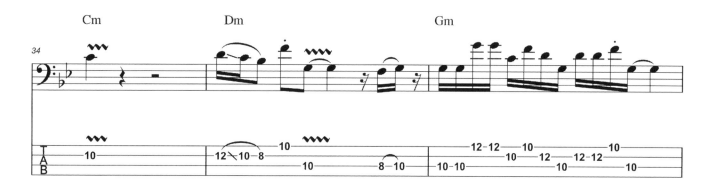

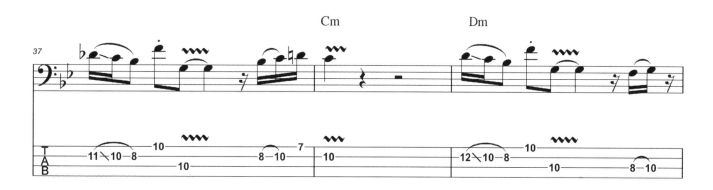

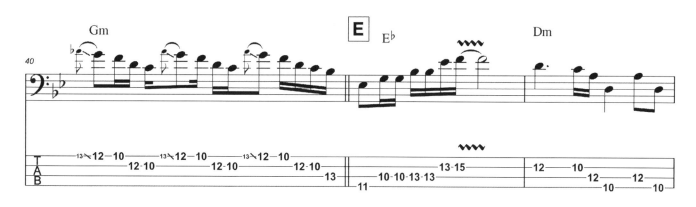

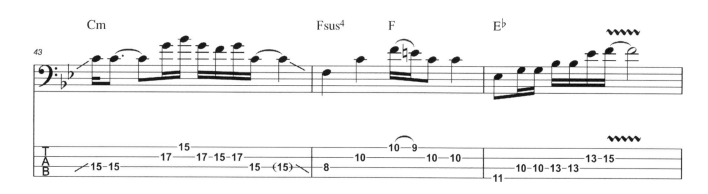

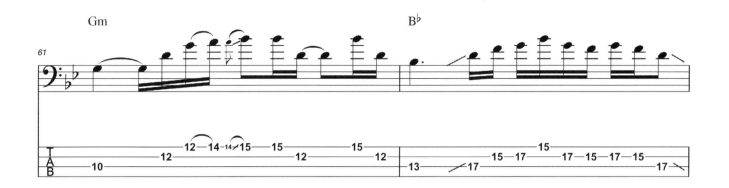

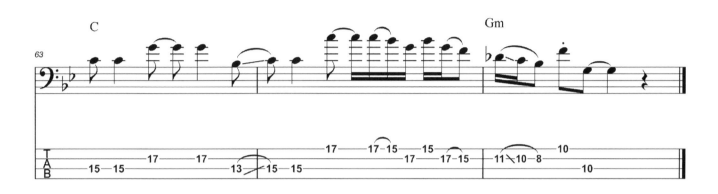

BILLY SHEEHAN

Billy Sheehan is one of the world's most creative rock bassists. Through his work with Dave Lee Roth, Talas, Mr. Big, The Winery Dogs and beyond, he has elevated rock bass playing to virtuosic heights that most of us can only dream of achieving. For years he has topped bass player polls and wowed audiences all over the world with his incredible technique yet remains keenly aware of the importance of being able to lay down a solid groove. His unique playing style is borne out of years of practice and playing live – Sheehan himself estimates that throughout his career so far, he has played well over 4000 gigs.

Billy Sheehan was born in Buffalo, New York on March 19th, 1953. After beginning his musical life playing his sister's guitar, Billy was first inspired to pick up the bass after hearing a neighbour practicing with a local band. Captivated by the low, rumbling tones of the instrument, Sheehan began learning on a Hagström FB bass, copping riffs not only from bass players like Tim Bogert (Vanilla Fudge) and Andy Fraser (Free), but from other instrumentalists such as Frank Zappa and Jimi Hendrix.

In 1970 Billy bought a Fender Precision bass, which he soon began to modify to suit his evolving playing style. Throughout the decade he made a living performing extensively in bar bands, something which he has often spoken of as being the perfect grounding for any aspiring professional bassist. Along the way he began to develop the technical mastery of the instrument for which he would later become renowned, often looking beyond the bass guitar for inspiration. Indeed, his first encounter with the tapping technique came when he witnessed guitarist Billy Gibbons play a basic tapping lick during a ZZ Top show. Intrigued, Billy began to experiment with a similar technique on the bass and quickly found that it enabled him to play fast, lead guitar-like runs with minimal effort. Before long, the technique had become a key part of his own skill set.

In 1972 Billy started Talas, a rock trio that was to become the perfect showcase for his unique approach to the bass. Free to explore the instrument within the generous working space the three-piece setting provided, Billy was soon wowing audiences in his hometown of Buffalo with his wild playing and even wilder solos. Besides his jaw-dropping command of tapping, he had begun to incorporate many other guitar-based techniques into his playing, including pinch harmonics, neck bending and the use of chords.

Talas released their self-titled debut album in 1979 and over the next few years began to build a strong local following. In 1980 they were offered the opportunity to open for Van Halen, which raised the band's profile further still and led to Billy becoming friends with guitarist Eddie Van Halen. By the time of 1982's *Sink Your Teeth Into That*, Talas had become extremely successful on a local level and Billy had made a name for himself as the hot young

bass player to watch. Tracks such as 'Shy Boy', 'Sink Your Teeth Into That' and the solo bass extravaganza 'NV43345' are superb examples of Sheehan's unbelievable playing from this era.

Talas toured with Van Halen again in 1984 and Billy's big break came soon after, when vocalist Dave Lee Roth quit to start his own group. Recruiting Billy, along with guitar virtuoso Steve Vai and drummer Gregg Bissonette, Dave's new band was to be the perfect home for Sheehan's virtuosity. Their first album, *Eat 'Em and Smile* was released in 1986 and was a huge hit around the world, both critically and commercially. Featuring the hits 'Yankee Rose' and 'Goin' Crazy', as well as Sheehan's composition 'Shy Boy', the album catapulted Billy to superstar status, making him a regular face on the cover of guitar/bass magazines. Vai and Sheehan had blistering solo spots during the band's live shows and often played complex unison lines within the songs themselves. A follow-up album *Skyscraper* was released in 1988 following a successful world tour, but musical differences led Sheehan and Vai to quit the group in 1989.

Billy immediately sought out a new project and with the help of Shrapnel Records owner Mike Varney, he put together Mr. Big with former Racer X guitarist Paul Gilbert, drummer Pat Torpey and vocalist Eric Martin. The band's self-titled debut was released in June 1989 and once again saw Billy laying down monster rock grooves as well as showcasing his extraordinary tapping techniques, often in unison with Gilbert. Excellent examples of Sheehan's playing from this album include 'Had Enough' (which opens with a tapped solo that features Billy's innovative take on the sweep picking technique) and 'Addicted to That Rush', an up-tempo rocker which features several stunning bass and guitar unison lines. Although the album was not a huge hit in the U.S., it was extremely successful in Japan and Asia.

Mr. Big's mainstream breakthrough came in 1991 with the release of their second album, *Lean Into It*. Interest in the band was sparked by the surprise success of the second single to be released from the album, the ballad 'To Be With You'. This simple, acoustic-based love song went to #1 in fourteen countries, somewhat ironic for a band credited

SELECTED DISCOGRAPHY

Talas – *Sink Your Teeth Into That*
'Sink Your Teeth Into That', 'Hit and Run', 'NV43345', 'High Speed on Ice', 'Shy Boy', 'King of the World', 'Outside Lookin' In', 'Hick Town'

Dave Lee Roth – *Eat 'Em and Smile*
'Yankee Rose', 'Goin' Crazy', 'Shy Boy', 'Elephant Gun', ' Tobacco Road', 'Big Trouble', 'Bump & Grind'

Mr. Big – *Mr. Big*
'Addicted to that Rush', 'Merciless', 'Had Enough', 'Blame It On My Youth', 'Take a Walk', 'How Can You Do What You Do', 'Rock and Roll Over'

Mr. Big – *Lean Into It*
'Daddy, Brother, Lover, Little Boy', 'Alive and Kickin', 'Green Tinted Sixties Mind', 'Voodoo Kiss', 'Never Say Never', 'Just Take My Heart', 'To Be With You'

Niacin – *Live! Blood, Sweat & Beers*
'Clean-Up Crew', 'Do a Little Dirty Work', 'Bullet Train Blues', 'Hell to Pay', 'Klaghorn', 'No Man's Land', 'Front and Center', 'Gelatin'

Niacin – *Time Crunch*
'Elbow Grease', 'Time Crunch', 'Stone Face', 'Red', 'Invisible King', 'Daddy Long Leg', 'Hog Funk', 'Outside Inside Out', 'Blue Wind'

Billy Sheehan – *Cosmic Troubadour*
'Toss It on the Flame', 'The Suspense is Killing Me', 'Don't Look Down', 'Dreams of Discontent', 'Taj', 'A Tower in the Sky', 'Long Walk Home'

The Winery Dogs – *The Winery Dogs*
'Elevate', 'Desire', 'We Are One', 'The Other Side', 'You Saved Me', 'Not Hopeless', 'One More Time', 'Damaged', 'Time Machine'

with some of the most gifted musicians in rock.

Over the next few years, Mr. Big released further studio albums, including *Bump Ahead* (1993) and *Hey Man* (1996), although changing musical times meant that they were unable to recapture the popularity they had achieved with *Lean Into It*. Paul Gilbert left the group in 1997, although the remaining members continued on for two subsequent albums with guitarist Richie Kotzen, before disbanding in 2002.

In the mid-nineties and in-between his commitments to Mr. Big, Billy began playing in a trio with drummer Dennis Chambers and B3 hammond organist John Novello. This unique group, named Niacin, released their self-titled debut album in 1996. Consisting of instrumental rock/fusion, the band created an unmistakable sound and Billy once again was able to make extensive use of the sonic space offered by the trio setting. Bass highlights from the album include 'Do a Little Dirty

Work', 'Bullet Train Blues' and Billy's strummed solo piece 'Clean-Up Crew'. Niacin followed their debut with a live album in 1997 and several subsequent studio albums in the years after.

Billy released his long-awaited debut solo album *Compression* in 2001. A song-based rock album, *Compression* featured Billy on lead vocals and also reunited him with guitarist Steve Vai on the track 'Chameleon'. An instrumental-based follow-up, *Cosmic Troubadour* was released in 2005, featuring some classic Sheehan grooves and solos. Highlights include the intricate chordal fingerstyle grooves of 'The Suspense is Killing Me', the up-tempo rock boogie lines of 'Don't Look Down' and the harmonics-laden 'Dreams of Discontent'.

Sheehan reunited with the original line-up of Mr. Big in 2009, releasing a greatest hits package which contained two new songs, 'Next Time Around' and a cover of the Argent song 'Hold Your Head Up'. Following a successful world tour, Mr. Big entered the studio in 2010, emerging later that year with their first album of new material in nearly ten years. Entitled *What If...* the new album successfully recaptured the classic Mr. Big sound, resulting in an

album that was well-received by their fans. The band undertook a world tour to promote the album in 2011.

Billy's next move was to form a new band, The Winery Dogs. With former Mr. Big guitarist Ritchie Kotzen and ex-Dream Theater drummer Mike Portnoy completing the trio line-up, the band released their self-titled debut in 2013. Featuring melodic, catchy songs that also showcased the virtuosity of the band's members, the album was well-received by their fans, and generated extensive praise from the press. Bass highlights from the album include 'Time Machine' and 'Not Hopeless', which features a blistering solo. The band toured heavily following the release of the album and their second effort, *Hot Streak* was released to widespread acclaim in 2015.

Having played the bass guitar now for over forty years, Sheehan is showing no signs of slowing down. Future projects with The Winery Dogs and Mr. Big are in the pipeline, and he continues to maintain a busy schedule of performances and masterclasses around the world. A tireless innovator, Billy is still developing new techniques to incorporate into his enviable technical arsenal, making him arguably the world's hardest working bass player.

Billy Sheehan with The Winery Dogs in 2014

BASS GUITARS

Although Billy's first instrument was a Hagström FB bass, it was with his 1969 Fender Precision that he really began to develop his signature sound. As his unique style began to form, Sheehan made various modifications to the instrument to accommodate this, starting with replacing the neck with that of a 1968 Telecaster bass. Inspired by the tone that Yardbirds bassist Paul Samwell-Smith coaxed from his Epiphone Rivoli, Sheehan bought a Gibson EB-O pickup, which he then added to his bass in neck position. Lacking the electrical know-how to correctly wire the pickup into the existing circuitry, he simply added a second jack output to the bass, in the process establishing what would become a huge part of his sound. From this point on, Sheehan used a dual amplifier system, sending the signal from the P-bass pickup to one amplifier and the signal from the EB-O pickup to another. Doing so meant that he was able to add distortion to the P-bass pickup to add a sharper edge to his tone, whilst retaining all of the low end through the EB-O woofer pickup. In addition to these crucial modifications, Sheehan also added a Hipshot D-Tuner, replaced the bridge, scalloped the upper frets for ease of string bending and permanently attached his strap to the bass using stove bolts. This bass – which was used continuously by Sheehan until the mid-eighties – was affectionately referred to as 'The Wife'.

After achieving wider recognition through his work with Talas and later Dave Lee Roth's band, Sheehan began working with Yamaha to create a signature instrument. The first iteration of this was a modified BB3000S which featured all of the modifications that Sheehan had made to his first Precision bass: an EB-O pickup in neck position, dual outputs, Hipshot D-Tuner, and scalloped frets. This instrument was rose blue in colour and is the bass that Sheehan was pictured with on the cover of *Guitar Player* magazine after winning the Bass Player of the Year award for the first time. Whilst touring with Dave Lee Roth during

the mid-eighties, Billy used this bass in conjunction with his original, modified Precision.

In the late eighties, Billy and Yamaha developed the Attitude bass, a signature instrument that again reflected all of the alterations that he had made to his original Precision. Billy began using the Attitude upon forming Mr. Big and has continued to use various iterations of the instrument ever since. Although there have been three versions of the bass over the past twenty-five years, the majority of the changes between models have been tweaks to the construction methods.

EFFECTS

Distortion is a big part of Billy's sound both live and in the studio and for many years was provided by a pair of Pearce G1 preamps. These have now been retired and he currently uses the EBS Billy Sheehan Signature Drive pedal. As well as distortion, Billy currently has an EBS Octobass sub-octave pedal and two MXR compressors in his rig. He also uses a crossover to remove a significant proportion of the low end from his distorted channel.

AMPLIFICATION

For many years Billy was an Ampeg endorsee, favouring AP6500 amps and 8x10 cabinets. He switched to Hartke amplification in 2011 and currently uses the HA5500 for his distorted channel and the HA1000 for his low end channel. He uses a combination of AK115 and AK410 cabinets, unusually preferring to use the 1x15's for his high-end tone and the 4x10's for his low-end tone.

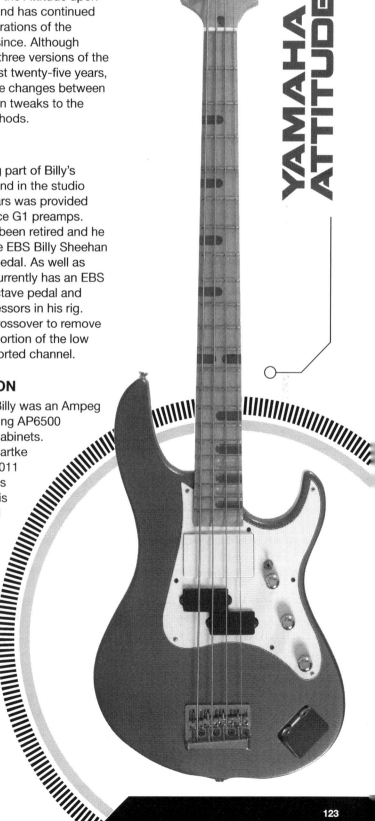

YAMAHA ATTITUDE BASS

PERFORMANCE NOTES

This is an up-tempo, aggressive rock track written in the style of Billy's work with The Winery Dogs and Mr. Big. In writing this piece, I was aiming to demonstrate several key elements of Billy's playing style – blistering unison runs, snarling rock riffs, artificial harmonics, and legato tapping techniques.

(Note that this piece is played with the low E-string detuned to D. You will need to retune it to E quickly later in the piece, so I recommend using a bass with a Hipshot D-tuner if possible.)

The intro is a fast, descending run that is played in unison with the guitar. This is performed mostly on the G-string, using pull-offs for a smoother, more legato sound. To play the opening bars, use the fourth, second and first fingers to fret the D, C and B♭ notes on the G-string. Each of these is pulled-off to sound an open G. Note that after the initial pull-off, the open G-string is played again by the picking hand to create a three-note grouping. It's important that you land on the A at the end of the first bar with your first finger, as this will mean that you can play all of the phrase in the second bar with the finger-per-fret technique. This whole phrase is then repeated, beginning now at the A at the fourteenth fret (bar 3). At the end of this bar, be sure to fret the E with the third finger of the fretting hand. The final part of this phrase is played using the same techniques. I recommend fretting the A at the end of bar 5 with the first finger – this will make all of the hammer-on/pull-off phrases in the next bar easier to execute.

After hitting the open low D-string at the end of bar 6, harmonics are played at the seventh fret of the D and G-strings (bar 7). Following these, you'll play the D at the seventh fret of the G-string and slide into a tapped trill in the upper register. This is very fast and is played in the same way that Billy plays the opening trill from the Mr. Big song 'Addicted to That Rush': whilst the first finger of the fretting hand holds the C at the seventeenth fret, the first finger of the picking hand and third finger of the fretting hand take turns to hammer-

on to the D at the nineteenth fret (see photograph below). Splitting the notes between two fingers like this means that tapped trills can be played very fast indeed.

At letter B the main groove enters. This is an eighth note-based line that uses a lot of hammer-ons and pull-offs to maintain a legato feel. When playing this part, I recommend fretting all of the notes at the third fret with the first finger and all of the notes at the fifth fret with the fourth. Covering three frets with four fingers in this way is very common for riffs such as this and is known as 'condensed fingering'.

At letter C, chords and artificial harmonics are played. The first chord is a C power chord and should be plucked with the thumb, first and second fingers of the picking hand. The next chord is an octave and is best plucked with the thumb and first finger. You should allow this chord to ring, then tap the notes shown in brackets in order to sound the harmonics. Note that you shouldn't tap these notes as you would when using conventional tapping technique, instead your finger should bounce off of the string. As you tap notes along the string (moving

towards the headstock) you will hear the harmonics going up in pitch. You shouldn't worry too much about hitting the exact frets shown in the TAB – this is more about the effect of artificial harmonics than specific pitches. You'll find that these will sound clearer if you are using some distortion in your sound.

At letter D, a new part is played, this time using conventional fingerstyle technique. This part is based around octaves and simple pentatonic phrases. The main challenge here is the speed, particularly when it comes to rapid-fire triplet part in bar 50. Billy uses a highly developed three-finger plucking technique which makes parts such as these a lot easier to execute.

Letter E is the 'chorus' part of the song and is based around the fingerstyle groove that was used in the second half of the intro – this part is followed by some simple root note-based lines. Be sure to allow the octave notes to ring above the lower notes in bars 63-66 as indicated.

At letter F a breakdown section begins. Whilst the guitar plays a funkier riff, the bass taps more

Fig. 1: Performing a tapped trill

artificial harmonics. These are played in the same way as those at letter C: fret the D on the G-string, then use the first (or second) finger of the picking hand to tap along the string bringing out harmonics – remember that you should be bouncing your finger, not actually pressing any frets down. There are no specific pitches required here, just tap up and down the string randomly using the rhythm indicated. You'll find certain parts of the neck are particularly strong with harmonics when fretting at the seventh fret – you should experiment with this technique in order to find the strongest and best sounding harmonics for this part.

At letter G the bass solo begins. I recommend playing the phrase in bars 83-84 as follows: fret the twelfth fret of the G-string with the third finger of the fretting hand and then use the fourth to hammer-on to the A♭. The first finger should already be fretting the F at the tenth fret ready for the pull-off that follows. Note that these first four notes are played in one stroke – only play the string once, then perform the notes using hammer-ons and pull-offs. The next four notes can then be fretted with the first and third fingers in the same position. In the next bar, fret the A with the third finger, the A♭ with the second and the G with the first, sliding this finger down to the F afterwards. You can then fret the D at the twelfth fret of the E-string with the fourth finger – this is a bit of a stretch but is a consequence of playing in drop-D tuning. After some hammer-on figures (bars 85

and 86), an ascending D minor pentatonic lick is played (bars 87 – 88). When performing this, fret all notes on the G-string with the first finger and all notes on the D-string with the fourth – this will ensure that your hand is in the correct position for the descending tapped part that ends the solo. This tapping lick is a lot easier to perform than it sounds and consists of two tapped triplets which are then moved downwards along the string, remaining within the D minor pentatonic scale. To play the first triplet, fret the A at the fourteenth fret with the first finger and have the fourth finger ready to hammer-onto the C at the seventeenth fret. Now, tap the D at the nineteenth fret with the first finger of the picking hand, pull-off to sound the A, then hammer-on with the fourth finger to sound the C. These three notes are the first triplet. The second triplet is played as follows: tap the D, pull-off to sound the C (which should already be fretted), then pull that off to sound the A. These two triplets are played fast, but after practicing them slowly in order to work on the coordination you should find this a lot easier than it sounds. The remainder of the tapped line is played using the same technique.

At letter H the guitar solo begins over an E minor tonality. After hitting the open low D-string at the end of the bass solo, you'll need to reach over and use the Hipshot D-Tuner (if you have one) to tune the string back up to E. The line during the solo is a typical Billy Sheehan-style

accompaniment part: root-based but with lots of minor pentatonic fills, slides, and chords. You'll need to detune to D again at the end of this solo section. Again this happens quickly, in this case whilst you will be fretting the C in bar 120.

The piece ends with a final 'chorus' section (largely the same as at letter E) and a repeat of the unison melody from the intro. After playing this, play the harmonics as written and bend the neck of the bass (gently!) to alter the pitch of the harmonics as heard on the track. Neck bending is best achieved with your fretting hand pressing on the back of the headstock and the picking hand pressing against the top forward bout of the body.

STYLE TIPS

- ○ Riffs and fills often built on blues and pentatonic scales
- ○ Use of artificial harmonics: these can be tapped as in this piece or played as pinch harmonics
- ○ Fast, legato tapping runs
- ○ Use of distortion
- ○ Use of string and neck bending techniques

SOUND ADVICE

This piece was recorded using an original Yamaha Attitude bass strung with Rotosound Billy Sheehan Signature strings, gauges .043, .065, .080, .110. I used both outputs when recording (as Billy does) and distortion was added to the P-bass pickup using the EBS Billy Sheehan Signature Drive pedal. The woofer pickup was recorded straight into the desk. These two signals were then compressed digitally, and a noise gate was used on the distorted channel.

In the absence of a dual output instrument, you will be able to achieve similar results using a Fender Precision bass (or similar instrument with a single pickup) and a distortion pedal, preferably the EBS Billy Sheehan Signature drive. You should also compress your sound quite heavily as Billy does.

In terms of technique, I recommend a fairly aggressive playing style – don't be afraid to really dig into these lines. It's worth remembering that a lot of Billy's sound comes from strength: heavy gauge strings played with power and aggression!

'WORKIN' LIKE A DOG'

Written by Stuart Clayton

Drums: Jason Bowld
Guitar: Charlie Griffiths
Bass: Stuart Clayton

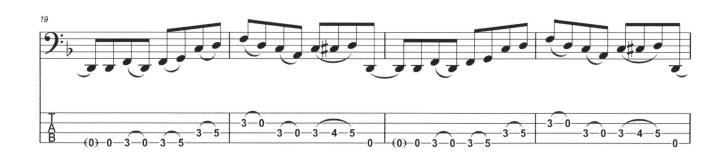

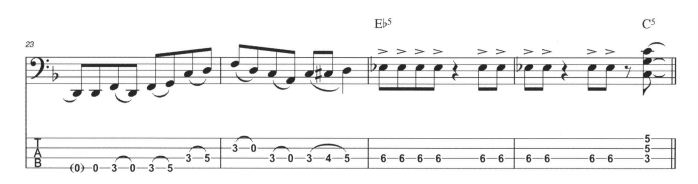

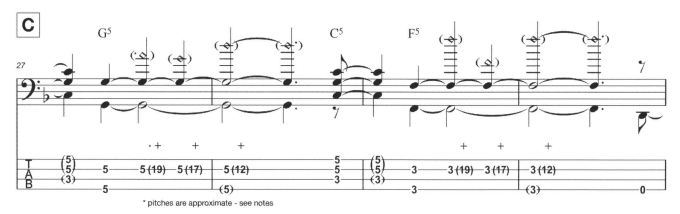

* pitches are approximate - see notes

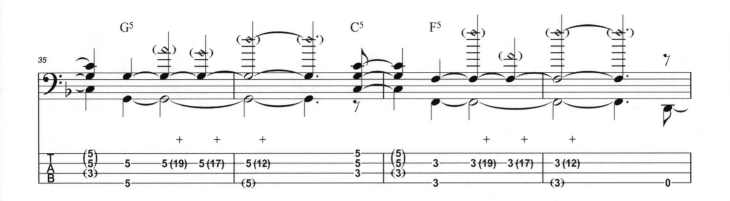

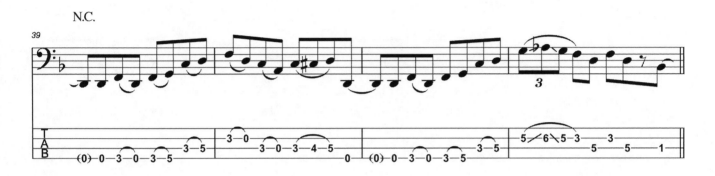

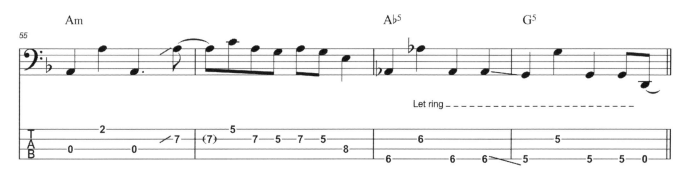

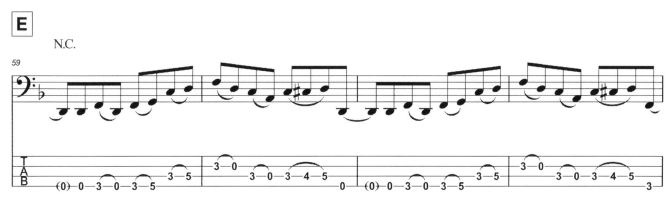

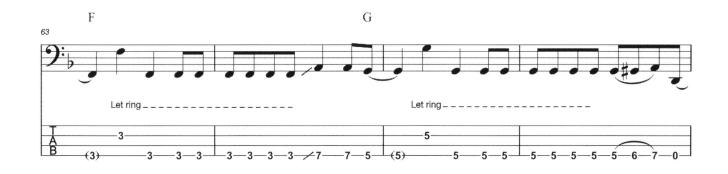

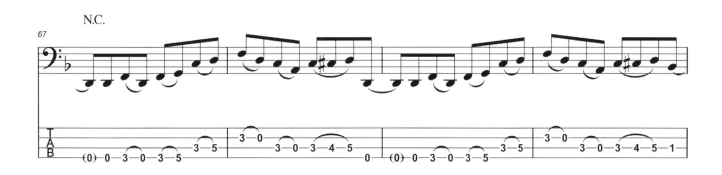

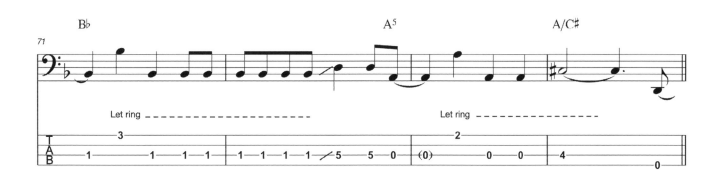

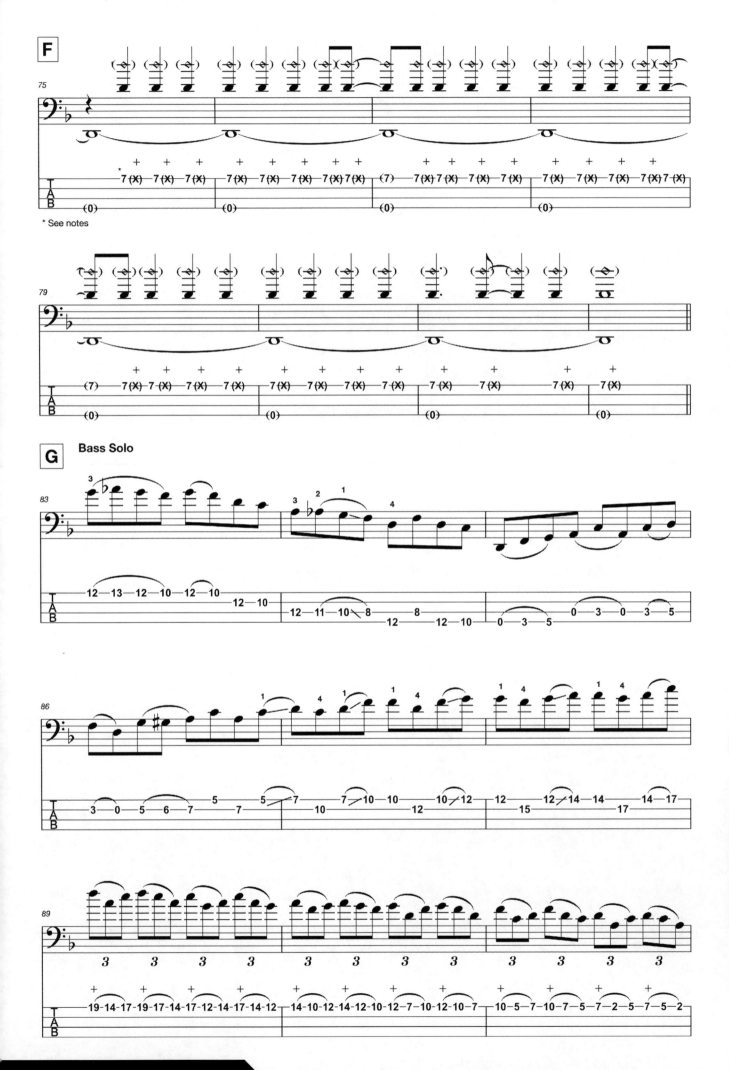

* See notes

G **Bass Solo**

H **Guitar Solo**

Half Time Feel

* Use D-Tuner to retune to E

a tempo

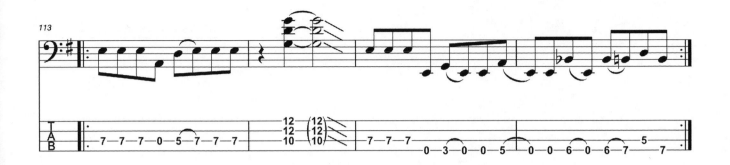

* Use D-Tuner to detune to E-string to D

I

N.C.

F   G

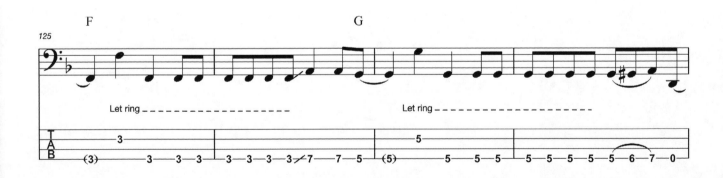

N.C.

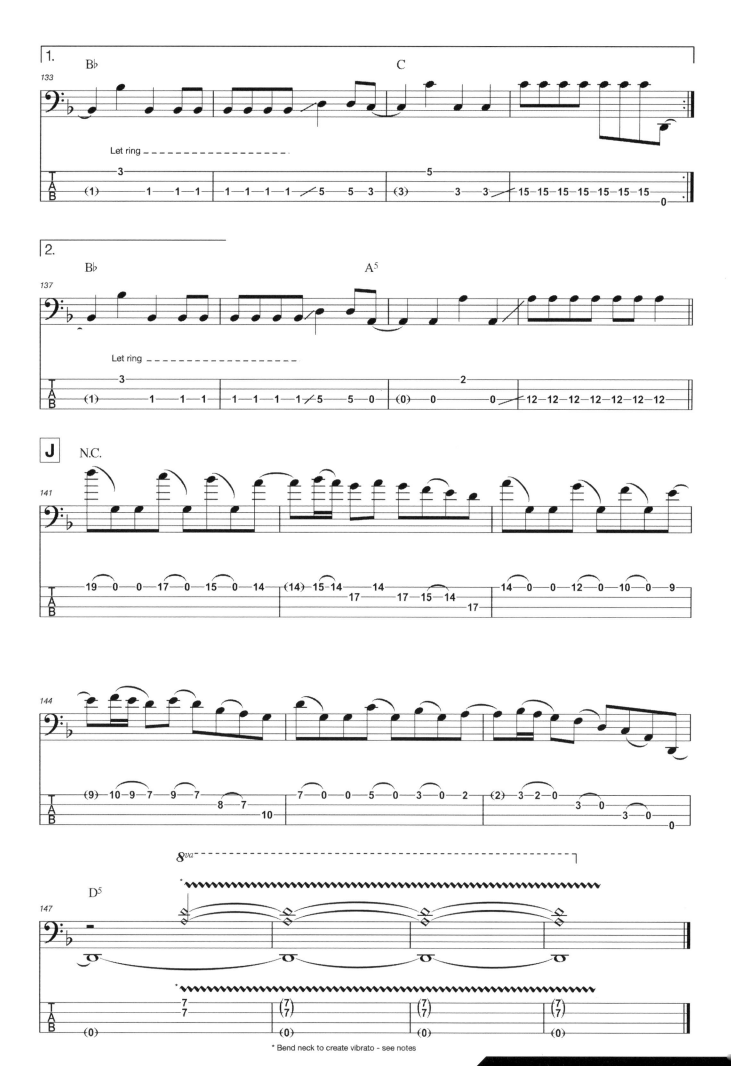

* Bend neck to create vibrato - see notes

STING

Unlike many of the bassists in this book, Sting is a household name, known to musicians and non-musicians alike thanks to a career in music that has few equals. With new wave/rock group the Police he became one of the world's best-selling artists, a feat that put four of the band's albums on *Rolling Stone* magazine's list of the 500 Greatest Albums of All Time. Whilst that would be an incredible achievement in itself, Sting has also had a successful solo career, won multiple Grammy awards, received two honorary doctorates, and been awarded a CBE from the Queen for services to music.

Gordon Matthew Sumner was born on 2nd October 1951 in Wallsend, Northumberland. Inspired by hearing his mother play the family piano, he developed an interest in music at a young age and began experimenting with the instrument himself. Unfortunately, when the family ran into money problems the piano was sold, putting a temporary stop to his musical efforts. Music had left a lasting impression however and a few years later, he became captivated by an acoustic guitar that was left at the family's house by a friend of his fathers.

As the instrument only had five rusty strings, he went to the local music shop and bought a new set, at the same time convincing his mother to buy him a basic guitar tuition book. He began to study the guitar intently, taking inspiration from the Beatles, who at the time were just beginning their domination of the pop charts.

When he was fifteen years old, Gordon went to see jazz/rhythm and blues band the Graham Bond Organisation at the Club a Go-Go in Newcastle. This particular incarnation of the group included future Cream members Jack Bruce and Ginger Baker, and although he was not sure if he liked the band's music, Gordon knew he was hearing something that was deeper and more complex than what he had been exposed to thus far. Over the course of the next year, he witnessed several other established acts at the club, including John Mayall's Bluesbreakers and Jimi Hendrix, both of whom had a significant impact on his guitar playing. During this time, he was also encouraged by some school friends to check out jazz musicians such as Thelonius Monk, Miles Davis, and John Coltrane, all of whom he studied intently.

In 1967 Gordon and his family moved to Tynemouth and he began attending a YMCA youth club in nearby Whitely Bay. Here, he became friends with several other musically inclined teenagers, including guitarist Ken Brigham and his brother Pete, who had made his own bass guitar. The three met regularly to learn songs and it was during this time that Gordon first began playing the bass. He was captivated by the instrument as soon as he picked it up and over the next few years would study it with enthusiasm, taking inspiration from bassists such as Paul McCartney, Jack Bruce, Phil Lynott and Carol Kaye.

Once he had finished school, Gordon began working, initially as a bus conductor, then as a building labourer and then as a tax officer. He eventually returned to education, enrolling on a three-year teacher training course, whilst he pursued music during evenings and weekends. During this time, he began working in a jazz group named Earthwise, then moved on to both the Phoenix Jazzmen and the Newcastle Big Band, where he learnt to read music. It was Gordon Solomon, the bandleader of the Phoenix Jazzmen that coined the nickname 'Sting': at the time he was known for wearing a black and yellow striped jumper which Solomon said made him look like a bee.

In 1973 the Newcastle Big Band were booked as the support act for fusion group Return to Forever's show at Newcastle Polytechnic. Blown away by Stanley Clarke's virtuosity on the bass, Sting was inspired to form Last Exit, a jazz fusion group in the same vein, but with vocals. Over the next few years, Sting began to refine his craft, mastering the bass guitar whilst also developing as a vocalist.

In 1976, he met Stewart Copeland, the drummer with progressive rock group Curved Air. Impressed with his performance with Last Exit, Copeland suggested that Sting contact him if he was ever working in London. By January of 1977, he had decided to move to the city to look for new opportunities. Once there, he immediately contacted Copeland, who had just split with Curved Air. Copeland had become enamoured with the burgeoning punk scene and was keen to put together a new group that would fit in. Although Sting was less taken with punk, he was able to see the potential advantage of adopting the style and so in early 1977 he and Copeland formed the Police with guitarist Henry Padovani. They quickly recorded the single 'Fall Out', which was written by Copeland and was released in May 1977 through Illegal Records. It failed to chart at the time, although it was well-received by the punk community.

During these early days of the Police, Sting and Copeland were also playing with a band called Strontium 90, where they met guitarist Andy Summers. Sting – who had been less than impressed with Padovani's performance thus far – convinced Copeland that they should recruit him for the Police. After Summers agreed to join the group, the trio were able to tackle more adventurous material, and Sting began to bring more of his own compositions to the band.

In late 1977 the Police recorded their debut album, *Outlandos d'Amour*, which was financed through a £1500 loan from Copeland's brother Miles. Upon hearing Sting's composition 'Roxanne', Miles immediately went looking for a record deal for the group, who were subsequently signed by A&M on the strength of the song. 'Roxanne' was released as a single in early 1978 but failed to chart. Because the song had failed to make its way onto the BBC playlist – presumably due to its subject matter – A&M began promoting it as having been 'banned by the BBC', which piqued the public interest somewhat. Ironically, the band's second single

'Can't Stand Losing You' *was* banned by the BBC due its cover artwork which depicted a teenage suicide. The song became a minor hit for the band, reaching #42 in the UK Charts. The band's third single, 'So Lonely' failed to chart upon release in November, but the band finally scored a hit with a re-release of 'Roxanne', which reached #12 in the UK the second time around.

The Police continued their successful streak in 1979 with *Regatta de Blanc*, an album which topped the charts in the UK and gave the band two huge hit singles, 'Message in a Bottle' and 'Walking on the Moon'. Both songs were written by Sting, who played probably his most-famous bassline on 'Walking on the Moon'. Across the Atlantic, success came a little later for the band: the two singles failed to chart, but the album reached #25 on the Billboard 200 Chart. However, the instrumental title track won the band their first Grammy, for Best Rock Instrumental Performance.

Zenyatta Mondatta followed in October 1980, with lead single 'Don't Stand So Close to Me' scoring the band their third UK #1 and going on to become the best-selling single of 1980. The album also won the band two further Grammys: the instrumental 'Behind My Camel' won Best Instrumental Rock Performance, while 'Don't Stand So Close to Me' won in the Best Rock Vocal Performance for Duo or Group category.

Throughout the early eighties the Police became arguably one of the world's biggest bands and the hits and accolades kept coming: 'Every Little Thing She Does is Magic' was their fourth UK #1 in 1981 and in 1982 the band won the Brit Award for Best British Group. In 1983, their hit song 'Every Breath You Take' won the Song of the Year Grammy, whilst their *Synchronicity* album topped the charts on either side of the Atlantic.

Such incredible levels of success rarely come without a price however and by 1984, tensions in the band

– notably between Copeland and Sting – were high. Consequently, the band decided to go on hiatus in order that each member could pursue other projects. By this time Sting had become one of the most famous musicians in the world and in addition to being the face of the Police, had also appeared in a number of films including *Quadrophenia* (1979), *Brimstone and Treacle* (1982) and *Dune* (1984).

Free to pursue other projects, in 1985 Sting put together a new band for his first solo album. Switching from bass to the guitar so that he could concentrate more on his vocals, he surrounded himself with a group of well-known jazz musicians including pianist Kenny Kirkland, drummer Omar Hakim and saxophonist Branford Marsalis. With session player Darryl Jones occupying the bass chair, the group recorded *The Dream of the Blue Turtles* and later embarked on a supporting tour, all of which was documented in the movie *Bring on the Night*. Although the album was not to match the success of Sting's albums with the Police, it nevertheless won several Grammy nominations and reached the top three in the album charts in the U.S. and the UK.

In 1986, the Police reconvened to play some concerts for Amnesty International and intended to enter the studio to begin work on a sixth album. Unfortunately, Copeland broke his collarbone in a horse riding accident before the band had the chance to begin writing, and so the aborted reunion resulted only in 'Don't Stand So Close to Me '86', a re-worked version of their earlier hit from *Zenyatta Mondatta*. The band split shortly after.

Throughout the eighties, Sting continued to pursue a successful solo career, while also working with artists including Dire Straits, Miles Davis, and Phil Collins. His 1987 album *...Nothing Like the Sun* yielded the hits 'Fragile', 'Englishman in New York' and 'Be Still My Beating Heart'. The album – on which Sting returned to the bass – again received multiple Grammy nods.

Sting's solo career continued on its upward trajectory during the nineties. The title track from his 1991 album

The Soul Cages won him another Grammy, whilst his 1993 album *Ten Summoners Tales* featured the hit song 'Fields of Gold', which is now one of his best-known tracks. This album in particular is notable for not only Sting's excellent song writing, but also his bass playing. Highlights include the odd-time grooves of 'Love is Stronger than Justice' and 'St. Augustine in Hell', the walking basslines in 'She's Too Good to Me' and the palm muted funk of 'Heavy Cloud, No Rain'.

On 11th September 2001, Sting had been scheduled to perform an internet concert held at his villa in Italy. However, as the band were preparing to go on stage, they learned of the devastating terrorist attacks in New York. Although they – and the audience – were stunned by the harrowing events of the day, the concert went ahead, although with a more sombre tone than had been intended. The resulting DVD and live album *All This Time* were dedicated to 'all those who lost their lives on that day'. The album is notable in that it features Sting on bass for most of the concert, alongside renowned upright bassist Christian McBride.

In 2002, Sting was inducted into both the Songwriters Hall of Fame and the Rock and Roll Hall of Fame as a member of the Police. In 2003 he received a CBE from the Queen, and in 2004 he published his memoir, *Broken Music*, which detailed his childhood and musical beginnings up to the point where he began achieving success with the Police. Throughout the decade he continued to pursue his solo career, notably straying from his established output with albums such as the R&B-tinged *Sacred Love* (2003) and *Songs from the Labyrinth* (2006) an album which heavily featured the music of the Elizabethan lutenist John Dowland.

In early 2007, rumours were circling that the Police would reunite to celebrate their 30th Anniversary. Opening the 49th Annual Grammy Awards in February of that year, the band performed 'Roxanne' and announced that they would embark on a world tour. The tour, which began in May, lasted for over a year, and was a huge success. Original guitarist Henry Padovani joined the band onstage for their encore at

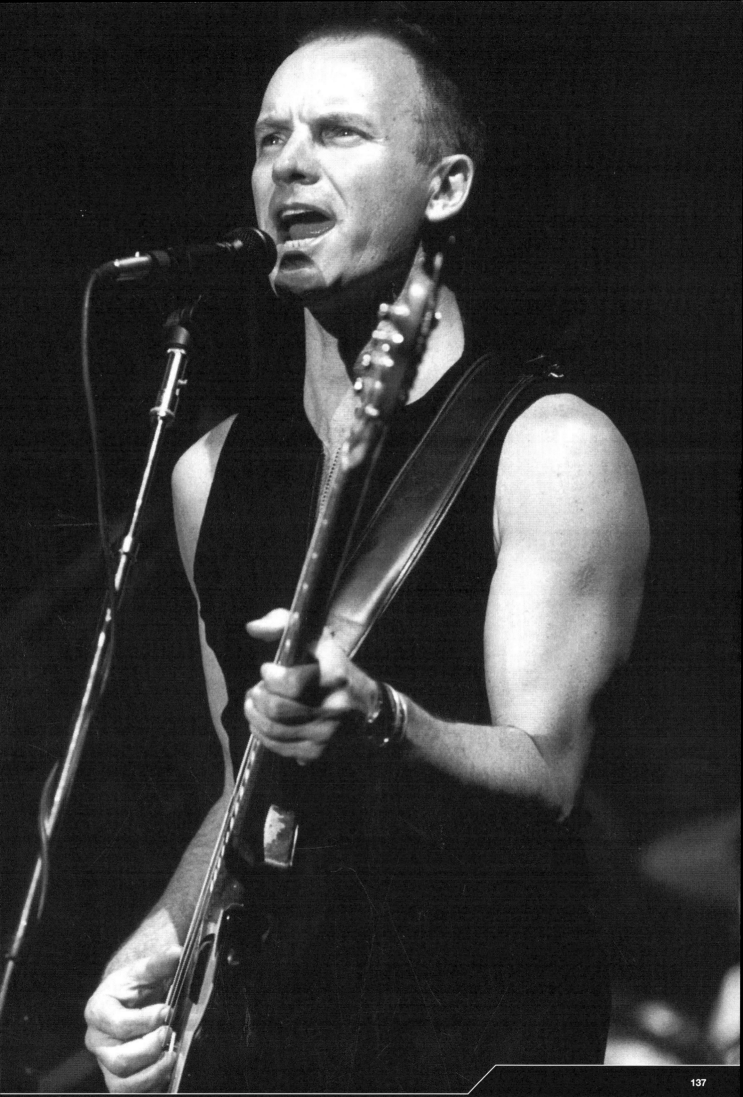

Sting on the Police reunion tour in 2008, with his '54 Fender Precision

the two shows in Paris, performing 'Next to You', the opening track from their first album. The band's final performance was at Madison Square Gardens, New York on August 7th, 2008. During the show they were joined by the New York Metropolitan

YOU MIGHT ALSO LIKE...

If you enjoy Sting's bass playing, be sure to check out the following bassists:

○ **Carol Kaye**
Giants of Bass: 60s - 70s

○ **Jaco Pastorius**
Giants of Bass: 60s - 70s

○ **James Jamerson**
Giants of Bass: 60s - 70s

Police Corp brass band for 'Message in a Bottle'. In addition to their huge catalogue of hits, the band also played cover versions of 'Sunshine of Your Love' by Cream and 'Purple Haze' by The Jimi Hendrix Experience in honour of the great rock trios that had inspired them as young musicians. A live show in Buenos Aires was filmed, and the DVD *Certifiable: Live in Buenos Aires* was released in late 2008.

In 2010 Sting released *Symphonicities*, during which he worked through material from his back catalogue backed by the Royal Philharmonic Orchestra. Throughout 2010 and 2011 he toured to promote the album and later released the live album *Sting... Live in Berlin*.

Throughout 2012/2013 Sting worked on the musical *The Last Ship*, which documented the demise of the shipbuilding industry in his

hometown of Wallsend. The musical debuted in Chicago in 2014 and later moved to Broadway, receiving two Tony Award nominations. Sting's eleventh solo album *The Last Ship* featured music from the show.

In 2014 Sting toured with fellow singer/songwriter Paul Simon on a joint tour titled *On Stage Together*. He then repeated the concept with Peter Gabriel in the summer of 2016.

In September 2016, Sting released *57th & 9th*, his first rock-orientated solo album for many years. The release of the album was preceded by the single 'I Can't Stop Thinking About You', which reached #2 on the U.S. Adult Alternative Song Chart. On the 12th November 2016 he played a concert for the reopening of the legendary Bataclan club in Paris. The club had been closed since it was attacked by terrorists the previous year.

BASS GUITARS

Sting's first bass was a 1962 Fender Jazz, which he purchased in Newcastle for approximately £150. At some point the original paint was stripped and a clear finish was applied. This was the bass that he used throughout his time with the Phoenix Jazzmen, the Newcastle Big Band and Last Exit. It was also used during the sessions for the first Police album, *Outlandos d'Amour*. Sting still owns the instrument and last used it live during the *Soul Cages* tour in 1992.

By the time the Police were recording their second album, *Regatta de Blanc*, Sting was using his Fender Jazz alongside a natural Fender Precision fretless with a maple fingerboard. In the late seventies he began using Ibanez Musician basses and owned both fretted and fretless models, both of which he used extensively during the early eighties.

During his time with the Police he also used Hamer Phantom and Cruise basses, a Hamer 8-string fretless, a Steinberger and a white Spector NS2 bass. He also often used his Z Bass – a Van Zalinge electric upright which he purchased in Holland in 1982 whilst the Police were recording *Zenyatta Mondatta*. This bass was used on several Police songs including 'Every Little Thing She Does is Magic' and later made an appearance on 'Moon Over Bourbon Street' from his first solo album *The Dream of the Blue Turtles*.

In the late nineties Sting began using a '54 Fender Precision (shown opposite) which then became his instrument of choice. As he liked it so much for live use, he had an exact replica built by the Fender Custom Shop, which accurately reproduced all dents and scratches on the original. This bass had a large white scratchplate, which he appears to have removed in recent years. Fender have released a Sting Signature Precision Bass, which is based on this instrument.

Sting used Rotosound Swing Bass Roundwound strings throughout his time with the Police, preferring a gauge of .040, .060, .080, .100. He later switched to DR Strings and currently uses DR Low Rider Nickel strings.

AMPLIFICATION

For many years Sting has used an Alembic FX-1 Preamp, Carver amplifiers and Clair Bros. cabinets. In recent years he has been using Avalon VT737SP and VT837 tube preamps and Lab Gruppen PLM20000Q power amps.

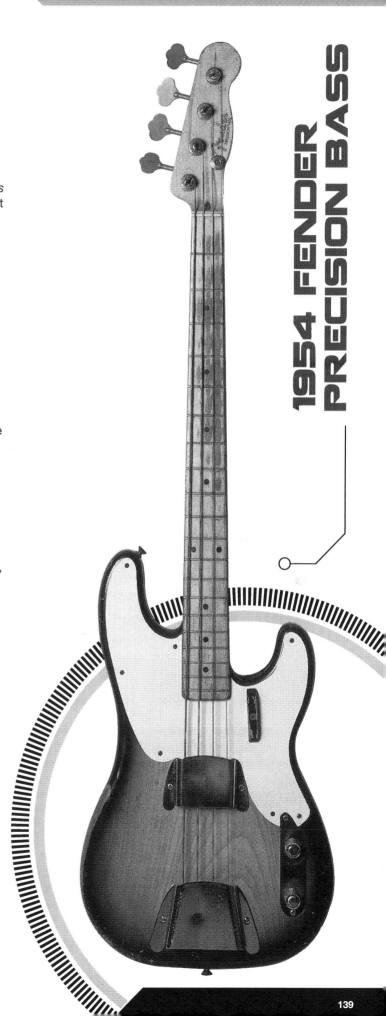

1954 FENDER PRECISION BASS

PERFORMANCE NOTES

'Stung' is a piece of music written in the style of Sting's work with the Police. Although this is essentially a fairly simple pop reggae tune, the bassline has some interesting quirks, all of which are common to Sting's playing with the band.

This track opens with a four-bar guitar intro which establishes the repeating two-bar chord progression which is used for several sections of the song. When the bass enters in bar 5, it plays a simple line, one that perfectly supports the chord progression. Although this line is heavy on chord tones, as one might expect, note that for the C^{sus4} and C chords in the second half of the second bar, no root notes are played. Instead, the melodic phrase begins on a D, moves up to E (the third of the C chord), then up to G (the fifth). This part works well despite the absence of a strong root note because it is very melodic and makes good use of other strong chord tones.

At letter A the 'verse' riff begins. This is similar in style to Sting's part on the classic Police song 'Can't Stand Losing You'. As the phrase begins, the bass rests on beat one, entering on the offbeat. A root-fifth-ninth figure is played here, both reflecting the guitar line from the intro and adding greater melodic interest to the bassline. For the D minor chord that occurs in the second half of the bar, no root note is played: instead, a low F (the minor third of the chord) and a C (the seventh) are played in the bass, quite radically altering the sound of the chord. Sting often uses non-root notes in his basslines, believing that the ability to do so – and therefore affect the harmony – is one of the main benefits to playing the instrument. This is something that he learnt from studying Paul McCartney's bass work with the Beatles. In the second bar of this sequence, the bass plays another melodic line. Again, you'll notice a rest on the downbeat of the first beat of the bar, as well as the absence of chord tones in the usual places. This line is repeated several times, with no variation – this is to reflect the fact that Sting rarely alters his parts significantly, as he is usually singing lead vocals at the same time. Overall, this line is very typical of Sting's work with the Police.

At letter B the 'chorus' part of the track begins. Here, the bass switches to a pumping, eighth note-based rock line. Note that the bass remains on the root note of the chord throughout each bar, moving to a different pitch on the final eighth note. These simple note choices help to ease the transitions between the chord changes.

In bars 33-36 a simple post-chorus phrase is played, reminiscent of the song 'Message in a Bottle'. When playing this section, be sure to acknowledge the staccato markings and take care to play the quarter note triplet as written.

After repeats of the 'verse' and 'chorus' sections at letters C and D, a new section begins at letter E. This acts as a 'middle 8' and as is often the case, features a sudden modulation to a new key centre (C# minor). The bassline here is based on a simple root-octave figure and is easy enough to play. This part leads into a repeat of the intro section and a final double chorus. The tracks ends with the post-chorus phrase that was used earlier in the song.

SOUND ADVICE

This track was recorded on a Fender Precision Bass, strung with heavy gauge flatwound strings, and played fingerstyle. The controls on the instrument were both set to full, and no EQ adjustments were made after the part was recorded.

Sting's tone is a simple one to replicate and can easily be achieved with either a Precision or a Jazz-style instrument.

Although Sting's lines are often quite simple to play, the real challenge with his music is playing them and singing the lead vocal part at the same time! If you're feeling brave, have a go at this with songs such as 'Bed's Too Big Without You', 'Spirits in the Material World' (both by the Police) or 'Love is Stronger Than Justice', and 'Seven Days', both from his 1993 solo album *Ten Summoners Tales*.

'STUNG'

Written by Stuart Clayton

Drums: Will Beavis
Keys: Stuart Clayton
Guitar: Gary Mitchell
Bass: Stuart Clayton

Pop Reggae ♩ = 130

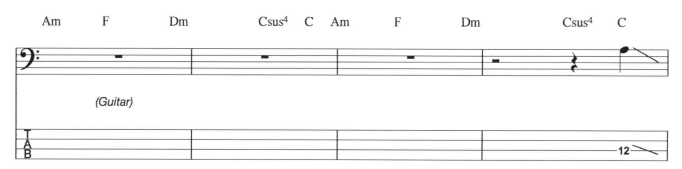

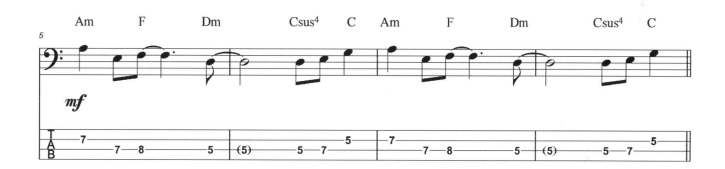

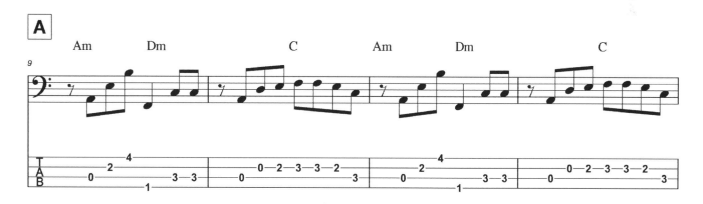

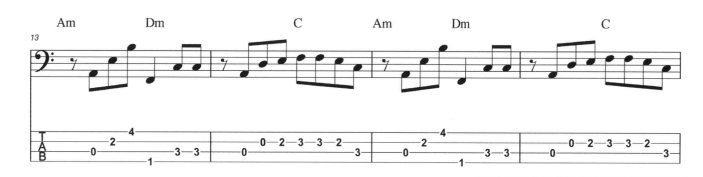

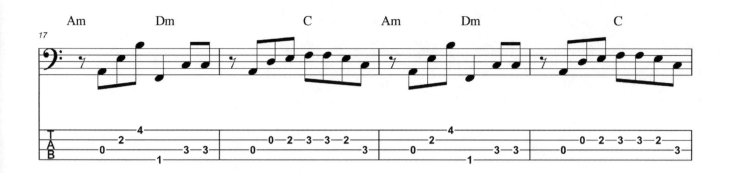

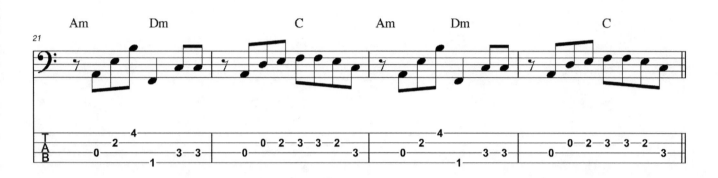

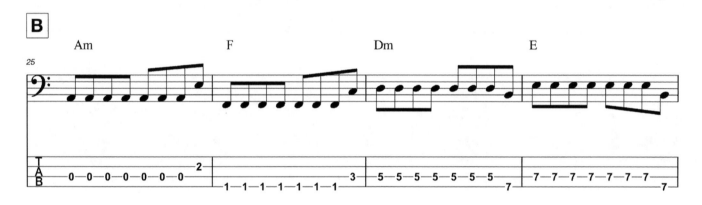

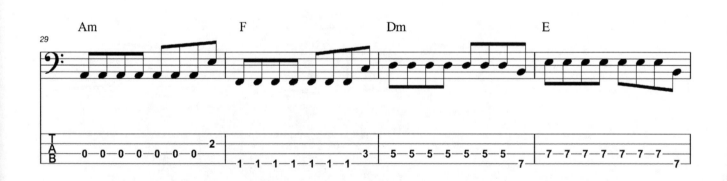

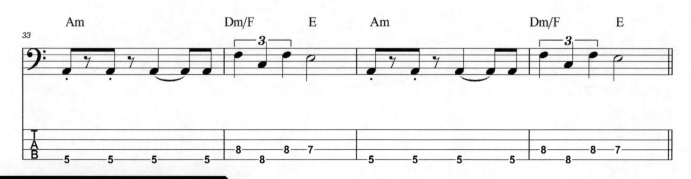

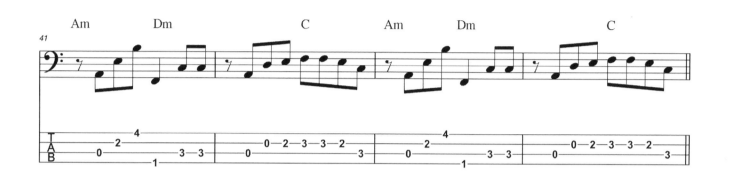

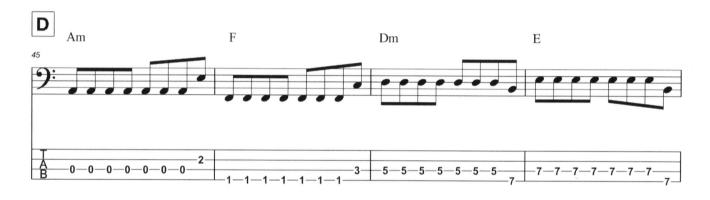

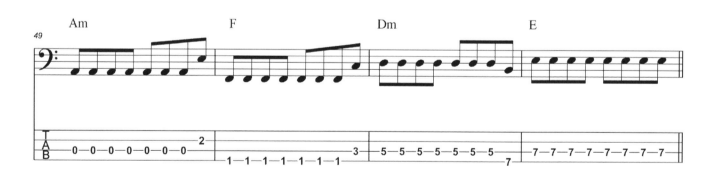

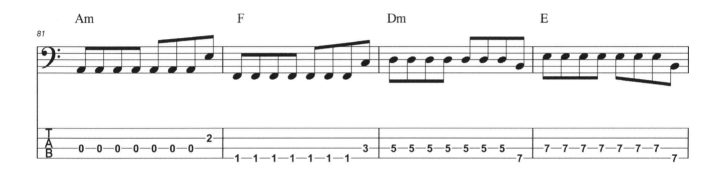

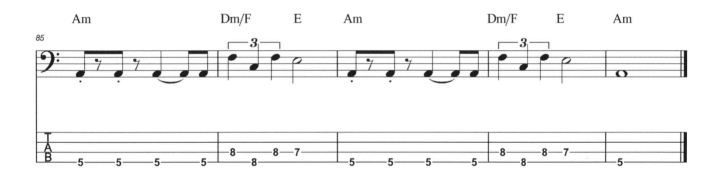

VICTOR WOOTEN

There can be no doubt that Victor Wooten is one of the most important figures in the history of the bass guitar. Through his work with Béla Fleck and the Flecktones and his own solo career, Victor's contributions over the last twenty years have pushed the boundaries of what is achievable on the instrument. He has inspired bass players from all over the world with his virtuosity and is the only multiple winner of *Bass Player* Magazine's Bass Player of the Year award. He has also been voted one of the 'ten most influential bassists of all time' and has two Nashville Awards for 'Bassist of The Year'.

Victor Wooten was born into a military family in Idaho on 11th September 1964. He spent much of his childhood living in Hawaii and California, before settling in Newport News, Virginia. His family was extremely musical (all four of his older brothers are accomplished musicians) and it wasn't long before Victor began playing bass in the family band. Astonishingly, Victor picked up the instrument at the age of 3, under his brother Regi's guidance. He made his playing debut with The Wootens at age 5, and during much of his childhood toured the nightclub circuit with the family band. Along the way he learnt countless songs and was able to continuously refine his abilities on the bass through the group's live shows. The Wootens progressed to the level where they were opening up for larger acts such as Curtis Mayfield and War, and in 1985 they recorded their own album, simply titled *The Wootens*.

Alongside his live work, Victor studied the work of bassists such as Larry Graham, James Jamerson, Bootsy Collins, Jaco Pastorius and Stanley Clarke. He also learned everything he could from his guitarist brother Regi – in fact, Victor has always been quick to credit Regi with showing him how to use his thumb like a plectrum and thereby laying the groundwork for his innovative double thumbing technique.

In 1988 Victor moved to Nashville in search of new musical challenges. Once there, he found work quickly and was soon introduced to banjoist Béla Fleck by mutual friend Kurt Storey. After an audition over the telephone, Victor was recruited by Fleck for his new band, Béla Fleck & The Flecktones. His brother Roy was also hired as the group's drummer, opting to instead provide the grooves through his Synthaxe Drumitar. The line-up of the new group was completed with the addition of Howard Levy on keyboards and harmonica.

After appearing on PBS's *Lonesome Pine Special*, The Flecktones were snapped up by Warner Brothers in 1990 and released their eponymous debut album to critical acclaim. Their highly original blend of jazz, bluegrass, fusion and everything in between made an instant impression on musicians all over the world, with Victor's bass work ensuring that the bass playing community tuned in. Whilst Victor is in superb form throughout, the band's debut album is notable for the track 'The Sinister

Minister' a memorable tune which is a jaw-dropping showcase for Victor's extraordinary slap techniques.

The Flecktones' second album, *Flight of the Cosmic Hippo* followed in 1991 and quickly climbed to the top of the U.S. Jazz Charts. This album boasts classic Flecktones tunes such as 'Blu-bop' and 'Sex in a Pan', a bass-orientated song that Victor often plays as a solo piece. The band also released a double live CD in the same year. Entitled *Live Art*, the album is a goldmine for fans of Victor's bass work: aside from a fantastic version of 'The Sinister Minister' the album also boasts an incredible bass solo from Victor featuring his arrangement of the traditional tune 'Amazing Grace' – another of his solo bass highlights.

The band's third album was 1992's *UFO Tofu* and was the last to feature Howard Levy, who left the band following its release. Rather than replace him, the Flecktones took the opportunity to continue as a trio, and integrated MIDI triggering technology into their arsenal to add further colours to their already impressive palette. Their first album with this line-up, *Three Flew*

Over the Cuckoo's Nest was the result. Throughout the nineties The Flecktones continued to release critically acclaimed albums whilst Victor also began to establish himself as a solo artist.

Victor's debut album *A Show of Hands* was released in 1995 and immediately turned the bass world on its collective ear. Completely unaccompanied and with no overdubbing, Victor presented a solo bass album that showcased the full extent of his abilities and significantly expanded the perceived boundaries of the 4-string bass guitar. Using a combination of his mind-blowing slap techniques, chordal playing, two handed tapping and everything in between, he worked his way through a selection of solo bass pieces that covered a wide variety of musical styles from funk and jazz to reggae and classical. From the funk grooves of the opening track 'You Can't Hold No Groove' to the rapid-fire arpeggiated passages of 'Classical Thump' Victor single-handedly revolutionised the slap and pop style, breathing new life into a technique that had become stale through the overuse of the same clichéd licks and patterns. It should be noted that

SELECTED DISCOGRAPHY

Victor Wooten – *A Show of Hands*
'U Can't Hold No Groove', 'More Luv', 'The Vision', 'Overjoyed', 'A Show of Hands', 'Classical Thump', 'Me & My Bass Guitar'

Victor Wooten – *What Did He Say?*
'What Did He Say', 'What You Won't Do for Love', 'Cherokee', 'Norwegian Wood', 'Naima', 'Sometimes I Laugh', 'The Sojourne of Arjuna'

Victor Wooten – *Palmystery*
'2 Timers', 'Cambo', 'The Lesson', 'Left, Right & Center', 'Sifu', 'Flex', 'The Gospel', 'Song for My Father', 'Us 2'

Steve Bailey & Victor Wooten – *Bass Extremes*
'A Chick from Corea', 'Stan the Man', 'Victor's Jam', 'Thumb Start My Harley', 'Emerald Forest', 'Donna Lee'

Béla Fleck & The Flecktones – *Béla Fleck & The Flecktones*
'Hurricane Camille', 'The Sinister Minister', 'Flipper', 'Mars Needs Women: They're Here', 'Tell It to the Gov'nor'

Béla Fleck & The Flecktones – *Live Art*
'Stomping Grounds', 'Lochs of Dread', 'Bigfoot', 'Flying Saucer Dudes', 'Vix 9', 'Improv/Amazing Grace', 'Blu-Bop', 'More Luv', 'The Sinister Minister'

Béla Fleck & The Flecktones – *Left of Cool*
'Throwdown at the Hoedown', 'Big Country', 'Let Me Be the One', 'Almost 12', 'Oddity'

Greg Howe, Victor Wooten & Dennis Chambers – *Extraction*
'Extraction', 'Tease', 'Crack It Way Open', 'Proto Cosmos', 'Lucky 7', 'Bird's Eye View'

while the album is one of the most technically complex that you are ever likely to hear from a bassist, Victor uses all of the techniques at his disposal with taste and maturity, always letting the music come first. It's little wonder then that *A Show of Hands* won *Bass Player* magazine's 'Record of the Year' award in 1996 and has since been nominated as one of 'Thirty Essential Bass Albums You Must Own.' With this recording, Victor quickly became the new figurehead of not only slapping and tapping techniques, but of high performance bass playing in general.

Victor followed the success of his debut with a second album, *What Did He Say?* in 1997. This time he allowed himself to use multiple bass overdubs and also employed a host of supporting musicians, including many members of his family. The album contains one solo piece, a tenor bass arrangement of the Beatles song 'Norwegian Wood', which is played with the two handed tapping technique. A superb performance of this track, as well as a mind-blowing rendition of 'You Can't Hold No Groove', can be seen on the *Bass Player Live 1998* DVD.

During the nineties, Victor collaborated with fellow bassist Steve Bailey on several *Bass Extremes* tuition projects. The first came as a book and CD set, featuring transcriptions of all of the pieces, as well as lessons on how to perform them. For fans of Victor's virtuosic techniques, this is an invaluable resource. Two further *Bass Extremes* CDs followed, each featuring several guest bass players such as Stanley Clarke, Oteil Burbridge and Anthony Jackson.

Throughout the 2000's Victor continued to release new albums whilst expanding his career in some surprising directions: as well as running regular bass tuition and nature camps, he set up his own label (Vix Records) and released a music tuition book entitled *The Music Lesson: A Spiritual Search for Growth Through Music*. Unusually

Victor with his Fodera Yin Yang bass

for such a project, Victor wrote the book in the form of a novel, the central character of which was a bass player. The project was later reworked as an audio book and has also been translated into several different languages.

2008 was a busy year for Victor, beginning with a new band project with fellow bassists Marcus Miller and Stanley Clarke. Named SMV, the group had evolved out of a performance at *Bass Player Live* in 2006, where Marcus and Victor had been asked to present legendary bassist Stanley Clarke with the *Bass Player* Magazine Lifetime Achievement Award. The three had then jammed through Clarke's signature tune 'School Days', with each indicating that they would like to continue to collaborate in the future. The result was an album – *Thunder* – which included original songs as well as covers of tunes from each of their back catalogues.

In the same year Victor released *Palmystery*, a new album featuring several intense jazz/fusion tunes including '2 Timers', a track which features members of his band playing in two time signatures at once. The album is also notable for the solo composition 'The Lesson', which he has played as part of his live bass solos for many years, and which was also a featured part of *The Music Lesson* project.

In 2011, to celebrate its fifteenth anniversary, Victor released a special edition of his debut album, *A Show of Hands 15*. The album was remastered and contained three bonus tracks: a new version of 'You Can't Hold No Groove' with JD Blair on drums, 'Flip Flop' and 'Live Solo #2'. He followed this with a dual release in 2012, *Words & Tones* and *Sword & Stone*.

After going on an extended hiatus in 2012, the Flecktones reconvened for a short summer tour in 2016.

Victor continues to record and tour as both a solo artist and sideman and regularly runs classes at Victor Wooten's Centre for Music and Nature at his Wooten Woods complex in Nashville, Tennessee.

YOU MIGHT ALSO LIKE...

If you love what Victor does, be sure to check out:

○ **Stanley Clarke**
Giants of Bass: 60s - 70s

○ **Marcus Miller**
See page 82

○ **Larry Graham**
Giants of Bass: 60s - 70s

BASS GUITARS

Victor's first bass was a Univox copy of a Höfner violin bass. He still owns this instrument and it can be seen on the front cover of his second album *What Did He Say?*. His second bass was a late 70s Alembic Series I and was his first 'good' bass.

Victor found his third bass in 1983, whilst recording with The Wootens in New Jersey. The producer for the session didn't like the bass he was using at the time and wanted him to use the studio bass, which Victor found uncomfortable. One of the studio staff mentioned that some friends of his – Vinny Fodera and Joey Lauricella – had just begun to build their own basses and so they went to investigate. Victor walked away from the meeting with his first of many Fodera basses, a 4-string Monarch Deluxe which to this day he refers to as his #1 bass. His original Monarch is built from curly and rock maple, Honduras mahogany, with an Indian rosewood fretboard. It has EMG pickups in a P+J configuration and Victor later added a Kahler tremolo bar. This bass has the serial number 037 and was his main instrument throughout the eighties and nineties. It was used extensively on his debut album *A Show of Hands* and for the first few Flecktones albums. Fodera now make a Victor Wooten Signature instrument, based on his original Monarch.

Victor's next bass was another Fodera Monarch, this time a standard model. This instrument had previously belonged to the LaBella String Company and had their logo inlaid into the body. This was replaced by a yin yang symbol and Victor's name when he began using it. This is Victor's tenor bass and is tuned a fourth higher than a regular bass: A-D-G-C.

In the late nineties, Victor began using a new Fodera bass: a Monarch with a Yin Yang symbol inlaid with contrasting woods on the top face of the instrument. The first of these basses was a fretless with an ebony and a holly wood top, whilst the second was a fretted instrument with an ebony and yellow wood top. Fodera make a Victor Wooten

Yin Yang signature model that as of 2016, is in its third iteration – the Deluxe Series III (see photo).

In addition to these main basses, Victor also has a Fodera with piezo pickups and stereo outputs and a Yin Yang 5-string with a Yamaha MIDI pickup. Also in his collection are a NYC Empire bass, a Kubicki Ex-Factor, Joe Compito 5-string fretless and 6-string fretted basses, a Keith Roscoe 5-string, a Conklin 8-string, a Nechville Banjo bass and a Taylor fretless acoustic. He also has a Conklin M.E.U electric upright and two upright basses, a Juzek and an Italian upright, built in 1781.

Victor strings his basses with Fodera strings, preferring a gauge of .040, .055, .075, .095.

EFFECTS

Victor has used several multi-effects units during his career, including the Ensoniq DP4, the Roland V-Bass system and the Boss GT-6B Bass Effects Processor. He also uses a Lexicon JamMan looper, a DigiTech Whammy, an EBS BassIQ and a Rodenburg volume boost.

AMPLIFICATION

In the early nineties Victor used ADA amps with MESA/Boogie cabinets. He later switched to a Walter Woods amplifier which he paired with Ampeg cabinets. During the early 2000s he favoured an Ampeg SVT-4PRO amplifier with Ampeg BXT-410HL4 and BXT-115HL4 cabinets. As of 2007 he has been using Hartke LH1000 amps and HyDrive 4x10 and 1x15 cabinets. In 2016 he began using the company's new Class D TX600 amp.

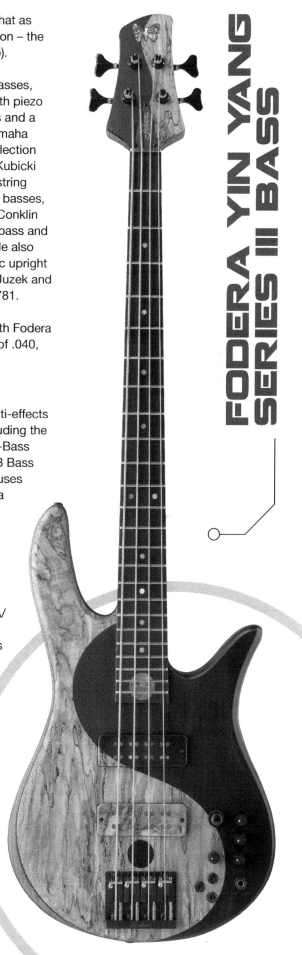

FODERA YIN YANG SERIES III BASS

As you'll hear, 'The Wicked Vicar' was inspired by the Béla Fleck & The Flecktones track 'The Sinister Minister', which features one of Victor's most popular lines. The instrumentation and arrangement used here were also very much inspired by the Flecktones, since the band is home to so much of Victor's best work.

The piece opens with a repeated four-bar bassline which establishes the main chord progression used throughout the song. The line here is played with basic slap and pop technique and should not prove too challenging. At letter B this bassline continues as the main melody line is played and the banjo provides a chordal accompaniment.

At letter C the bassline begins to become more active, with triplet pops used to both reinforce the harmony and add rhythmic interest. These are performed by slapping the lower note with the thumb, then popping the two upper notes in quick succession with the first and second fingers of the picking hand. Note that in the final bar of the sequence (bar 12) you will be popping a note on the D-string, then slapping another on the same string shortly afterwards.

At letter D the main melody returns, with the bass playing the simple line that opened the piece. At the end of the second repeat however, the bass becomes much more active, playing the Bm7 and B7 arpeggios using open string hammer-on phrases in a sixteenth note rhythm. This sets up the E section, which is based on this technique. When performing this line, it's important to note that the open strings that begin each hammer-on phrase are not always integral to the chord itself but are sometimes merely 'jumping off' points for the hammer-ons. The same chord progression is followed here, but with the bass outlining simple chord voicings using the open-hammer-pop technique. You can afford to allow the notes to ring into one another when playing this part as the chordal effect of this is not undesirable. When playing the Bm7 and B7 chords in bar 21 the fingerings are a little tricky. I recommend the following: fret the D

at the seventeenth fret of the A-string with the second finger and the B at the sixteenth fret of the G-string with the first. Then, on beat two, fret the F♯ at the sixteenth fret with the first finger and the B at the same fret with the second. The final D of the second beat should be fretted with the second finger. Remember that all of these notes are preceded by open strings, so there is time for the fingers to jump around as needed. On beats three and four, fret the D♯ at the eighteenth fret of the A-string with the second finger, the B at the sixteenth fret of the G-string with the first and the A at the nineteenth fret of the D-string with the third.

At letter F a unison melody is played with the banjo. This is played with conventional fingerstyle technique and uses the E minor pentatonic scale. This is a relatively simple part (compared to the rest of this piece!) and the only real potential problem you'll encounter is with the line in the fourth bar of the sequence (bar 27). On the third beat, I recommend fretting the G at the twelfth fret of the G-string with your first finger, then sliding this same finger up to the A two frets higher. Once there, perform the hammer-on to the B with the third or fourth finger, then use the first finger of the picking hand to

tap the E at the twenty-first fret. The co-ordination required here can be tricky, so be sure to practice this part slowly to begin with.

At letter G with have a short interlude section which is reminiscent of a part Victor plays in the tune 'Sex in a Pan', a song which he also frequently performs solo. To play this line, pluck the opening double stop chord of each bar with the thumb and first finger of the picking hand. The bass note in each bar will need to ring as you perform the rising melody line on the G-string. Note that the second note of each phrase is performed with a hammer-on and the third is tapped by the picking hand. After playing these notes, you will need to slide into the double stop chord with the picking hand and tap a new bass note with the fretting hand. For the F△7 chord, the picking hand should slide up to the E and A at the fourteenth fret of the D and G-strings with the first and second fingers. As this happens, tap the F at the eighth fret of the A-string with a finger of the fretting hand.

At letter H the bass solo begins. This opens with an E minor pentatonic-based riff that is uses some different time signatures and is played with the palm muting technique. To

Fig. 1: Performing an upstroke with the thumb

palm mute, rest the edge of your picking hand across the strings just in front of the bridge. You'll need to experiment with the amount of pressure you exert on the strings, but the desired effect is a heavily muted sound. When playing this line, all notes on the A and D-strings are best played with the thumb (not slapped, just plucked), whilst all notes on the G-string should be played with the first finger. This four-bar riff is played twice. At bar 36 the riff continues, now played with the slap technique. Some double thumbing is required alongside conventional slap technique – any notes shown with an upward pointing arrow in the notation guide between the staves are to be played with thumb 'upstrokes'. To use the double thumbing technique, slap the string as you would normally, but allow the thumb to 'pass through' the string and come to rest on the next string. You can then bring the thumb upwards, plucking the string as you do (See Fig. 1). You'll find that double thumbing – which is essentially like using your thumb in the same way that you would use a pick – is easier with a lower string-to-body distance. This is why some bassists install a 'ramp' under the strings.

In bar 43 a descending fill is played, beginning with a sixteenth note triplet on the same note. This is played by slapping the note with the thumb, performing an upstroke, then popping, all on the same note. This can be challenging to do to begin with, but latter parts of the solo will use this technique heavily.

At bar 44 a new slap part begins, using conventional slap technique, although with some double popped notes and a few thumb upstrokes. Bar 47 features a classic Victor Wooten lick: sixteenth note triplets performed using the open-hammer-pop technique. To play this line, slap the open A-string, then hammer-on to the E at the seventh fret with the first finger of the fretting hand. This is followed by a popped ghost note on the G-string. Then, slap the open D-string and hammer-on to the B at the ninth fret with the fourth finger of the fretting hand. You should then barre across with this finger for the popped E at the same fret. You'll see that you are essentially slapping a 'power chord' of root-fifth-octave. This shape is then moved down the neck on subsequent beats.

In bar 52 a new lick begins. This is based off of a triplet technique that Victor commonly uses, and which can be heard in the bass solo from 'The Sinister Minister'. Here, triplets are played using thumbed downstrokes, upstrokes and pops. The popped notes are always on the G-string, but the slapped notes will be either on the A, D or G-strings. I recommend practicing this idea with ghost notes to begin with: down-up on the A-string then pop the G-string, down-up on the D-string then pop the G, down-up-pop on the G-string and finally, down-up on the D-string and pop the G. This repeating right hand figure is very challenging to play initially, so practice it slowly to begin with. At bar 54 this technique is used to

begin playing through the main chord progression from the piece. The chord voicings used here are similar to those used in the E section and I recommend familiarising yourself with the required fingerings before playing them with this unusual slap technique. Once the chord sequence is complete you will find yourself in the upper register of the instrument. Beginning in bar 58, you will then play through the chord progression in a descending motion, using the same technique.

The bass solo is followed by the re-introduction of the main bass figure that opened the piece, followed by a repeat of the main melody. The open-hammer-pop riff is reused at letter K and is followed by a repeat of the unison line at letter L. The Interlude line at letter M is used to bring the piece to a close by adding a final chord, Em^7. This chord is arpeggiated by strumming across the strings with the thumb.

SOUND ADVICE

I recorded this track using a GB Guitars Rumour 4-string. This is an active, modern sounding instrument with a powerful onboard preamp. I set the pickup selector and all tone controls in the centre position as this results in a nice, transparent tone that works perfectly for pieces like this. Some very minimal EQ tweaks were made in Logic once the part was recorded and a little compression was used to even out the sound. It's important to note that the majority of the recorded tone came from the natural sound of the instrument and the way it was played. This instrument also has a 'ramp', a 3mm piece of Perspex beneath the strings between the neck and the front pickup. This reduces the string-to-body distance and means that the thumb doesn't snag when playing upstrokes with the double thumbing technique.

When playing this piece, I recommend using an active bass, preferably with two humbucking pickups. Set the EQ flat to begin with (as I did) and then make small tonal adjustments from there. A healthy dose of compression can also help even out your playing, particularly with techniques of this nature.

'THE WICKED VICAR'

Written by Stuart Clayton

Programming: Stuart Clayton
Guitar: Steve Banks
Bass: Stuart Clayton

Funk/Bluegrass ♩ = 125

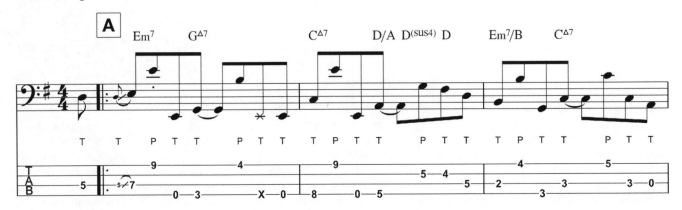

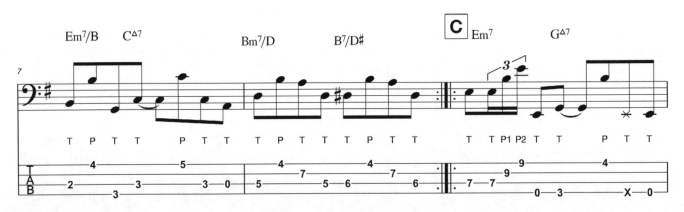

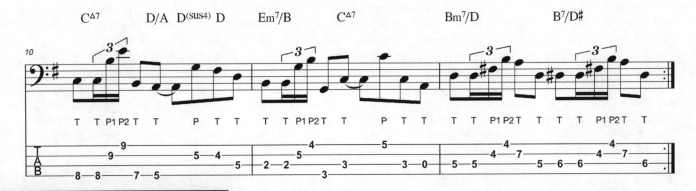

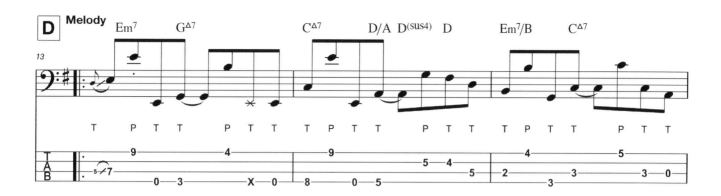

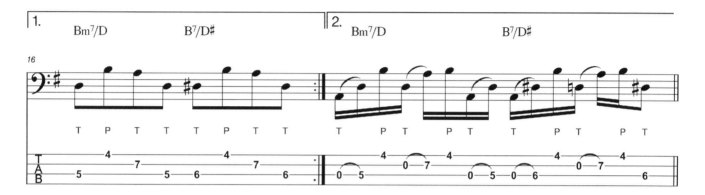

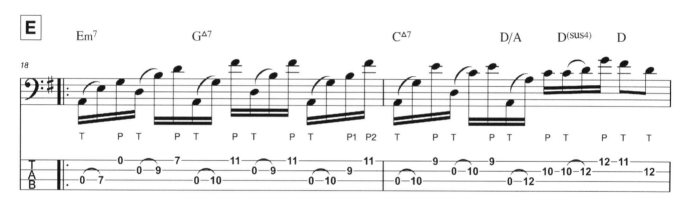

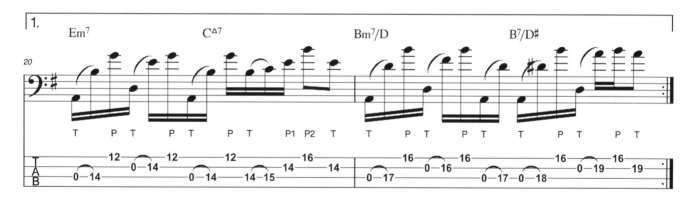

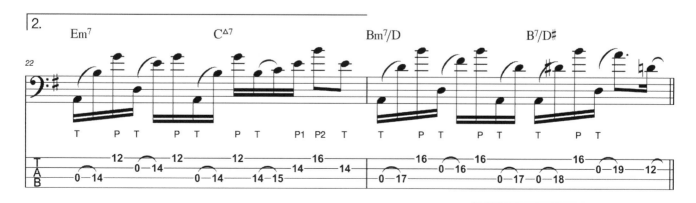

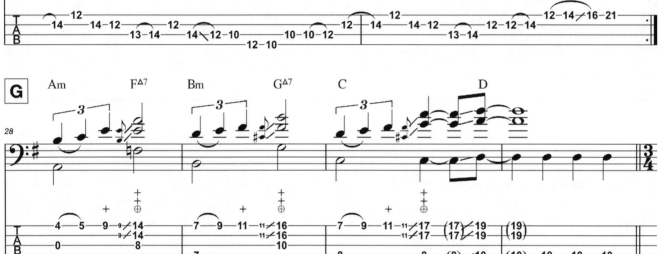

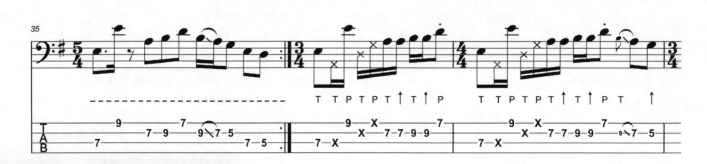

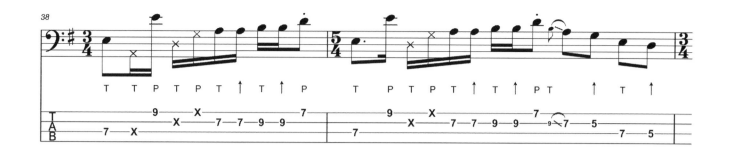

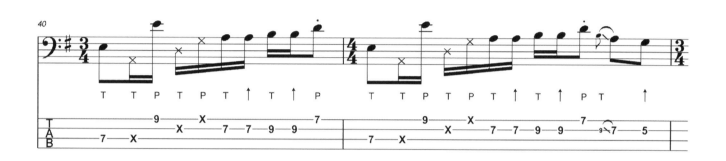

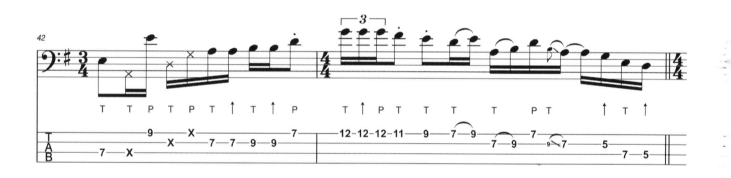

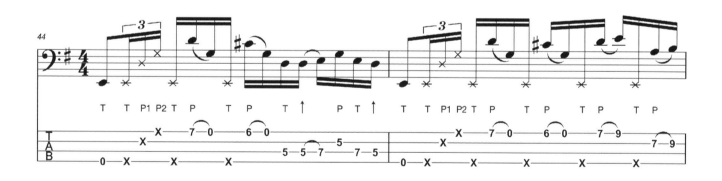

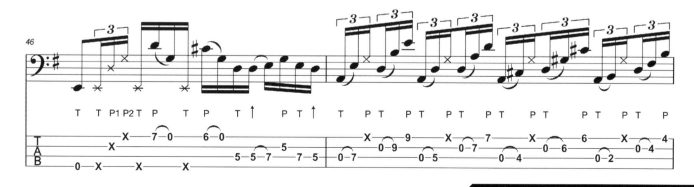

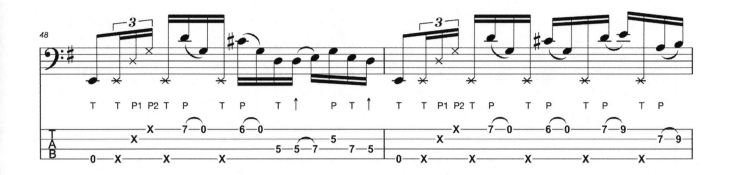

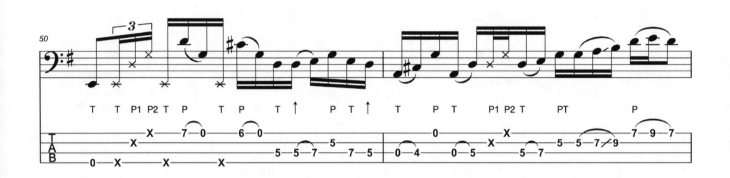

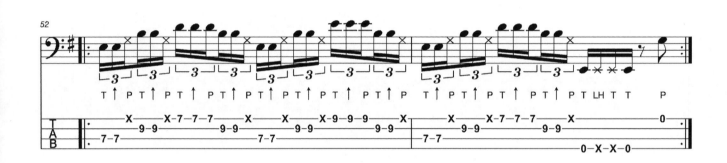

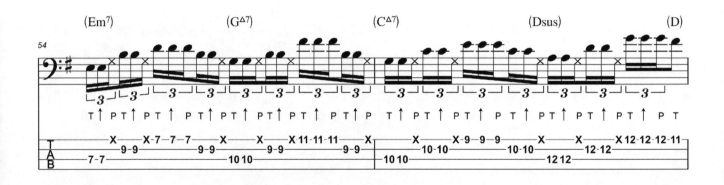

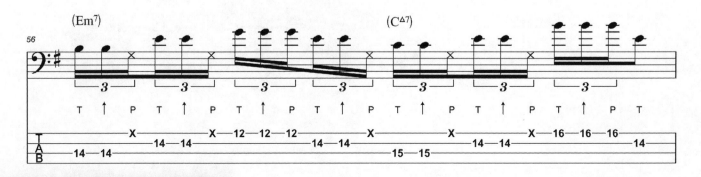

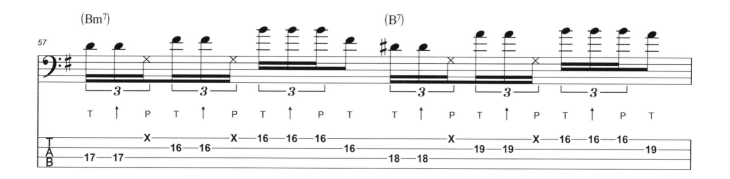

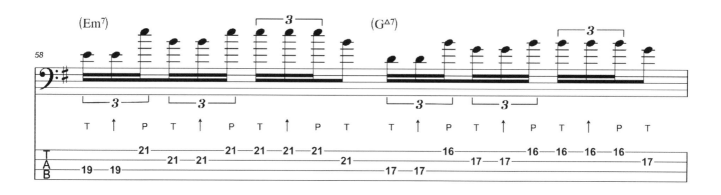

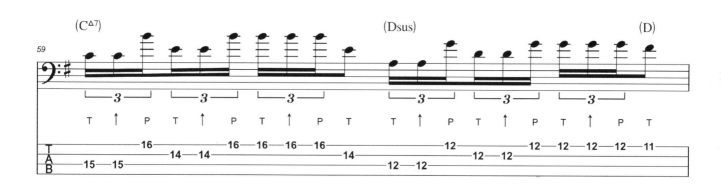

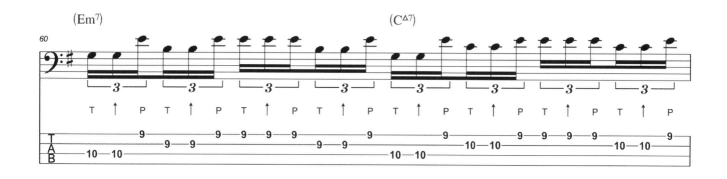

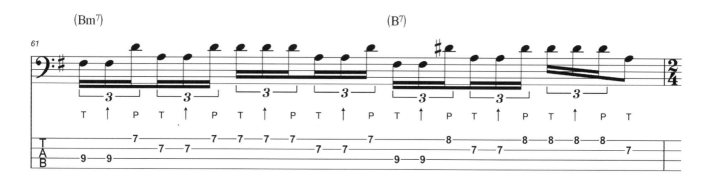

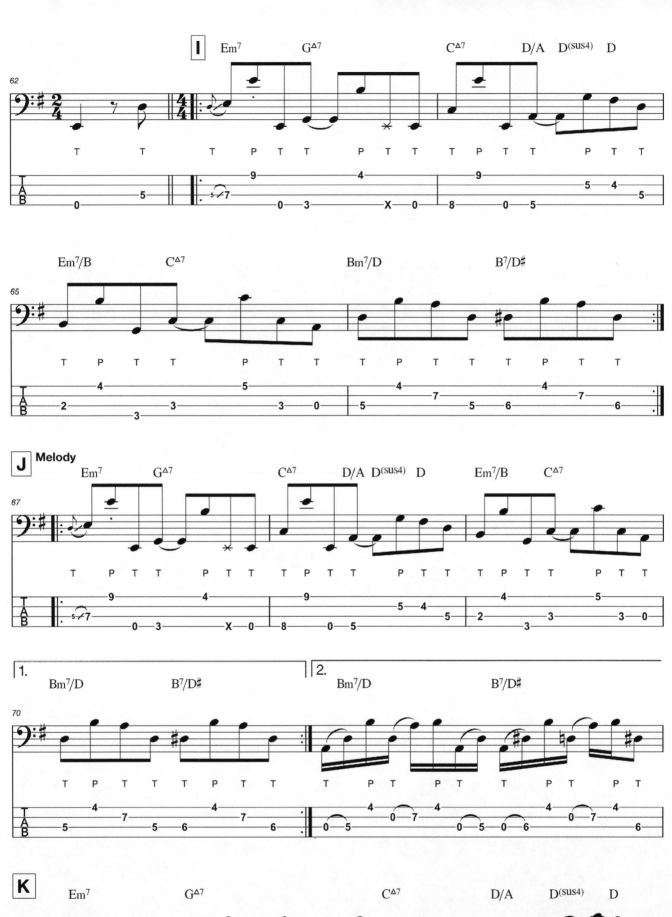

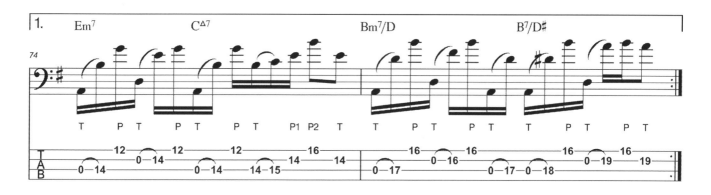

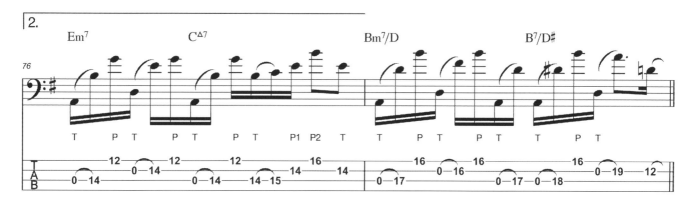

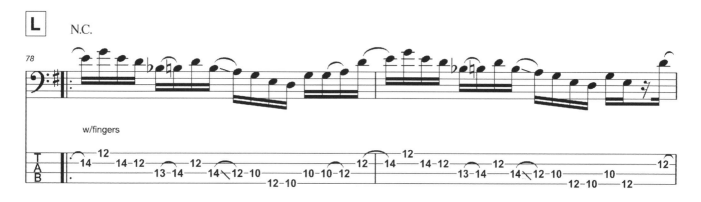

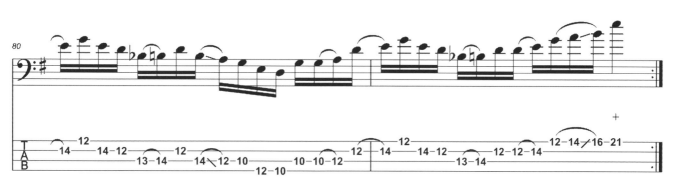

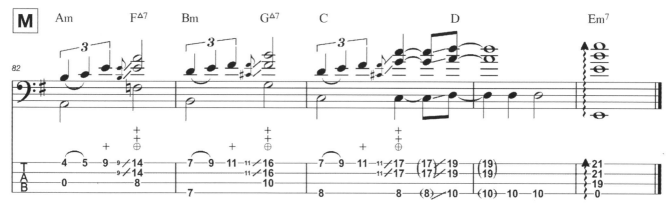

STUART ZENDER

Through his work with Jamiroquai in the early nineties, Stuart Zender cultivated an enviable reputation as one of UK's most influential bass players. His infectious, funk-driven bass work was undoubtedly a key part of the band's sound and has been much missed since his departure at the peak of their success in 1998. Since then he has lent his low-end talents to a range of other artists including Lauryn Hill, Omar, Stevie Wonder and Incognito. Now working as both a session bassist and a producer, he remains as popular as ever with aspiring funk bassists all over the world.

Stuart Zender was born on March 18th, 1974 in Sheffield, South Yorkshire, but moved to the United States with his family at the age of seven. He grew up in Norristown, Pennsylvania, just outside of Philadelphia, a city with a notable musical heritage and the birthplace of a great deal of funk and soul music. This environment was a huge influence on Stuart as a young boy, as was being part of a musical family: his father was a pianist and his uncle a flamenco guitarist.

Stuart and his family returned to the UK when he was fifteen and he found work as a lighting engineer with the circus troupe Archaos. Although he had begun his musical life playing the drums, he also began playing bass in various bands including Fabulous, a punk band formed by NME journalist Simon Spence and photographer Martyn Goodacre. Stuart's early influences on the bass included bands such as Ozric Tentacles, Red Hot Chili Peppers, and Weather Report. The latter group were an important influence on him as a teenager, so much so that he studied and learnt the entirety of their iconic *Black Market* album in just two weeks.

Stuart's break came in early 1993 after meeting singer Jay Kay through Archaos drummer Nick Van Gelder. After a few years of fronting his own group Natural Energy, Jay had auditioned as the vocalist for the Brand New Heavies. Although unsuccessful, he had become enamoured with the acid jazz/rare groove sound and had subsequently recorded the single 'When You Gonna Learn' with musicians from the Acid Jazz label. The song caught the attention of several of the major labels and Jay found himself the subject of a record label bidding war. Eventually signed to Sony, Jay recruited Stuart and Nick to join him and keyboard player Toby Smith in his new group, Jamiroquai. The name of the band was a portmanteau of 'jam session' and 'Iroquai', the name of a Native American tribe. Augmented with a two-piece horn section, a DJ and the didgeridoo talents of Wallis Buchanan, the band recorded the *Emergency On Planet Earth* album when Stuart was just nineteen.

The first single from the album, 'Too Young to Die' was released in March 1993 and fared well in the UK charts, peaking at number 10. The band's debut album, *Emergency on Planet Earth* was even more successful, hitting the top of the UK charts upon its release in August 1993. The impact this album had on bass players upon its release was immense: Zender's funk-fuelled lines on tracks such as 'Hooked Up', 'If I Like It, I Do It', 'Music of the Mind' and 'Whatever It Is, I Just Can't Stop' were undeniably infectious, bringing to mind all of his main influences – Jaco Pastorius, Flea, Mark King, Larry Graham, and Paul Jackson. Unsurprisingly, the album

was voted one of the 50 best bass albums of all time (along with the two other Jamiroquai albums that Stuart played on) by the readers of *Bassist* magazine in 2000.

The bands second album, *The Return of the Space Cowboy* was released in 1995 and saw the band developing further both as performers and writers. By this point, Stuart was also developing quickly as a bassist and had expanded his tonal palette to include the use of bass effects pedals. Tracks such as 'Just Another Story' and 'The Kids' are notable examples of this and feature his use of the Boss ME-8B and Mutron pedals, both of which would soon become a regular part of the Zender sound. The album was another huge success for the band and yielded several hit singles including 'Half the Man', 'Stillness in Time' and 'Space Cowboy', which was particularly successful in the U.S., reaching #1 on the Dance Chart.

Jamiroquai's third album *Travelling Without Moving* was released just a year later in 1996 and quickly brought the band to worldwide attention. Hit singles such as 'Virtual Insanity', 'Cosmic Girl' and 'Alright' were huge hits both in the UK and internationally and all featured killer lines from Stuart. Further bass highlights could be found in the Latin jazz workout of 'Use the Force', the gorgeous low-end throb of 'Everyday', the effects-soaked 'High Times' and the album's title track, 'Travelling Without Moving'.

Unfortunately, internal conflicts had begun to rear their heads within the

band by this point and Zender made the decision to part ways with the group following an argument over writing and production credits.

After leaving Jamiroquai Stuart began working as a session bassist, collaborating with his partner Melanie Blatt (of girl group All Saints), and playing on songs for hip-hop artists Lauryn Hill and D'Angelo. Sessions with soul singer Omar also led him to record bass on a song for the legendary musician Stevie Wonder.

After a few years during which he and Melanie raised their daughter, Stuart re-emerged in 2006 playing bass for acclaimed producer Mark Ronson. Zender appeared on the songs 'Stop Me' and 'Apply Some Pressure' from the hit album *Version*, which consisted of Motown-style cover versions of popular songs. When Ronson went on tour to promote the album, Stuart was hired as the band's bassist and musical director.

Over the last decade Stuart has continued as a session musician. In 2008 he played on 'Cold Shoulder' from Adele's acclaimed album *19*, and in 2010 he was a guest on the song 'Lowdown' with funk group Incognito. He worked with Incognito again in 2016, guesting on two songs from the band's *In Search of Better Days* album: 'Love Born in Flames' and 'Echoes of Utopia'.

In addition to his recent work with Incognito, Stuart has kept busy with studio work, producing, and playing on 'Everybody Needs Love' by Zak Abel and 'Love Shoes' by The Barberettes.

SELECTED DISCOGRAPHY

Jamiroquai –
Emergency on Planet Earth
'Too Young to Die', 'Hooked Up', 'If I Like It, I Do It', 'Music of the Mind', 'Emergency on Planet Earth'

Jamiroquai –
Travelling Without Moving
'Virtual Insanity' 'Cosmic Girl', 'Use the Force', 'Everyday', 'Alright', 'High Times', 'Travelling Without Moving'

Jamiroquai –
The Return of the Space Cowboy
'Just Another Story', 'Manifest Destiny', 'The Kids', 'Mr. Moon', 'Scam', Space Cowboy (Stoned Again Mix)'

Incognito – *In Search of Better Days*
'Love Born in Flames', 'Echoes of Utopia'

WARWICK STUART ZENDER BASS

BASS GUITARS

Stuart's first bass was an unidentified budget instrument, which he used with the various bands he worked with before joining Jamiroquai. Upon joining the band, he purchased a Warwick Streamer Stage 1 with a natural finish, which was then used for the entirety of *Emergency on Planet Earth*. He then remained a Warwick user for several years, moving to Streamer Stage II basses shortly after the recording of the band's second album. He had two very memorable models built for him, the first of which was the chrome 'Ender' bass, which had green fretboard LEDs. The second was the 'Iroquai bass', which was decorated with the pattern from a Native American blanket worn by Chief Joseph of the Iroquai tribe, from whom the band took part of their name. This bass had red fretboard LEDs. Unfortunately, both of these instruments were stolen during the nineties and Stuart has often stated that he is keen to have them back. In addition to these instruments, whilst in Jamiroquai he also owned an 8-string Warwick bass and another Stage II in white, with blue LEDs. This latter bass was restored for him by Warwick in 2015.

During recording sessions for the second Jamiroquai album *The Return of the Space Cowboy*, Stuart also used an Alembic Essence bass and a '74 Fender Jazz Bass. The Alembic bass was later stolen from his car.

Whilst working with Mark Ronson in 2008, Stuart began using a Gibson Les Paul bass strung with flatwound strings. He then reverted to Warwick in 2010, with whom he developed a striking signature instrument. The Stuart Zender Signature Bass was based on the Streamer I with a deeper cutaway for upper fret access – Stuart had actually cut a section out of the body of his original Streamer bass to make playing in the upper register easier. The body shaping is a little more extravagant and the fretboard is decorated with large, triangular fret markers, which were a nod to the triangular pattern of his old Iroquai bass. There is also a large, stylised 'SZ' motif at the twelfth fret.

Stuart also regularly uses a '63 Fender Precision bass, which he can be seen playing in the video for the Incognito track 'Love Born in Flames'.

EFFECTS

Stuart used effects heavily during his time with Jamiroquai, most commonly an envelope filter effect. This was usually provided by Boss ME-6B and ME-8B multi-effects units – good examples of Stuart's use of these effects can be heard on 'The Kids' and 'Just Another Story', from *The Return of the Space Cowboy*. In 2017 Ashdown collaborated with Stuart on the 'Funk Face', a new pedal which features both fuzz and wah effects.

AMPLIFICATION

During the early part of his time with Jamiroquai, Stuart used SWR amplification, later moving to Warwick. He used the Wamp 400 head with 410-80 cabinets for several years, before switching to a Trace Elliot V-Type setup. During the 2000s he used an Ampeg rig for a while before switching to a Warwick Jonas Hellborg signature bass rig.

'Zender Jazz' is a piece written in the style of the music Stuart recorded with Jamiroquai on their first three albums.

After a short drum intro, the bass enters at letter A with a four-bar groove. This line is based around an E⁷ chord: note the double chromatic passing notes that ascend to the third (G♯) and fifth (B) of the chord in the first bar. This idea is continued into the second bar with an ascent from the seventh (D) to the root (E), followed by a melodic phrase that makes use of a 'shake'. To play the shake, fret the G at the fifth fret of the D-string with your first finger and shake the note from side to side, crossing from G to the G♯ at the sixth fret. This is similar to a trill, but because it is played with one finger it has a different sound. When playing the hammer-on from F♯ to G♯ in the third bar of the sequence (bar 7), I recommend fretting the F♯ with the first finger and the G♯ with the fourth. You can then use the first finger to jump across to the G-string and play the E at the ninth fret. The phrase that occurs in the fourth bar is best played with the first finger of the fretting hand on the F♯ at the fourth fret of the D-string – your fingers will then be in position to play the G, G♯ and E as well, using the finger-per-fret technique. The E is followed by an open A-string, which will give you a chance to shift your hand down to the second fret.

At letter C a 'pre-chorus' section begins. In the first bar, the bass plays a root-octave-ninth figure that was often used by Zender in Jamiroquai's music. Be sure to play the ghost notes as written here as they are important to the part. In the second bar of the sequence (bar 14), the bass plays a busier line that makes heavy use of the blues scale. note that the legato phrase on the G-string is to be played in one stroke: after playing the G at the twelfth fret, slide up to the A♭, back to the G quickly, then pull off to sound the F at the tenth fret. The line then descends through the D blues scale. After a repeat of the first bar of the sequence, this section of the song ends with some simple octave figures which set up the transition into the 'chorus' part of the song.

The bassline at letter D is an octave-based groove that is reminiscent of Zender's lines on tracks such as 'Cosmic Girl' and 'Alright'. Note that from the root note of each chord change, the bass follows a root – second – third motif, which reinforces the harmony. When playing this part, the ghost notes are performed by raking backwards with the fingers of the picking hand. This section of the song ends with a three-bar tag that features some descending chords. The lower register of a 5-string is required to play these notes, although they can easily be transposed up an octave if you don't have a 5-string bass.

The bass parts at letters E, F and G are repeats of earlier sections of the song, with no variations.

At letter H a new part begins, which is performed with the slap and pop technique. This line follows the chord progression from the D and G sections of the track (the 'chorus' part) and is heavily syncopated. Note that accurately playing the rests between the notes is vital to the groove here, so listen closely to the audio when learning this part. Your slap technique and timing will need to be very accurate here as it can be very challenging to play these syncopations individually. Note that you are briefly required to switch to the fingerstyle technique for the three-note motif at the end of the third bar of the sequence (bar 50).

The final part of the song is a closing 'chorus' section and is played with the slap technique. Watch out for the shake in the fourth bar of this line.

SOUND ADVICE

This track was recorded using a Sei Flamboyant 5-string bass. I used both pickups but favoured the neck pickup slightly. All controls on the instrument were set flat, although some minor tweaks to the EQ were made after the part was recorded. The bass was also slightly compressed digitally.

Zender's tone is classic funk, and a very similar sound can easily be found using either Precision or Jazz-style basses. If you are using a Jazz bass, I recommend favouring the neck pickup for a fatter, darker tone – this will work well for both the fingerstyle and slap elements of this piece. Although it wasn't used on the track, you might want to also experiment with using an envelope filter effects for the chorus sections.

Remember that just as important as the sound are the stylistic touches: the shakes, the staccato notes, the correct performance of rests etc. Take care to follow these closely in the score as they will help with the overall feel of the line.

'ZENDER JAZZ'

Written by Stuart Clayton

Drums: Will Beavis
Keys: Tom O'Grady
Guitar: Steve Banks
Bass: Stuart Clayton

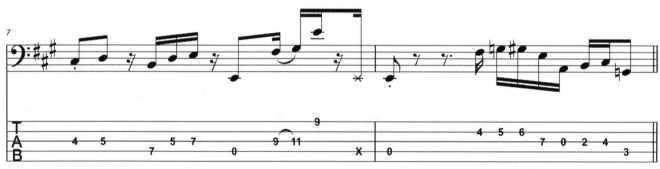

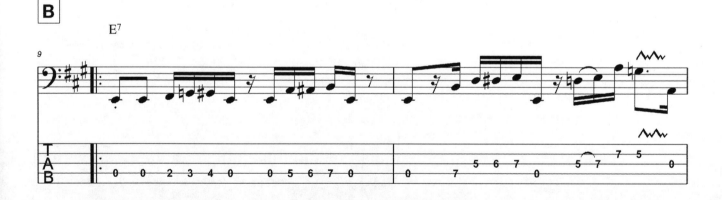

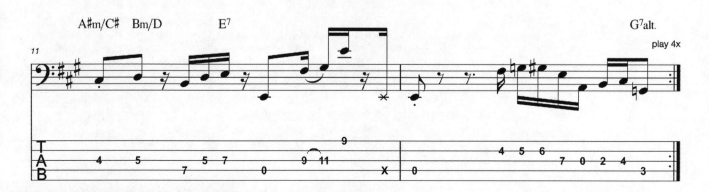

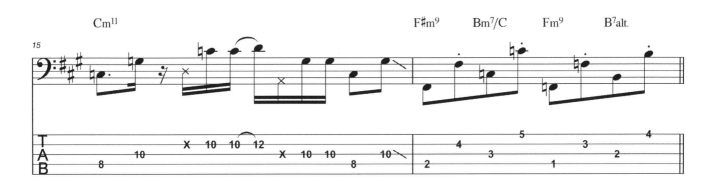

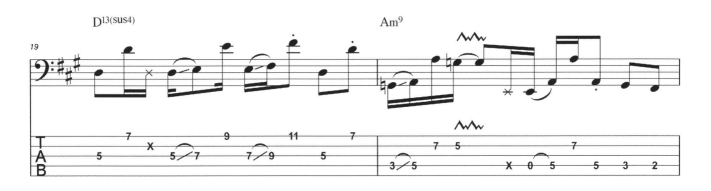

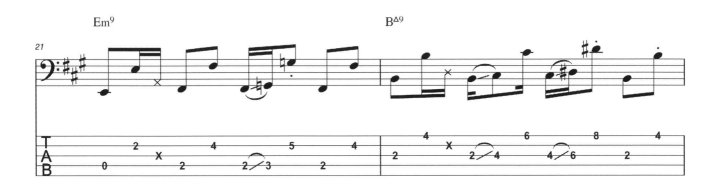

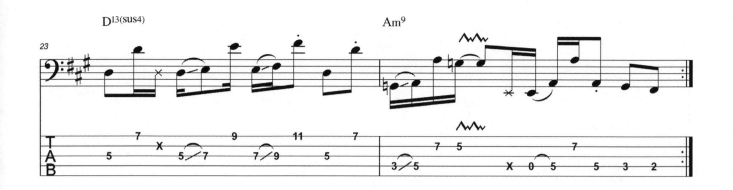

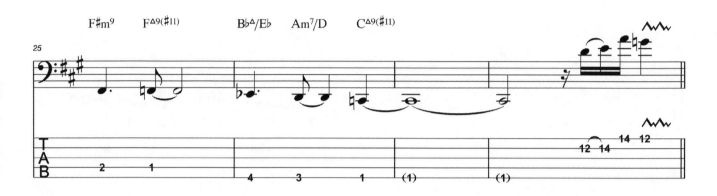

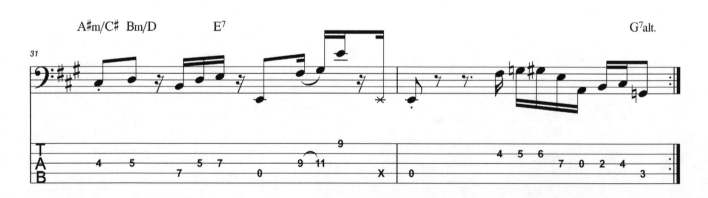

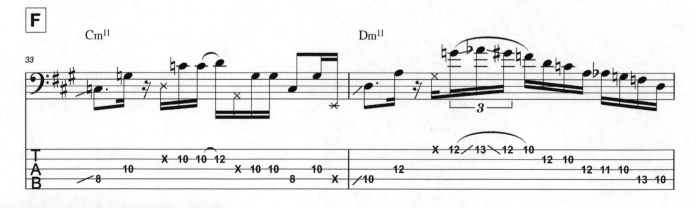

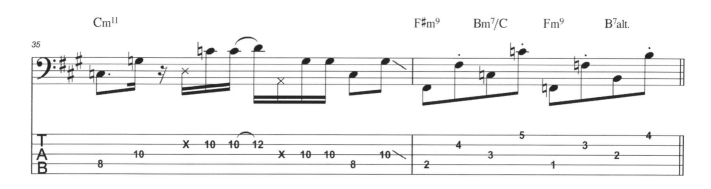

G

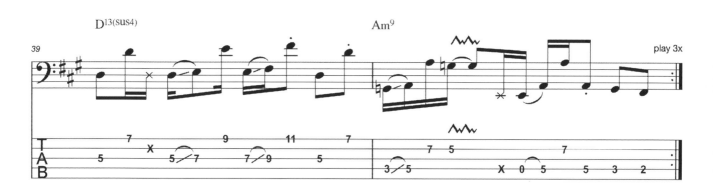

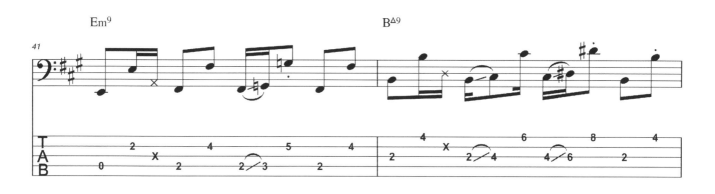

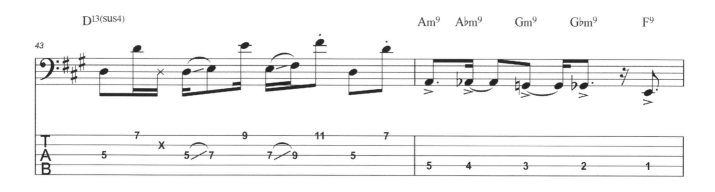

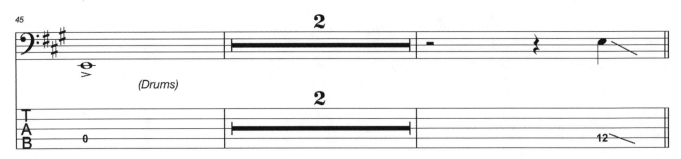

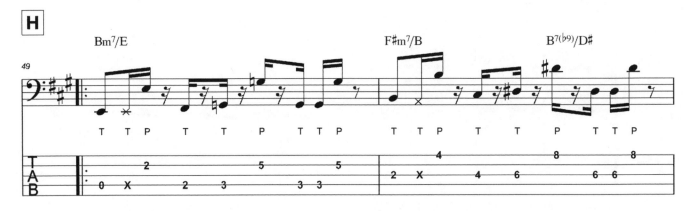

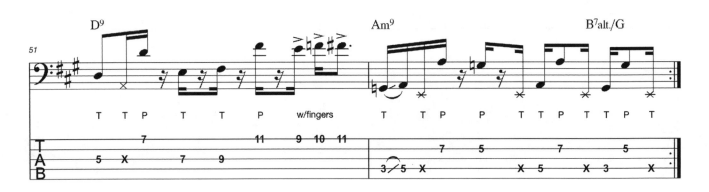

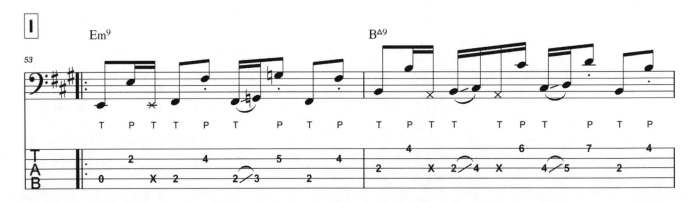

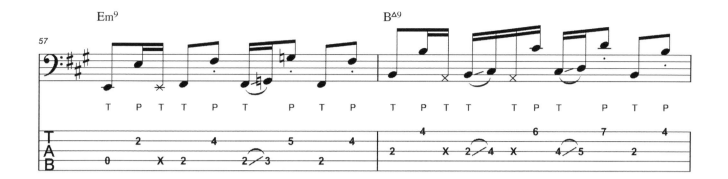

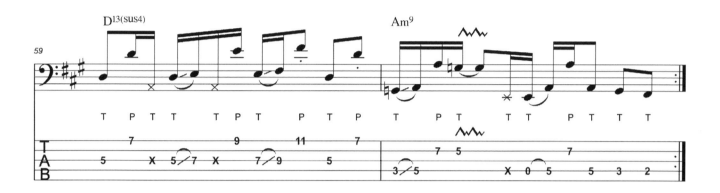

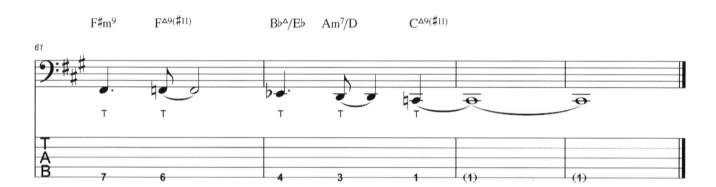

Bassline Publishing Transcription Books

The following transcription books are available from Bassline Publishing

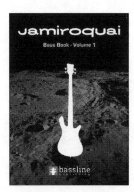

**The Jamiroquai Bass
Book - Volume 1**

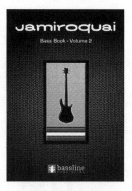

**The Jamiroquai Bass
Book - Volume 2**

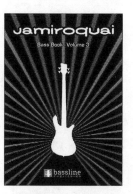

**The Jamiroquai Bass
Book - Volume 3**

**The Jamiroquai Bass
Book - Volume 4**

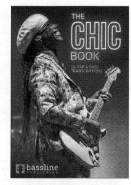

**The Chic Book - Guitar
& Bass Transcriptions**

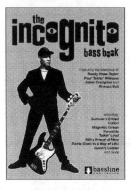

**The Incognito
Bass Book**

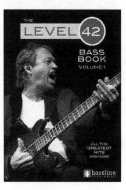

**The Level 42 Bass
Book - Volume 1**

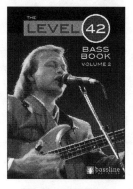

**The Level 42 Bass
Book - Volume 2**

**The Level 42 Bass
Book - Volume 3**

**Level 42 -
A Physical Presence**

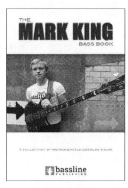

**The Mark King
Bass Book**

**Stuart Hamm -
The Early Years**

**Stuart Hamm -
Outbound & Beyond**

**Stu Hamm
The Book of Lies**

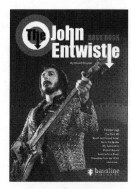

**The John Entwistle
Bass Book**

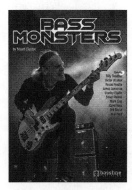

Bass Monsters

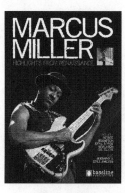

**Marcus Miller
Highlights from
Renaissance**

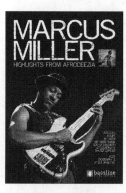

**Marcus Miller
Highlights from
Afrodeezia**

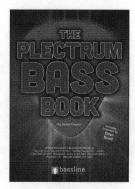

**The Plectrum Bass
Book**

**The Brothers Johnson
Bass Book**

Available to order from **www.basslinepublishing.com** and from **amazon**

Bassline Publishing Theory & Technique Books

The following theory and technique books are available from Bassline Publishing

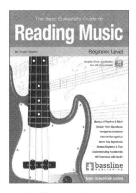

The Bass Guitarist's Guide to Reading Music - Beginner Level

The Bass Guitarist's Guide to Reading Music - Intermediate Level

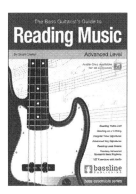

The Bass Guitarist's Guide to Reading Music - Advanced Level

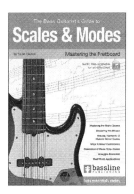

The Bass Guitarist's Guide to Scales & Modes

Play Bass

Ultimate Slap Bass

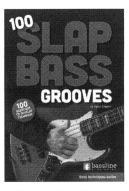

100 Slap Bass Grooves

Ultimate Tapping for Bass Guitar

Plectrum Technique for Bass Guitar

Advanced Studies for Bass Guitar

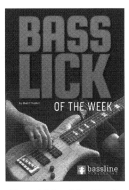

Bass Lick of the Week

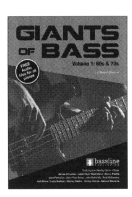

Giants of Bass Vol. 1 - 60s & 70s

Giants of Bass Vol. 2 - 80s & 90s

The Bassist's Guide to Injury Management, Prevention & Better Health - Vol. 1

The Bassist's Guide to Injury Management, Prevention & Better Health - Vol. 2

Available to order from
www.basslinepublishing.com
and from

ALSO AVAILABLE BASSLINE PUBLISHING VIDEO COURSES

After many years of writing a popular series of bass guitar tuition and transcription books, author and leading bass educator Stuart Clayton has created a series of instructional video courses. These are available via subscription to users all over the world.

Informed by Stuart's extensive experience as a teacher at one of the UK's top music schools, these courses are broken down into short, manageable lessons, with clear, attainable goals. Users can subscribe monthly or annually - subscriptions can be cancelled at any time.

MONTHLY* Subscription £7.99 per month
ANNUAL* Subscription £89 per year

Video Courses include:

Giants of Bass
Each course contains a full play-through of the piece, followed by section-by-section lessons on how to play in the style of well-known bassists including Billy Sheehan, Bootsy Collins, Carol Kaye, Flea, Mark King and many more.

Learning the Modes
This series of courses takes each of the modes and breaks it down into detail. Each course covers approaches to playing the mode all over the fingerboard and a range of exercises that it to use, so that you can hear the unique sound that each one offers.

Slap Bass
Beginner, Intermediate & Advanced
These courses are based on the popular *Ultimate Slap Bass* book and cover everything you need about this technique!

Scales and Arpeggios
Learn using the 'content over patterns' theory, avoiding the use of patterns and box shapes, and instead focuses on the notes.

Plectrum Course
This is a crucial technique to master for any professional bassist and this course is the perfect place to start.

Song Tutorials
Popular songs are broken down, section by section. Includes: 'Tommy the Cat' (Primus), 'Forget Me Nots' (Patrice Rushen), 'The Machine Stops' (Level 42), 'Hump de Bump' (Red Hot Chili Peppers) and more.

Tapping
Tapping is a rather unconventional technique, but in the right hands, it can be a valuable musical tool. Learn finger dexterity exercises, muting, and the best way to set up your bass for this technique.

New courses added regularly!

www.basslinepublishing.com